Anabaptist Ways of Knowing

Published in association with Eastern Mennonite University

Anabaptist Ways of Knowing

A Conversation About Tradition-Based Critical Education

Sara Wenger Shenk
Foreword by Nancy Murphy

Publishing House
the new name of Pandora Press U.S.
Telford, Pennsylvania

copublished with
Herald Press
Scottdale, Pennsylvania

Cascadia Publishing House orders, information, reprint permissions:
contact@CascadiaPublishingHouse.com
1-215-723-9125
126 Klingerman Road, Telford PA 18969
www.CascadiaPublishingHouse.com

Anabaptist Ways of Knowing
Copyright © 2003 by Cascadia Publishing House,
Telford, PA 18969
All rights reserved.
Copublished with Herald Press, Scottdale, PA
Library of Congress Catalog Number: 2003043435
ISBN: 1-931038-16-3

Book design by Cascadia Publishing House
Cover design by Merrill R. Miller

The paper used in this publication is recycled and meets the minimum requirements of American National Standard for Information Sciences—Permanence of Paper for Printed Library Materials, ANSI Z39.48-1984. All Bible quotations are used by permission, all rights reserved and unless otherwise noted are from *The New Revised Standard Version of the Bible*, copyright 1989, by the Division of Christian Education of the National Council of the Churches of Christ in the USA

Library of Congress Cataloguing-in-Publication Data
Shenk, Sara Wenger, 1953-
  Anabaptist ways of knowing : a conversation about tradition-based critical education / Sara Wenger Shenk
    p. cm.
  Includes bibliographical references (p.) and index.
  ISBN 1-931038-16-3 (alk. paper)
  1. Mennonites--Education. 2. Education--Philosophy. I. Title

LC486.M4S54 2003
371.829--dc21

2003043435

12 11 10 09 08 07 06 05   10 9 8 7 6 5 4 3

*To Chester and Sara Jane Wenger,
wellsprings of a deep knowing
drawn from the source—
ancient and yet fresh every day.*

CONTENTS

Foreword by Nancey Murphy 11
Introduction: Remember Who You Are 13

1. A CONGREGATIONAL PORTRAIT OF CHANGING PRACTICES • 23
Training in Good Habits
Bodily and Social Memory
Changes in Mennonite Lived Religion: Congregational Portrait
Congregational Profile Summarized
Conclusion

2. ANABAPTIST PERSPECTIVES ON "KNOWING" • 37
Anabaptist Theology
Descriptive Overview of Anabaptists
Anabaptist Distinctives Relevant to Education
  Discipleship: Patterning Our Lives on Jesus Christ
  Hermeneutical Community: Discerning Truth Communally
  Ecclesiology: Tradition for Transformation
Educational Implications

3. CLASSICAL *PAIDEIA* AND ANABAPTIST DISTINCTIVES • 60
Classical Greek Notions of Paideia
Early Christian Notions of Paideia
Paideia and Theological Education
Critical Retrieval of Paideia
  An Alternative Paideia
  Paideia and the Ideal of the Good
  Paideia and Intellectual and Moral Virtues
  Paideia and Critical Inquiry

4. OTHER VOICES:
A "KNOWING" CONVERSATION WITH THE ANABAPTISTS • 78

Overview of Ways of Knowing
Voices Invited to the Table
   Introducing Michael Polanyi
      Key Polanyi insights relevant to a tradition-based, critical educational theory
         Personal knowledge
         Bodily roots of tacit knowing
         Indwelling
         Society of Explorers
         Tradition and religion
         Concluding thoughts on Polanyi
   Introducing Rebecca Chopp
      Key Chopp insights relevant to a tradition-based, critical educational theory
         Person-centered education
         Ekklesia
         Practices as sites of learning
         Theology as "saving work"
         Concluding thoughts on Chopp
   Introducing Nancey Murphy
      Key Murphy insights relevant to a tradition-based, critical educational theory
         Relationship between science and theology
         Role of tradition and formative texts
         The priority of the ethical and theological to intellectual life
         Practices characteristic of the Radical Reformation heritage
         Concluding thoughts on Murphy

5. AN EMERGING CONSENSUS ABOUT "KNOWING" • 119

Exploring New Paradigms
Knowing and Tradition
Knowing and Ethics
Knowing As Narrative In Action
Knowing and Intuitive Imagination
Communal Knowing As Disciplined Discovery

**6. WEAVING A THEORY OF EDUCATION
FROM THE CONVERSATIONAL STRANDS • 133**

Constructing a Theoretical Framework
Defining the Purpose
A Formative Paradigm
How Do We Know?—Philosophical Assumptions
   The Traditional Roots of Knowledge
   The Spiritual Roots of Knowledge
   The Communal Roots of Knowledge
   The Bodily and Tacit Roots of Knowledge
   The Intuitive And Imaginal Roots of Knowledge
   The Rational Roots of Knowledge
   The Ethical Roots of Knowledge
   The Practical Roots of Knowledge
Educational Settings
   The Church
   The Family
   The School
Strategies And Methodologies
   Reimaging Communal Ideals
   Indwelling Narratives And Practices
   Communal Moral Discernment As a "Society of Explorers"
   Revitalizing Core Practices
   Reflecting on Practice
Conclusion

Glossary   165
Notes   171
Bibliography   197
Index   201
The Author   211

Foreword

Stephen Toulmin wrote in his *Cosmopolis: The Hidden Agenda of Modernity* that the formal doctrines underpinning the thought and practice of modernity followed a trajectory with an Omega shape: "After 300 years we are back close to our starting point."[1] Toulmin argues that modernity really began with the tolerance and mild skepticism of the Renaissance, with its interest in the timely, the local, the particular, and the practical. The quest for universal, certain, theoretical knowledge begun by René Descartes has been a long detour from which we are only now returning.

I, too, would emphasize ways the modern quest has come nearly full circle, but I see better options than a return to skepticism. Jeffrey Stout describes modernity as a flight from traditional authority.[2] The Enlightenment accounted for its own origins in terms of the rejection of religious superstition and mankind's daring to think for himself (I use the masculine advisedly). Toulmin and Stout, each in his own way, trace it instead to the desperate need to resolve bloody disputes when Protestant and Catholic authorities disagreed. Stout argues that the resources devised for this purpose created an epistemological crisis for theology from which it has never recovered. If modernity *was* a child begotten by Christian strife, it would have been poetic justice if modern standards of rationality had resulted in the death of Christian belief. Yet God's justice is not "poetic," and the church has outlived its recalcitrant child.

If indeed modernity began with the rejection of tradition—the quest (in Toulmin's words) to begin with a clean slate—we have closed the circle in Alasdair MacIntyre's recognition of the tradition-dependence of all rationality. "To be outside all traditions is to be a stranger to enquiry; it is to be in a state of intellectual and moral destitution...."[3]

Another feature of modern reason has been its dualistic attempt to detach cerebration from the life of the body. Current feminist thinkers (Shenk draws largely from the work of Rebecca Chopp) recognize the extent to which knowledge begins with our *embodied* presence in the world. Confirmation for this claim comes from a variety of sources, most powerfully from the work of George Lakoff and Mark Johnson, who argue that all of reason's categories are extensions of metaphors based on bodily experience in the physical world.[4]

We who are involved in theological or church-related education often have much to celebrate in such developments. One who celebrates and puts them to good use is Sara Wenger Shenk. "The long dark night honoring those who engaged primarily in detached rational thinking" has come to an end (p. 157). Drawing on a wealth of current resources, she has devised an approach to education that draws its strength from the particular, the practical, the timely, and the local. This pedagogy recognizes its indebtedness to tradition, understood as the social and critical embodiment of the community's formative texts. She translates an epistemology rooted in the traditional, the spiritual, the communal, the bodily, the intuitive, the ethical, and the practical—along with the rational—into strategies for education that stress reimaging our communal ideals, indwelling narratives and practices, communal moral discernment, and revitalization of family and church practices.

Shenk promotes this vision with a sense of urgency. Just as the secular world has been returning from its detour in search of universal rationality, her research shows that her own Anabaptist tradition has been rapidly losing touch with the traditional formative practices that have been an important source of its identity. Yet Anabaptism is rich in resources for an approach to knowledge appropriate to our postmodern world: communal reading of the biblical texts, discernment, theology developed in response to live issues in the church. I share Shenk's sense of urgency but also her enthusiasm for promoting an authentically Anabaptist epistemology and pedagogy. I am honored to have my voice included among the resources she has so skillfully woven together.

—*Nancey Murphy, Professor of Christian Philosophy*
Fuller Theological Seminary, Pasadena, California

Introduction: Remember Who You Are

I don't know when it began, but it became a frequent practice in our home. As the children left for school, I would say to them, "Remember who you are!" I never said it without feeling a quiet joy, grateful for knowing something about who I am. And I said it thinking that perhaps our children would also be reminded that they are "somebody"—somebody with a special history, with an identity worth celebrating.

I am intrigued that they didn't ask me, "What do you mean, Mom? What am I supposed to remember about who I am?" An unspoken potency was bound up in the understanding we shared. "Remember who you are!" seemed to suggest that who we are is worth remembering and has everything to do with how we carry ourselves into the wider world.

As I reflect on why I would remind our children of this, I think I was inviting them to call to mind several aspects of their identity. I was reminding them to remember what family they belong to—that they are Wenger Shenks and that we have a unique history, special practices, and core commitments that shape who we are as family. I was also reminding them that we belong to a distinctive community of faith, a community that shares a special history of pain and hope, recognizable practices, and a confession of faith which define us as "in the world but not of the world."

The times in which we live may be particularly suited to remember who we are and draw enormous energy from that memory. These are exciting times—times when persons who draw strength and identity from a particular peoplehood may be uniquely prepared to "seize the day." Postmodernity and its disenchantment with "scientific certainties" and universal explanations, offers us a splendid opportunity to speak truth out of our own history as a minority people. In my case, that special history derives from the Anabaptists and their radical identification with Jesus Christ and the early Christian church. "Communities of conviction," as educator Craig Dykstra calls us, bear within ourselves a long historical tradition that is deep and rich, a potent legacy that equips us to be an oasis in the desert of this age.

We live in a time of great foment and shifting loyalties. "Postmodernity," some call it. "Post-Christian" or a "culture of disbelief," others call it. Whatever one chooses to name the current era, it seems clear that we in the so-called West are at a turning point in how we choose to construe our reality. Much of what is called "postmodern," suggests Nancey Murphy, is actually nothing but a recognition of the failure to find indisputable foundations for universal knowledge.[1] Foundationalism, as a philosophical approach to knowledge, demanded certainty and decontextualization simply not available to most human endeavors.

Among theologians and philosophers there is more and more widespread acknowledgment of the importance of taking context into account. Nonfoundationalist theologians speak about confessing Christian affirmations as uniquely and finally true, but they acknowledge that this truth must be confessed or professed as there is no such thing as absolutely secured knowledge. Knowledge is "particular and perspectival," and as such is always contestable. Truth, then, can be lived, believed and witnessed to only from a specific perspective or point of view.[2] And so, in "remembering who we are" we actively own our perspective and offer its unique texture to the fabric of our world.

POSTMODERNITY AND TRADITION-BASED, CRITICAL EDUCATION

The discussion in this book can be thought of as a table conversation about how to remember who we are; a conversation about education, and about personal and communal formation. I will serve as the primary host of the conversation, though I am really serving on behalf of the contemporary heirs of the Anabaptists, most specifically the Mennonites. As the host of the conversation, I have invited multiple guests to share their perspectives, particularly as they relate to educational approaches.

I feel a profound urgency to engage in this conversation. The urgency grows out of a nagging concern that narratives and practices, which in earlier generations were deeply formative for our community life, are rapidly and uncritically being discarded. In the conversation, I will share the distinctive confessional priorities that, in my view, relate most directly to educational priorities. And then, keeping those distinctive priorities in mind, I will invite interaction with the other voices at the table, hoping to shed light on ways to reformulate an educational vision and give direction for the educational mission of other particular Christian communities like my own Mennonite community.

Questions of how we come to know move to the forefront in discussions about education—what can we know, how do we know it; and the related ethical question, what is it good to know? The emerging awareness in many circles is that we are far more limited in what we can know rationally or empirically than the Modern era led us to believe. Education theorists are giving evidence that questions and answers about how we come to know are more multi-faceted than previously thought, breaking us out of the narrow tunnel vision of rationalist thinking ushered in by the Enlightenment.

As is characteristic of unstable, dynamic times, when basic assumptions about truth and how we know truth are open for reevaluation, attempts are being made to provide new conceptual frameworks to examine the questions. Some of the most fruitful attempts take us back to a tradition-based community in a critical, dialectical relationship with the individual and his or her needs and visions; a faith community that knows itself to be a distinctive, minority group with unique practices and purposes in relation to the larger society; a community that while attempting to faithfully steward a living tradition, is open to ongoing prophetic critique.

My contention in this conversation about education will be that the early Anabaptist stance toward knowing truth resonates with much of the current thinking about how we come to know in its emphasis on the traditional, spiritual, ethical, communal, bodily, and practical ways of knowing. Such a stance can provide important insights for guiding us in envisioning educational and formational priorities for the coming years.

An approach to education from within a tradition-based community will underscore the social nature of human life with particular focus on life practices. Community practices express a basic appreciation of the importance of a personal, participatory knowing that must be nourished by tradition and communal experience. Central importance will be given to narratives and practices as providing identity and meaning to the community and its members.[3]

Philosopher Alasdair MacIntyre argues that knowledge and truth are rooted in culture and need a narrative context to become intelligible. "Narrative history of a certain kind turns out to be the basic and essential genre for the characterization of human actions," he asserts. An action requires a context to be intelligible. Behavior, he claims, can only be characterized adequately when we know its setting, the beliefs that informed it and the long and short term intentions of that behavior. Behavior and communication, according to MacIntyre, only become intelligible by finding their place in a narrative informed by the past, living in the present, and moving toward the future.[4]

In trying to make sense of the future toward which we're moving, a human is essentially a story-telling animal, argues MacIntyre, a teller of stories that "aspire to truth." Deprive children of stories and "you leave them unscripted, anxious stutterers in their actions as in their words."[5] The story of a life is always embedded in the tale of the communities from which we derive our identity, he continues, suggesting that in this way possessing an historical identity and a social identity coincide. And he notes that what a person is is in large part what the person inherits. MacIntyre argues convincingly that for our human communities to thrive, we must give vigilant attention to the tradition of the virtues and the narratives and practices that sustain our community life together. To put it bluntly, our salvation lies in our traditions and it is the exercise of the relevant virtues that sustains and strengthens our traditions.[6]

Murphy suggests that no philosopher has done more to show a helpful way beyond the current crisis about truth claims than MacIntyre and the tradition-based rationality and morality he outlines in his work. She claims that MacIntyre provides an alternative to the demand for universal reason and to the cynicism and relativism that show up when such a search is found to be futile. It is our traditions that give us the resources for justifying our actions as well as our truth claims, he argues. Outside of all tradition one is morally and intellectually destitute. He also believes it is possible for traditions to compete meaningfully with one another, and occasionally to argue, in the public forum, that one tradition is rationally superior to its rivals.[7]

The work of George Lindbeck has also been helpful in recognizing the value of concrete religious traditions and reclaiming the value of particular and local traditions and practices. He has stressed the formative power of language and the liturgy of the church, as well as the regulative role of doctrine and argues that "to become religious involves becoming skilled in the language, the symbol system of a given religion. To become a Christian involves learning the story of Israel and of Jesus well enough to interpret and experience oneself and one's world in its terms."[8]

Lindbeck argues (along with many others), that followers of Christ have something to say to the world only to the extent that they can produce communities which embody a distinctive way of life. He claims that religious communities are likely to contribute more to the future of humanity if they preserve their own distinctiveness and integrity than if they yield to homogenizing tendencies. Thus the primary task of the church is to be faithful to the Christian narrative to preserve its own distinctive integrity. But, and here is a cautionary note, it is also important to remind ourselves that the quality of our knowing will depend on whether our community participates in a larger reality than its own life-forms. If we don't remember that the language we speak is capable of referring to realities beyond the language itself, our truth claims may collapse into "mere convention, opportunistic instrumentalism, and sectarian ethnocentrism."[9]

If we accept the assertions of Lindbeck and other scholars of religion and culture that *particular,* traditional communities of faith can provide the most potent resource for embodying a distinctive Christ-like life in postmodernity, what must characterize a given church community so it can actively remember its own story while becoming a community "for the world?"[10]

How can we draw strength from a particular tradition, a particular story, while cultivating a lively critique of that tradition so as to keep it vital in changing times? It is timely to re-vision education as both tradition-based and critical.[11] As followers of Christ we must come once again to understand ourselves as a resourceful minority. It is in embodying a distinctive way of life modeled on the teachings of Jesus that we will recapture the missional and transformative purpose that has characterized educational endeavors during some of its most generative eras. And we will observe that critical reflection on the ways in which the traditions are embodied is essential to keep them vital.

A Particular Faith Community

The Anabaptist-Mennonite approach has been to expect its traditional narratives and practices to serve a central formative function in the life of the community. While they seldom expressed themselves with elaborately formulated, explicit theology, they have been guided by an implicit theology, a set of firm convictions and practices for which they have risked, and sometimes paid, their lives.[12] They sought to model their communal, social and personal practice according to Jesus' life as the norm with the assistance of the Holy Spirit.

The ethical and philosophical concerns of their approach have been to maintain a unity of faith and practice because it is in following Jesus more closely that we come to know God and God's purposes more truly. Mennonite theologian Tom Finger notes that the early Anabaptists stressed Jesus' teaching and example far more than did other religious groups of their time.[13] They affirmed that only one committed to following Jesus in concrete practices of daily life can know the truth about God's purposes. This affirmation has been called a distinctive emphasis within the sixteenth century on the nature and method of knowing.[14]

Heirs of the Anabaptists have emphasized the need for unity of faith and practice. Their traditional church-centered communities have maintained a degree of strength in large part because of a profound commitment to maintain the unity of faith and practice and also to remain distinct as a church community from the larger society.[15] It is their distinctive emphases in conversation with early Greek notions of *paideia* and recent philosophical thinking that will guide my construction of a tradition-based and critical approach to education for postmodern, particular Christian communities.

Fayette Veverka, a Catholic educator, raised the question which is central to my sense of urgency about the need to formulate an approach to education for Mennonites and for other particular Christian communities: "If education is a community building enterprise, how do we educate when the very definition of what it means to be a people is at stake?" Out of her Catholic context, she was suggesting directions for education that resonate with where my own thinking is going as a Mennonite. She spoke of educational strategies that include cultural practices that "embody" and "enact" religious traditions.[16]

I approach this conversation about education from the vantage point of my own personal history as a daughter, a granddaughter, a sister, a wife, a mother, a neighbor, a teacher, a pastor and as a woman involved in theological education. I approach it as a practical theologian who wants theology to help make sense of everyday, down-to-earth realities. And I approach the topic in an informal sense as an ethnographer, one who loves to study people amid their lives and the complexity of their relationship; to look, listen and observe people within the web of forces that impact their lives—their walls, their loves, their enemies, their celebrations and work, what they wear and what they long for.

I also come from many generations of Mennonite families who originally emigrated to the United States from Switzerland and Germany. My family has for several generations been deeply involved in education. My own experience has included relating to educational realities cross-culturally, in Ethiopia, the former Yugoslavia and in a variety of different cultural and educational settings in the United States. This conversation about how we come to know and about education represents for me an opportunity to reassess some of the strengths and limitations of the traditions that have largely formed me. I will hope to critically retrieve those aspects of the traditions which continue to have potential for shaping a vital educational vision able to address present communal and cultural challenges.

Anabaptist Ways of Knowing

Chapter 1

A CONGREGATIONAL PORTRAIT OF CHANGING PRACTICES

Our discussion in this chapter and subsequent ones could be characterized in part by a conversation around a dinner table. It is the concerns of the Anabaptists and their Mennonite heirs which will give direction and momentum to the conversation. And I have invited many others to the table to converse with each other and with us about the meaning of education and strategies for discerning and practicing truth. Among those present are Paul Connerton, Alasdair MacIntyre, Plato, Michael Polanyi, Rebecca Chopp, and Nancey Murphy.

The purpose of the conversation is not to shape some new theoretical edifice that is logically symmetrical and absolutely grounded in immovable foundations. It is rather to gather together vibrant strands from several traditions along with intriguing threads from recent experience, and with the threads of the Anabaptist story, to design a beautiful and practical pattern for ongoing communal educational endeavors.

As primary host of this conversation, I see the purpose for this table gathering as emerging from a nagging concern that practices deeply formative for the faith community I know best are rapidly being discarded. Deemed too ethnic, quaint, or rigid, they are crowded out by sports, TV, and a multitude of other options.

My sense is that the Mennonite church community, not unlike other faith communities, has come through a generation and more of heavy critique and suspicion of its faith tradition and has gone far toward dismantling its ethnic isolation and sectarian-like exclusivity.

My concern is that many of the practices essential to the educational faith priorities of the community are being uncritically discarded along with the ethnic characteristics of the community. If some practices have been discarded as no longer relevant to maintaining our church community life, what are the implications for community life? Have we paid enough attention to whether or not our current practices are illustrative of what we confessionally claim ought to characterize our church community? Are there practices which might be reclaimed or adopted to more clearly embody who we say we are confessionally? To get a concrete feel for what the discussion is about, I will share a profile of changes in practices across several generations in the life of one congregation.

But before looking at the congregation, I want to hear from several voices describing some of the dynamics at work in personal and communal formation. My hunch at the outset of this conversation is that in our engagement with educational concerns as a community, we have underestimated the function of patterned bodily practices and internalized ritual behaviors and the powerfully formative substratum of knowledge they provide. If it is the case that this internalized substratum of knowledge out of which our conscious language and behaviors flow has been severely undermined or contaminated, then a conversation about education ought to address ways to renew the wellsprings of communal life.

Training in Good Habits

Aristotle, like Socrates and Plato, addressed a central problem of educational philosophy: how is virtue (temperance, courage, wisdom and justice) to be acquired? He didn't seem satisfied with the simple theory that the possession of knowledge was adequate to make one virtuous. He argued that there are three factors involved in the formation of virtuous behavior: nature, habit, and reason.[1]

In his discussion of virtue, Aristotle divides virtue into two corresponding groups—the intellectual virtues and the moral virtues, or "intellectual excellence and goodness of character."[2] The intellect, he said, is chiefly fostered by education, but moral goodness or character is formed mainly by "training in habit." Moral virtues, he says, are not formed in us by nature but are developed in the *training* of our natural capacity. We are made good by being trained in good habits.

Aristotle emphasizes that we are formed in good character not by attaining knowledge in the abstract about what virtue *is* but by *becoming* virtuous. We learn by doing. It follows then, that a person becomes just by acting justly, says Aristotle, and self-controlled by acting with self-control. There is no way for a person to become virtuous except by virtuous conduct. Socialization or habituation in the moral virtues provides the grounding, then, for the development of the intellectual virtues, according to Aristotle.

For Aristotle, moral goodness is formed by training in habit. It follows then that any serious concern about educational priorities will pay attention to the rhythm of daily practices as powerfully formative in the lives of children and adults.

Bodily Social Memory

In a fascinating study entitled *How Societies Remember*, social scientist Paul Connerton argues that bodily social memory is an essential aspect of social memory that has previously been badly neglected in research and writing about memory. Images of the past and knowledge of the past are conveyed and sustained by bodily rituals and practices.[3] Yet when traditions have been studied, the focus has usually been on the transmission of written texts.

What is handed down in the form of a text within a culture, however, is transmitted like nothing else that comes down to us from the past. It is detached both from its producers and from any specific addressees and can lead a life of its own, enjoying relative cultural autonomy. And yet we have assumed that such "inscribed" practices should be the privileged form for the transmission of a society's memories.[4] We can't, however, underestimate the importance and persistence of the bodily aspects of social memory, he argues, and he suggests that *every group will entrust to bodily automatisms the values and categories they are most anxious to conserve*. They will know how well the past can be kept in mind by a habitual memory sedimented in the body.[5]

In making his case, Connerton emphasizes that to study the social formation of memory is to study those "acts of transfer that make remembering in common possible." He carefully looks at certain acts of transfer that are found in both traditional and modern societies. He singles out commemorative ceremonies and bodily practices as "acts of transfer of crucial importance." These are not the only constituents of communal memory, he notes, observing that informal narrative histories form a basic activity of everyday life and are a feature of all social memory. But he focuses on commemorative ceremonies and bodily practices because it is the study of these, he argues, that leads us to see that images and knowledge of the past are conveyed and sustained by (more or less ritual) performances.[6]

Christianity stands or falls with the tie that connects it to its historical origin, he argues. It originated in a definite historical moment and at all subsequent points in its history it "explicitly and elaborately refers back to that moment." Christianity is not primarily an exposition of an abstract doctrine or the recapitulation of a myth. It teaches that God has intervened in history and that the vocation of the Christian is to remember and commemorate the history of that intervention. And he contends that there's not a prayer or an act of devotion that doesn't refer back directly or indirectly to the historical Christ.[7]

We preserve versions of the past by words and images but we also preserve the past in our bodies. Many forms of "habitual skilled remembering" illustrate a keeping of the past in mind that, without advertising its origin, nevertheless re-enacts the past in our present conduct. "In habitual memory the past is . . . sedimented in the body," he contends.

Habits are more than technical abilities, Connerton argues. When we think of habitual behavior like walking, swimming, typewriting, we think of habits as technical skills with varying degrees of complexity. But the word habit gives us a way of referring to the kind of activity in which a cluster of features are collected together to form a practice: "an activity which is acquired in the sense that it is influenced by previous activity; which is ready for overt manifestation; and which remains operative in some subdued way even when it is not the obviously dominant activity." A habit, he suggests, is "a knowledge and a remembering in the hands and in the body; and in the cultivation of habit it is our body which 'understands.'"[8]

Changes in Mennonite Lived Religion: Congregational Portrait

The contributors to a recent book entitled *Lived Religion in America* use an approach they call "lived religion," a shorthand phrase that has long been current in the French tradition of the sociology of religion but is relatively novel in the American context. One of the goals of the authors' study was to encourage reflection on "practice" as the center or focus of the Christian life.[9] They suggest that while we know a great deal about the history of theology, we know next-to-nothing about religion as practiced and little about the everyday thinking and doing of lay men and women.[10]

No single key unlocks the door to lived religion, editor David Hall contends, though one term—*practice*—does have particular importance. He struggles to give it a definition. Perhaps "culture in action," he suggests.[11] "Religion" is best approached, say the authors, by meeting men and women in their daily tasks and in all the spaces of their experience. They invite a redirection of religious scholarship away from traditional constructs of "Protestantism," "Catholicism," and away from the denominational focus toward a study of how particular people in particular places and times live with the religious idioms available to them in culture.[12]

What might some of the change in practices look like in one particular Mennonite congregation that I'm familiar with? Profiling change represented in one congregation won't give us a comprehensive sense of changes underway in the broader faith community but it will provide several concrete illustrations for our further conversation. The congregational portrait that follows is not meant to be a scientifically representative study of changing trends in Mennonite lived religion at large. It simply gives a sampling of changing practices over several generations currently represented in one congregation.

The congregation I've chosen to profile is a relatively affluent, multiple-staffed congregation many of whose members are associated with Eastern Mennonite University in Harrisonburg, Virginia. This congregation has a sizable population of older adults, most of whom were raised in Mennonite homes. It also has a burgeoning population of middle-aged and younger adults who were also raised in Mennonite homes and are currently raising their children in the Mennonite church context.

My purpose in examining the faith-related practices of members of one congregation was to contrast the practices of three to four generations of Mennonites and in so doing, illustrate how the frequency and reported significance of those practices have changed over time. I developed a questionnaire that listed 20 core practices that have been a vital part of Mennonite family life and 16 practices that have been a vital part of church life (see below). I asked 20 to 25 persons of my parents' generation (60-85 years of age) how frequently they engaged in these practices in their childhood and then how frequently they engaged in these practices with their own children. I also asked how significant they felt these practices were to their family and church life. I asked 20 to 25 persons of my generation (30-50 years of age) the same two sets of questions related to the same lists of practices: frequency and perceived significance as it relates to their childhood and now to life with their own children both at home and at church.

I asked whether respondents were associated with the Mennonite church in their childhood and whether they are currently members of a Mennonite church to ascertain whether their engagement in practices as children and as they raised their children was likely to have been in a Mennonite community context.

I was hoping to receive at least 15 questionnaires in each age group that were usable according to my criteria and was pleased to receive 16 in each age group which were appropriate for further analysis. All of the 32 respondents were raised in Mennonite homes and churches and raised or are raising their children in Mennonite homes and churches.

Overall, the frequency comparisons proved to be more interesting than those related to significance. There are, however, observable changes in the perceived significance of the practices which appear to correlate with the frequency findings.

My hypothesis for the study was that there are certain observable core family and church-based practices which are regularly engaged in by persons across three to four generations represented in the sample. I also anticipated that there would be a decline in the frequency of many core practices particularly among those parents currently raising their children. I asked the significance questions hoping to find some meaningful correlation between the way practices were regarded and the frequency of their occurrence, anticipating that decreasing regard for the practices will likely be confirmed by a declining frequency of those practices.

There was strong confirmation overall that the home and church-based practices selected for testing are practices that have been engaged in across the three to four generations, at least on a weekly or occasional basis. And there was strong confirmation that, though the frequency rates have changed, many of these practices have played a significant role in family and church life throughout the time covered in this study.

Below are the practices I identified for study.

Family Based Practices

Family worship
Mealtime prayer
Family meals
Family singing
Bedtime prayers
Family service activity
Hospitality to others
Parents quoting Scripture for guiding children
Parents telling or reading Bible stories
Conversations about faith within family
Money given to church-related efforts
Meals with persons of other races or socio-economic levels
References to being "separate from the world"
Simplicity in attire emphasized
Modeling of forgiveness and reconciliation
Sunday as day of rest
Support for MCC (Mennonite Central Committee relief/development agency) or mission work expressed
Frugality in lifestyle modeled
Peaceful alternatives to war taught

Church-Based Practices

Attendance of church functions
Communion
Baptisms
Footwashing
Person's invited to publicly testify
Sunday school participation
Small Group participation
Women involved in leadership

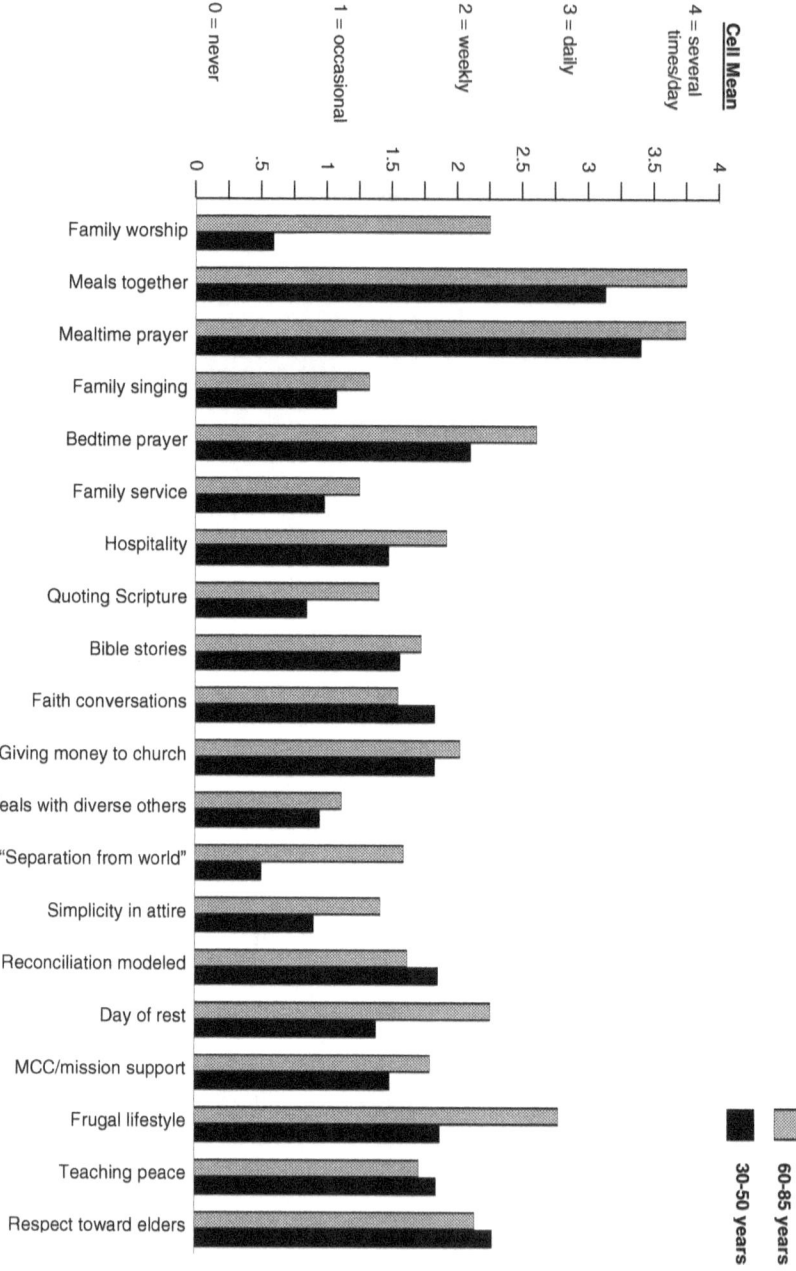

FIGURE 1
Frequency of Family Practices compared by generation: how the earliest and most recent generations were raised
Cell Bar Chart, Split by: Generation

Scripture memorization modeled
Group Bible Study for discernment about how to live
Worshiping with persons of other races and socio-economic levels
Expectations that sex belongs only in marriage expressed
Singing together
Opportunity for public confession of sin
Public story-telling of "Mennonite stories"
Public story-telling about heroic "peace-makers"

Figure 1 (opposite page) is helpful in mapping the changes in frequency of a given practice from the earliest generation represented in our study to what is currently the situation with parents now raising their children. The contrast is between the frequency of practices in the older group's childhood homes in the 1920s-40s and the frequency of practices in the homes of those currently raising their children.

Figure 1 confirms that the overall trend in home-based practices did move in the direction I anticipated, toward less frequent engagement in the selected practices. All but four of the practices show a lower frequency rate in present practice. Eight of those practices show a remarkably lower frequency rate. The most dramatic decline in frequency is in family home-based worship, moving from more frequent than weekly in the childhood homes of the older group to midway between occasional and never among parents currently raising children. The second most dramatic decline in frequency of home-based practices is in reference to being separate from the world. Frugality in lifestyle is the third most dramatic decline, moving from being modeled on a daily basis to a weekly basis.

The decline in meals together moved from several times daily toward a daily average. Bedtime prayers are more likely to be weekly now than daily. Scripture is now only occasionally quoted for guidance in everyday life rather than being used on a weekly basis. Emphasis on simplicity in attire also declined. Sunday is now urged as a rest day more occasionally than weekly.

It is also intriguing to consider those practices which appear to buck the trend. Four practices show a higher frequency rate among parents currently raising children—though the increase is very slight. Family conversations about faith moved slightly closer to weekly. The modeling of forgiveness and reconciliation seems slightly higher as does teaching

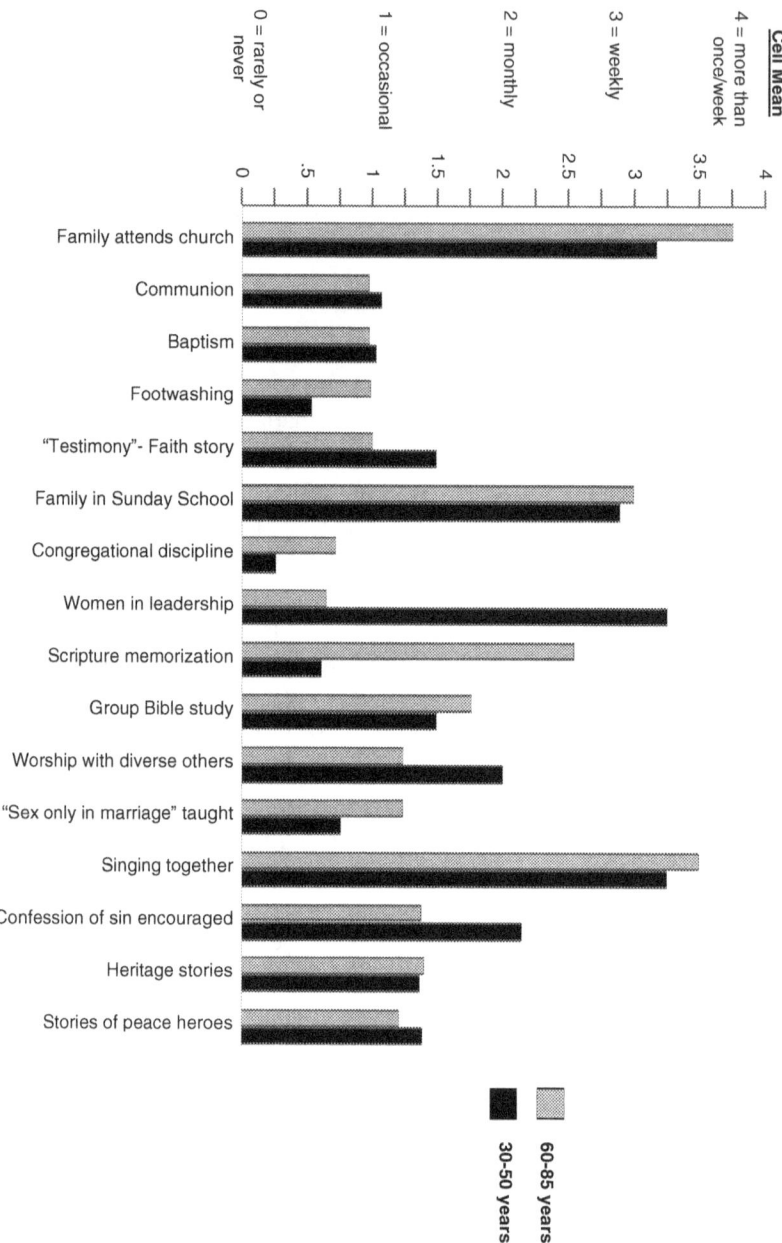

FIGURE 2
Frequency of Church Practices compared by generation:
how the earliest and most recent generations encounter church practices
Cell Bar Chart, Split by: Generation

about peaceful alternatives to conflict, both moving slightly closer to weekly. And finally, there appears to be a slight increase in respectful address of elders.

The most notable drop off in frequency of practices was by the middle-aged group in raising their own children. Within this group, most of the decline in the frequency of core practices over the last three-four generations has occurred among those currently raising their children. While there has been a slight decline in the frequency between childhood homes and raising children by the older group, the most dramatic change comes between the childhood homes of the middle-aged parents and how those parents are currently raising their children.

The trend toward lower frequency of selected practices is weaker in church-based practices (Figure 2, opposite page). Only nine of 16 practices showed some decline in frequency with much of that decline being only minimal. The most dramatic decline was Scripture memorization. Group Bible study declined, as did teaching about sex in marriage.

Seven of the practices selected have increased in frequency. Testifying or sharing faith experiences shows a remarkable increase. Women in leadership has jumped dramatically. Also showing a remarkable increase is worship that connects members with persons of other races and economic levels. A similar increase is confession of sin, which would likely reflect the increased use of liturgical resources that make confession of sin a regular part of the worship sequence.

The significance ratings almost all fall within the undecided to positive to very positive range. I had anticipated more negative readings. It may be that another way of setting up the contrast would have achieved a broader range of perspectives. We can still observe some interesting features, however.

The feature on significance of home-based practices that I found most interesting was the contrast between the significance indicated by the older group in how they raised their children and the significance indicated by the middle-aged group in how they regard the way they were raised. While both groups' assessment remains in the positive or very positive range, the middle-aged group has less positive regard for the practices prevalent in their childhood home than those from the generation who raised them have about practices used in raising their children. While the differences are not large, in nearly every practice the middle-aged group regarded the practices used in their childhood as less positive than the older group's assessment of the practices they used in raising children who would now be middle-aged. Singing remained the same, and frugality of lifestyle, interestingly enough, is slightly more positively regarded by the middle-aged generation, but all others show some decline in significance. It appears that there may be some meaningful correlation between the lowered significance assessment on the part of the middle-aged group and the decline in frequency of many home-based practices.

The middle-aged group was also more ambivalent about the church-based practices in their childhood but showed an increased positive regard for the significance of these same practices as they now raise their children.

The differences between how the older and middle-aged groups regard the church practices are really quite minimal overall. But an intriguing aspect worth noting is that the middle-aged group are reporting a higher positive regard in at least six of the items than did the older generation. Those items are practicing footwashing, testifying or sharing faith experiences (the biggest increase), disciplining a wayward member, women's involvement in leadership, confession of sin, and hearing Mennonite heritage stories.

Congregational Profile Summarized

Some tentative conclusions that appear warranted by this analysis could be summarized. In general, those home-based practices selected for inclusion in this study are less positively regarded than they were two and three generations ago and are being engaged in less frequently than they were in the previous two generations. Most notable in their decline in frequency are family based worship experiences, meals together, bedtime prayers, Scripture used as a normal part of daily parental guidance, talk about being "separate from the world," emphasis on simplicity of attire and lifestyle, as well as Sunday urged as a day of rest. The few exceptions to the decline in frequency appear to include practices that show a keener awareness of the need for open, honest conversation about faith and for efforts at reconciliation, peacemaking and respectful treatment of elders. They may reflect a higher regard for relational dynamics, a greater willingness to listen and relate across our differences, and some embarrassment about conflicts in a sectarian past.

Overall, both groups still hold relatively high positive regard for most practices at home and at church. There is however, some movement across the board by the middle-aged group toward greater ambivalence than the older group about the positive significance of home-based practices. This contrasts, however, with some higher positive regard for a variety of church-based practices by the middle-aged group which suggests there may be a recovery or revitalization at work in worship and the corporate life of this church. Those home-based practices regarding which the middle-aged group felt the most ambivalence in relation to their own childhood homes were family worship, emphasis on separation from the world, and valuing simple attire. They continue to be most ambivalent ("undecided," the middle response between negative and positive) about those three in raising their own children.

Overall, the findings of the study confirmed my hunches about the declining frequency of a variety of faith-based practices in at least one congregation. One would have to look deeper and broader to provide a reliable analysis of factors contributing to the decline in many practices and the increase in frequency and significance of others. I'm not surprised by the lowered frequency and regard for separation talk and emphasis on simplicity and frugality. I anticipated the decline in family worship/prayer/Scripture use/Sunday practices though I am somewhat mystified about why the worship piece has declined so precipitously. It may suggest a number of things, including negative experiences with family worship, or discomfort with personal expressions of faith and an inability to integrate them in an authentic way into everyday life. The higher frequency and positive regard for a variety of home and church-based practices suggest some positive momentum toward revitalization of life-giving practices in that church.

Conclusion

If human communities want to thrive, according to Alasdair MacIntyre, we must give attention to the tradition of the virtues and the narratives and practices that sustain our community life together. Our thriving depends on our traditions and our traditions are sustained and strengthened by the exercise of the relevant virtues.[13]

What faith-based daily and regular practices will replenish the wellspring of tacit, tradition-based knowledge out of which can flow a quality of life that will honor God and equip us and our children to be truthful, courageous, just and loving? In addition, how can we critically and imaginatively engage in those practices so they serve to free rather than oppress our flourishing? This we will continue to explore in subsequent chapters.

Chapter 2

ANABAPTIST PERSPECTIVES ON "KNOWING"

David Tracy suggests that we rely on the historical process of public exposure and discourse to help with discerning what may become a "classic" expression of meaning that stands the test of time. In examining the particular classical genius of each tradition we may arrive at a more universal understanding of truth. Allowing one's own particularity to be tested in public is not with a view to losing the genius of that particularity, but in order, potentially, to deepen it and to allow it to inform others' traditions.[1]

Tracy appropriated Hans Georg Gadamer's idea of the "classic." A classic is an expression of the human spirit, born of a particular context and time. It opens up and focuses some dimension of experience with such "engaging power and depth that persons from other times and contexts find themselves addressed, expanded, and informed by it." For Tracy, the work of practical theology is to bring Christian classics into critical correlation with interpretations of present situations that need to be addressed. His correlational approach speaks to the postmodern experience of religious pluralism. It does this by "reasserting the integrity of particular religious traditions as mediating relatedness to the Ultimate."[2]

This chapter will be an examination of Anabaptist "classic" distinctives that are helpful as we reflect on our ways of knowing and their relevance for theorizing about tradition-based, critical education. It will identify distinctive Anabaptist theological affirmations and point toward their educational implications. And later, these confessional distinctives will be brought into conversation with the others invited to the table to examine their broader implications for educational theory and strategy.

Anabaptist Theology

Anabaptist scholar Robert Friedmann discusses the frequent question of whether the Anabaptists had a theology or whether it was simply the case that they were theologically unsophisticated either through choice or through circumstance. His conclusion was that Anabaptism is theological in the same sense that the Synoptics are theological, not in a formal sense but in the sense of an implicit theological awareness and coherence. A movement of such strength, he suggests, would be unthinkable without a definite theological foundation, which is implied in all the doings and witnessing of the Anabaptists.[3]

Mennonite theologian Thomas Finger argues that an Anabaptist constructive theology can only be done "in Anabaptist perspective" because it isn't possible to develop a coherent constructive theology from the historical, descriptive material available from the early Anabaptists unless one selects among its elements by means of criteria derived elsewhere. Normative criteria don't emerge unambiguously from within the narrative. Early Anabaptism when historically understood, can't provide the full content nor the clear norms needed for a contemporary constructive theology, he suggests, but can provide a perspective from which it can be done.[4]

The early Anabaptists themselves pointed toward a historical source to which they sought to be faithful—the New Testament church, which itself pointed for its source to the "grace of God actualized through Jesus' life, death, and resurrection." And it was to Scripture that they looked for the overarching narrative of God's activities in the world, so Scripture was understood by early Anabaptists to point to the ultimate theological norm, "with the focal point being Jesus' life, death, and resurrection."[5]

Descriptive Overview of the Anabaptists

There are broad characterizations that are generally used to describe what is often referred to as the "radical reformation." The Anabaptists of the sixteenth century were named such because they repudiated their own infant baptism and were rebaptized as adult believers, which was at that time, an act of civil disobedience. They came to reject the medieval synthesis of Constantinian Christendom and sacramentalism and called people to radical discipleship, to patterning their lives on the radical ethic of Jesus as demonstrated in "the way of the cross." Rather than church structure or doctrine being paramount in their minds, their life together in gatherings of committed followers of Jesus was modeled on what they understood to be the character of the early church. They were missionary in their zeal, and passionately committed even amid widespread persecution by Protestants and Catholics. While refusing to bear arms to defend their faith or swear oaths they encouraged obedience of legitimate government. Their concerns about the separation of church and state, about freedom of conscience and about voluntary church membership have continued to germinate and bear fruit in many other contexts.

Anabaptism took shape in the sixteenth century within the broader contours of the Protestant Reformation. It was a movement of religious and social reform deeply committed to the careful study of Scripture by laity and clergy alike and convinced of the Scripture's authority and relevance in all matters of faith and daily life. In their insistence that the Bible was the final arbiter of religious debate, argues historian John Roth, the Anabaptists didn't differ significantly from other Protestant reformers. Rather, they parted company with the magisterial reformers on the question of how the truths of Scripture were to be interpreted and applied.[6]

Because Anabaptism was a lay and not a clerical movement, every believer was in essence, a priest and a minister, argues historian Walter Klaassen. While that view was central to the Reformation in Wittenberg, Zurich, Geneva, and Canterbury from the beginning, it was taken further by Anabaptists than by anyone else. And since every believer was a minister, every believer had to be equipped to witness. A believer could not be a witness without a profound sense of being a believer by personal choice, by baptism, by Bible study, by congregational process. This was the secret of Anabaptism's growth.[7]

Despite many shared convictions, which we will by and large focus on in this chapter, it is also necessary to acknowledge the great diversity present both in the early Anabaptist movement and among the descendants of that movement. "Ask twenty Anabaptists what they believe and you will probably get twenty different answers," suggested Mennonite theologian Marlin Miller. This diversity, he said, stems from differences among the earliest Anabaptists, from the varied countries that played host to the Anabaptists before they moved to North America, and from recent developments on the American scene. Also complicating any attempt to identify what Anabaptist-Mennonites believe is the reality that Mennonites and other Anabaptist groups have usually stressed *living* the faith, giving more weight to Christian practice than to standardized doctrinal formulations.[8]

Many varied attempts have been made over the years to interpret the meaning of the radical reformation for a new generation of would-be Anabaptists. One of the most significant in this century was the publication in 1944 of *The Anabaptist Vision*, by Harold S. Bender, historian, theologian, church administrator and one of the most visible Mennonite leaders of his day. The essay was originally presented as an address in 1943 at Columbia University to the American Society of Church History of which Bender was then president. It laid out Bender's interpretation of Anabaptist beginnings in the sixteenth century and the distinctive genius of the Anabaptist movement.

According to Bender, the Anabaptists' understanding of the gospel differed from their Catholic and Protestant counterparts in three important ways: 1) they viewed the church as a voluntary fellowship rooted in the local gathering of believers; 2) they insisted that true faith must find tangible expression in daily discipleship; and 3) they held to an ethic of love and forgiveness, modeled on the life of Christ, which extended even to the enemy.[9] This vision profoundly shaped the identity of the Mennonite church during the last half of the twentieth century. For more than fifty years, suggests Roth, Bender's Anabaptist Vision has served as a symbolic theological anchor within the Mennonite church. In the era following WWII, as Mennonites became increasingly acculturated into the mainstream culture, Bender's summary of Anabaptism's essential features became a lodestar for leaders throughout the church.[10]

In the decades following Bender's article, however, Anabaptist scholarship pursued significant new developments.[11] A field of study that had been largely dominated by theologians has grown to include social historians who looked more closely into the economic and political context within which the Anabaptist movement began. What appeared in Bender's and his contemporaries' rendering of an Anabaptism that provided "a normative standard against which other sixteenth, as well as twentieth-century expressions of faith might be judged, has given way to a view of Anabaptism whose boundaries were much more fluid and dynamic than earlier scholars were willing to concede."[12]

After acknowledging the diversity present among the earliest Anabaptists and their descendants, Miller suggested that all Anabaptists, nevertheless, share a number of Christian convictions about belief and practice:

- Believing in Jesus as Son of God and Savior can never be separated from following him in everyday behavior.
- Baptism is reserved for those who confess their faith in Jesus Christ and commit themselves to live as his disciples.
- The Scriptures, not creeds or traditions, provide the primary standard for faith and life.
- God's saving grace in Christ results not only in newness of life for the individual but also creates and sustains the church, a community called to radical discipleship and service.
- Discipleship in the new community obligates members to invite unbelievers to accept the Christian faith, love the enemy, reject war and violence, and seek peace in the church and in the world.[13]

Miller remarks that whatever their deficiencies, the Anabaptists remind us that the church must get on with the "radical, risky business of being Christ's disciples."[14] And yet it is readily apparent to any astute observer that the Anabaptism of the sixteenth century can't simply be transplanted to the twenty-first century. Mennonites, at least in North America, are not being persecuted as the Anabaptists were. We live in a remarkably different world with some similar challenges and many that appear very dissimilar.

What elements of the tradition are to be preserved today, asks Klaassen, if we are to understand ourselves to be a part of it? Not everything in the tradition was good. Which aspects can be considered vital and essential for today and which not? We should have the courage of the Old Testament writers, he asserts, who did not hesitate to blame their ancestors for unfaithfulness, even as they praised them for having faith.[15]

Anabaptist Distinctives Relevant to Education

Of the many varied features that are generally acknowledged to characterize the Anabaptist legacy, there are several that I will argue are especially helpful for educational theory and strategy relevant to the times in which we live. It is the responsibility of every new generation of educational theorists to review the traditions and cultural legacies of the past, especially those of which one is steward by virtue of proximity and in-depth acquaintance, to critically retrieve those aspects which can provide relevant criteria for guiding education in this time. What is retrieved and highlighted will likely vary in each generation, because of the different needs of each era. It is an awe inspiring opportunity to stand on the shoulders of those who have gone before and gather into a new coherent whole gleanings from the stories of their commitments, failures, passions, sacrifices and extravagant gestures of faithful living.

I will gather gleanings from the Anabaptist legacy which I deem particularly helpful for reflecting on how we come to know, into three primary clusters. The first cluster for critical retrieval will include the meaning and relevance of the Anabaptist emphasis on discipleship, particularly as it relates to "indwelling" the story of Jesus, patterning our lives on Jesus' life, and joining ethical and epistemological dimensions of experience which lead toward deeper knowing.

The second cluster of characteristics for critical retrieval will include what has been referred to as "the hermeneutical community," or the interpreting community, widely acknowledged as a significant contribution of the Anabaptists. Particularly relevant to our discussion will be the examination of what it means to discern truth within the community and how traditional root metaphors, stories and practices become powerfully formative as they interact with current community experience.

The third cluster of gleanings will come from an Anabaptist ecclesiology or understanding of church. What might it mean educationally to think in terms of a tradition-based, prophetic church which nurtures its own members in a distinctive community while working to resource and transform the larger culture? How might cultural practices that "embody" religious traditions as well as critique them, serve an educational purpose? And what might it take to enable a deep participatory knowing nourished by tradition, communal experience, and social responsibility?

Discipleship: Patterning Our Lives on Jesus Christ

There is widespread agreement among Anabaptist scholars that discipleship was one of the central concepts of Anabaptist faith and theology. In Harold Bender's classic essay, *The Anabaptist Vision*, he states that

> First and fundamental in the Anabaptist vision was the conception of the essence of Christianity as discipleship. It ... meant the transformation of the entire way of life ... so that it should be fashioned after the teachings and example of Christ. The Anabaptists could not understand a Christianity which made regeneration, holiness, and love primarily a matter of intellect, of doctrinal belief, or of subjective 'experience' rather than one of the transformation of life.[16]

J. Lawrence Burkholder, Mennonite philosopher, says that the central question for the early Anabaptists was: "What does it mean to follow Christ? Or, what does it mean to submit life in its totality to the claims of the kingdom of God?"[17] Furthermore, he asserted, "The uniqueness of Anabaptism lies in its conviction that Christianity is much more than reflection upon Christ as the divine Being who invaded time, and it is more than the appropriation of benefits of the divine drama of the cross. Christianity is the concrete and realistic 'imitation' of Christ's life and work in the context of the kingdom of God."

Menno Simons, the sixteenth-century Dutch Anabaptist leader, chose 1 Corinthians 3:11 as a key verse and theological motto: "For no one can lay any foundation other than the one that has been laid; that foundation is Jesus Christ." Over time, this foundation became the basis for the Anabaptists' growing conviction that the life, death, and resurrection of Jesus Christ must be central for understanding salvation, the church, Christian ethics, and eschatology. Marlin Miller argues that the "Anabaptists like to stress that Jesus is both the Son of God by whom we are saved through faith, and the Lord who has exemplified in his earthly life and ministry the way Christians are called to live in this world. This emphasis on Jesus Christ as both Savior and Lord has usually included efforts to interpret his saving work in terms that provide the basis for both salvation and ethics."[18]

Sixteenth-century Anabaptist understandings of Christ were generally compatible with orthodox understandings, suggests Miller. They affirmed both the divinity and humanity of Jesus Christ and that salvation comes through his atoning death on the cross. However, in describing these affirmations they usually described them using biblical categories, making little constructive use of the traditional dogmatic vocabulary. Their preference for biblical terms, writes Miller, has had both positive and problematic consequences for Mennonite theology and ethics since the sixteenth century.

On the positive side, he said, this preference contributed to the Anabaptist and Mennonite teaching about Jesus as the "model and example for believers." While affirming Jesus' divinity they emphasized his humanity, teaching, and actions. While teaching his atoning work on the cross, they emphasized "Jesus' way of the cross as the model for Christian discipleship."[19]

Finger affirms the same distinctives about an Anabaptist understanding of Christ. The major Anabaptist emphasis was not on Christ's "nature" or "person," but "on the function of Jesus as model and example."[20] A study of Anabaptist-Mennonite confessions reveals that their primary emphasis is on following the teachings and example of Jesus.[21]

Many so-called "high Christologies" tend to omit mention of Jesus' commands, not making his authority concrete enough. Jesus functions for Mennonites as "one to be followed in concrete discipleship, not only as an object of worship or an ultimate salvific agent."[22]

Miller observes then that the pattern for a life of discipleship is "the perfect humanity of Jesus Christ." This means that the life, teachings, and cross of Jesus Christ constitute the defining "pattern for shaping the Christian's life in the world." [23]

When Jesus' teaching and example are made central, it follows then that the faithful life won't be understood primarily as giving assent to correct doctrinal beliefs, even though right teaching will be important. Nor will the life of faith be characterized primarily by "an inner attitude abstracted from any visible expression," although an attitude of trust will be essential. "The life of faith is rather understood primarily in terms of a commitment to 'following Jesus in life.'"[24]

The Anabaptists couldn't accept Luther's distinction between "public" and "private" person, or between secular and sacred vocations, due to commitment to follow Jesus in all of life, in the church and in their occupations, in the family and in relation to governments. They understood Jesus' teaching in the Sermon on the Mount as well as Paul's ethical admonitions as given and intended to shape Christian conduct.[25]

If Jesus is not a model for conduct, argues John Howard Yoder, the theological significance of his humanity may be diminished: "What becomes of the meaning of incarnation if Jesus is not normative man?"[26] Jesus reveals the true nature and vocation of human beings.

The 1995 *Confession of Faith in a Mennonite Perspective* includes eight articles on themes common to the faith of the wider Christian church such as the Trinity, Scripture, Creation, Sin and Salvation. The *Confession* includes eight articles on the church and its practices. And the third set of eight deals with discipleship and the Christian life. The article that leads off the discipleship section of the *Confession* affirms that

> We believe that Jesus Christ calls us to take up our cross and follow him. Through the gift of God's saving grace, we are empowered to be disciples of Jesus, filled with his Spirit, following his teachings and his path through suffering to new life. As by faith we walk in Christ's way, we are being transformed into his image. We become conformed to Christ, faithful to the will of God, and separated from the evil in the world. . . .
>
> In all areas of life, we are called to be Jesus' disciples. Jesus is our example, especially in his suffering for the right without retaliation, in his love for enemies, and in his forgiveness of those who persecuted him. Yet, as we follow Jesus, we look not only to the cross, but through the cross, to the joy of the resurrection.[27]

Clearly, within the Anabaptist tradition, modeling one's life on the life of Jesus occupies a central place. This concept has far ranging educational implications.

What does it mean to identify so closely with someone that one's life is shaped by that life? What does it mean to "indwell" the Jesus story bodily, embodying that story and the Spirit of Jesus in ways that transform one's life and spirit?[28] What would it mean to be so immersed in scriptural narrative that its language and metaphors become the primary shapers of our imagination and practices?

It is very evident from their writings that the Anabaptists formed much of their thinking and speaking from the Scriptures. Willard Swartley suggests that despite their diverse origins and character, the Anabaptists were convinced that Scripture is true and powerful—"able to demolish strongholds and perform the work of regeneration in the believer's life." Any cursory reading in primary sources, he says, leaves this overwhelming impression. This conviction about the Scriptures sustained them amid persecution and suffering, especially for practicing baptism on confession of faith and for eschewing the use of the sword.[29]

Swartley cites a study that points out an interesting correlation between George Lindbeck's "intratextual" proposal and Menno Simon's use of Scripture. He observes that it is clear that Menno "understood himself and his experience through or by means of the Scripture." Menno doesn't seek to understand the text on the basis of his experience, but he "locates and situates himself in the story and the claims of those texts to understand himself."

Swartley observes that the extent to which the Anabaptist writers "steeped themselves in Scripture is overwhelming." He quotes historian John C. Wenger who speaks of the biblicism of the Anabaptists. "Amazing is not too strong a word," he said, "for the fact is that untrained lay brethren often proved more than a match for the Roman Catholic doctors of theology who interrogated them." Because they steeped themselves in Scripture to derive self-understanding, guidance, and empowerment, the text lived in them; and they lived in the text.[30]

Miller observed that the Anabaptists approach to Bible study in which they made the church body the locus for biblical interpretation nurtured a broadly based love of and familiarity with the Bible among them. Reading the Bible in the context of a congregation of believers means a foundational commitment to have our theology and church life shaped by the biblical vision rather than trying to adjust the Bible to a theology and church life formed primarily by other sources.[31]

This immersion in Scripture grew out of desire to live faithful lives of discipleship. The desire to know the Scriptures so well that one's life is conformed to the language, metaphors, practices and vision of Scripture was an all consuming passion for the Anabaptists. Becoming a disciple of Christ meant "indwelling" the story and the reality of Christ to such an extent that one would come to know Christ and become like Christ.

A classic Anabaptist affirmation, stated by Hans Denck, an early Anabaptist leader reads, "No one can truly know (Christ) unless he follow him in life, and no one may follow him unless he has first known him."[32] Mennonite historian Irvin B. Horst described this as an epistemological principle and a distinctive emphasis within the sixteenth century on the nature and method of knowing.[33]

Finger observes that in Christian tradition, mystics have sometimes emphasized a personal relationship with Jesus that appears unrelated to following his commands. Activists have sometimes emphasized following his commands without regard to a personal relationship. In the Anabaptist approach, however, knowing and doing are inseparably intertwined. "Only those who know Jesus as the one who calls and sustains them can really do his commands. Yet one can know him more fully and intimately only by walking in his way."[34]

Ted Koontz, professor of ethics and peace studies, argues that "the early Anabaptists were motivated first and foremost by encounters with God, encounters which transformed them primarily 'from the inside out.'" He contends that the Anabaptist martyrs didn't choose to face suffering simply because they read the New Testament and were intellectually convinced that they should follow Jesus and take up the cross. What led them to the kinds of lives they lived wasn't a literal reading of the text and a decision to follow the texts. Rather, what changed them was an encounter with God.[35]

The 1995 *Confession of Faith in a Mennonite Perspective* has added an article on "Christian Spirituality," which appears to be an acknowledgment of the recent recognition that too many earlier interpretations of Anabaptism neglected to recognize the extent to which a relationship with Jesus Christ undergirded ethical behavior. It says, "We draw the life of the Spirit from Jesus Christ, just as a branch draws life from the vine. Severed from the vine, the power of the Spirit cannot fill us. But as we make our home in Christ and Christ abides in us, we bear fruit and become his disciples."[36]

The educational implications of a tradition's central focus on discipleship are many. While examining the strengths of the tradition for critical retrieval, there will also need to be a critical look at who determines the meaning of discipleship. Who defines what should characterize discipleship? Mennonite theologian Lydia Harder reminds us that the traditional approach to biblical interpretation has contributed to making male discipleship normative for the meaning of the term, subsuming female experiences of discipleship. In Mennonite tradition this led to an understanding of discipleship that was largely associated with crossbearing, self-denial, obedience, and servanthood, characteristics that challenged the expectations of a patriarchal society for men, but affirmed what was already expected of women.[37]

With this critical concern in mind we will explore the possibilities for education that an emphasis on discipleship suggests. We will look at what it may mean to commit oneself to follow the "Jesus way," to "indwell" the Jesus story, "to abide in Christ." And we will look further at how discipleship functions as the arena where ethics and epistemology are joined, where "practicing" the Jesus life leads to a deeper knowing. We will also look at how discipleship is defined and who participates in the defining process.

Hermeneutical Community: Discerning Truth Communally

Designating the local congregation as the "locus of interpretation" was arguably the most important and distinctive Anabaptist contribution to sixteenth-century hermeneutics or biblical interpretation, argues Stuart Murray in his recent, exhaustive survey of Anabaptist hermeneutics. The community was "the focal point" of Anabaptist biblical interpretation, the context for every believer's engagement with Scripture, and the setting for their reliance on the Holy Spirit. Contemporary discussion about biblical interpretation has both recovered this emphasis and suggested important refinements and developments."[38]

The interpreting community for the Anabaptists, "was the congregation of believers meeting together around Scripture to learn how to live as disciples." Elements deemed essential for participation in the community of interpretation were "the participants' commitment to discipleship, the communal context, the authority of Scripture and the goal of application." Murray illustrates how all these elements have been reemphasized in the contemporary rediscovery of community-based interpretation.[39]

The Anabaptists offered a coherent and distinctive approach to biblical interpretation in the sixteenth century, Murray argues. The basic principles can be discovered from the writings of Anabaptist leaders and the practice of Anabaptist congregations. Six convictions characterized their approach:

- Scripture was sufficiently clear for all believers to be enfranchised as interpreters.
- Scripture must be interpreted in the light of Jesus Christ, its focal point.
- The New Testament must be accorded priority and the Old Testament interpreted in the light of the New.

- The Holy Spirit was the interpreter, whose guidance must be actively sought.
- Only those committed to discipleship and obedience to Scripture should expect such guidance.
- The congregation was the hermeneutic community where all believers could contribute to the interpretive process and where the Spirit's guidance was anticipated.

Although these principles were not consciously synthesized into an integrated system, they overlapped, refined and qualified each other.[40]

Murray suggests that the conviction that Scripture was clear enough for ordinary Christians to understand and apply without the assistance of education, philosophical or theological expertise, clerical guidance or ecclesiastical tradition, was in practice qualified by other convictions:

> Scripture was clear, they taught, when it was read communally and under the tuition of the Holy Spirit. Such clarity could not be expected, however, by individuals reading it alone or by those who neglected the Spirit's help. Anabaptists actively relied on the Holy Spirit as the interpreter who would lead believers into the truth and whose teaching was more helpful than education or theological expertise. And they located interpretation in a communal context, where the right of individual interpretation was safe-guarded but where the results of such interpretation were open to challenge and correction. Furthermore, this communal context must consist of those who were committed to discipleship. Scripture was clear only to those who approached it with a right attitude, with a commitment to obedience, rather than curiosity or merely intellectual questions.[41]

The question must be asked, however, whether interpretation of Scripture really worked this way in Anabaptist communities. To what extent were these principles implemented and adhered to? Was community discernment and life enhanced by following these principles of biblical interpretation?

Mennonite historian John Roth observes that over the past forty years the basic principles of Anabaptist biblical interpretation have been restated and amplified in numerous articles and monographs. These various efforts to capture the essence of Anabaptist hermeneutics have much to commend them, he says, and as "ideal type" summaries they provide useful analytical categories.⁴² But, speaking as a social historian, he asks whether such summaries may conceal as much as they reveal. He offers a short critique of traditional scholarly interpretation, highlighting the reality of Anabaptist diversity as an often fragmented movement characterized by deep hostility and divisions within and among various groups. He illustrates how among various groups, a shared set of interpretive principles did not yield a common mind on a whole set of theological questions, including such crucial matters as ecclesiology, child nurture, mutual aid, and missions. The general literature on Anabaptist approaches to biblical interpretation has tended to blur the diversity and even intramural hostility among Anabaptist groups.

Roth also asks whether these principles were ever actually implemented in the life of the congregations and communities they served. The point here, he said, is not to deny that the principle of the "hermeneutical community" found expression among the Anabaptists but to ask how the ideal actually worked itself out in practice? Among other things, Roth suggests that an insistence on "Anabaptist literalism" as a principle separating them from Catholics and Protestants overshadows the ways in which elements of tradition, creed, charisma, and the authority of office also shaped the Anabaptist reading of Scripture in decisive ways.⁴³

After acknowledging that the Anabaptist movement was clearly more diverse than the composite summary of interpretive principles would imply Roth asks what, if anything, was distinctively "Anabaptist" about their interpretation of Scripture. He suggests a new model for understanding Anabaptism—particularly as it coalesced during the last half of the sixteenth-century—and the place of interpretive principles within the movement. Using historian David Sabean's work on village culture, which challenges traditional scholarship's tendency to define community in structural, functional, or normative terms, he suggests that rather than describing the Anabaptist use of Scripture in fixed, normative hermeneutical principles, we describe them as "a series of arguments or debates into which participants were drawn precisely because they agreed on the importance of the issue being debated." The summary of Anabaptist hermeneutics compiled by the traditional historiography is helpful, he suggests, in that it points toward "a frame of reference within which discussions and disagreements regarding proper biblical exegesis took place."⁴⁴

While the ideal that Scripture should be interpreted by a gathered body of earnest Christians was and is a powerful concept, it is also inherently problematic, acknowledges Roth. In practice, it has raised a host of questions. What is the role of the trained expert? What prevents community-based interpretation from degenerating into a "least common denominator" approach to Scripture? How is authority to be legitimized? What is the place of charismatic leadership? How is tradition integrated into the active process of discernment? Who decides when consensus has been reached?

Despite all these fundamental tensions, the ideal of congregational involvement in the process of spiritual discernment has persisted, Roth observes, and it continues as a focus of debate, renewal, and even as a principle of unity. To the extent that various groups continued and continue to take these principles seriously by debating and discussing them, they are part of a shared conversation that can legitimately be described as Anabaptist. To define the Anabaptist use of Scripture in terms of tensions, argument, and debate does not negate the importance of the ideal. But it does suggest a more dynamic model for understanding biblical interpretation that drew the spiritual ancestors of the Mennonites into a common conversation, though not always a common mind.[45]

Roth appears to be affirming the role of tradition to suggest an ideal, frame the issues, and provide the root metaphors and core commitments in which a serious, shared conversation can meaningfully take place. What he describes resembles MacIntyre's definition of a living tradition as "an historically extended, socially embodied argument." What sustains and strengthens traditions? MacIntyre asks. What weakens and destroys them?[46] The argument, in this case, appears to be primarily about how to best interpret and apply the formative texts of a community.

Swartley observes that it is striking how much the distinctive features of an Anabaptist hermeneutic are "hot" topics in current hermeneutical discussions. The Anabaptist emphasis on congregational or community discernment as an essential part of interpretation has many resounding echoes in the current role of community in understanding and living the faith story. In addition the Anabaptist emphasis has a strong contribution to make in three contemporary arenas: against the reign of individualism; as correction to the chasm that has opened between scholars and lay people; and as antidote to postmodern emphasis on deconstruction.[47]

We must beware however, he cautions, that we don't claim too much from a movement that had its own internal problems, and whose approach to biblical study was defined by specific issues in the sixteenth century socio-political environment. Yet, neither should we discount their insight and contribution for we do gain insight from them for a whole array of issues.[48]

Harder makes some observations which must be brought into consideration for a critical retrieval of the Anabaptist model of interpretation, particularly as we reflect on its significance for an educational theory. She observes that while Mennonites have spoken of a "hermeneutics of obedience," some others, most notably Elizabeth Schüssler Fiorenza, argue for a "hermeneutics of suspicion." Though Mennonite obedience and feminist suspicion appear to be opposite approaches toward the Bible, both speak of authority in the context of communities of experience and practice which emphasize particular commitments and biases.[49] Biblical study that includes critical awareness must include study not only of the text but also of the interpreter and her/his commitments. A "hermeneutics of suspicion" which asks critical questions about how the social context has affected all interpretations must be held together with the commitments of the community to be faithful disciples. Harder demonstrates how both critical suspicion and the disciples' commitment to follow Christ may work together to help with discernment.[50]

Harder argues that the shaping of biblical interpretation by community experience within the context of communal discernment around Scripture can lead to biblical interpretation which transforms as well as biblical interpretation which justifies the status quo. The notion of a "hermeneutics of obedience" allows an ambiguity to remain in the definition of discipleship which can easily serve as a justification of oppressive practices as well as an expression of willingness to be shaped by God's Spirit. Obedience can be defined as including radical servanthood as well as submitting to conventional norms. Because the interaction between tradition and current experience can serve either to confirm presuppositions and prejudices already held or to challenge the community to new faithfulness, the question of *who participates* in the interpretive discourse is of vital importance.[51]

Harder points out that Mennonites have emphasized the importance of testing interpretations with others in the church congregation in light of their experience as disciples seeking God's will. So, within the interpreting community, the question of who we choose as our primary conversation partners is of critical importance. How the discernment takes place in the community may well depend on the dialogue partners who are invited to participate in the community discourse. By including males and females differently in its discerning community the Mennonite community has sometimes failed to apply their own commitment to include the full community in discerning the Scriptures.[52]

Murray also acknowledges that there are certain aspects of contemporary community-based interpretive models implemented by various individuals or movements which introduce elements that Anabaptists either rejected or failed to consider. These need to be considered lest it be thought that the Anabaptist model is adequate for contemporary interpretation. He acknowledges that while the Anabaptist model represented a radical alternative in the sixteenth century and its contemporary influence is highly significant, it has several limitations which must be addressed if the full potential of congregationally based interpretation is to be realized. He makes these suggestions for improving on the model:

- The community of interpreters need not exclude scholars. The relationship between scholars and local congregations will need to be worked out carefully, but their involvement has tremendous benefits.
- The community of interpreters need not exclude those who have studied Scripture in earlier generations. It's appropriate to be wary of according them too much authority, but earlier interpreters should be admitted into the present community of interpreters. This community can be seen as a transtemporal community.
- The community of interpreters should include persons from diverse social, political, and cultural backgrounds, lest a local congregation not recognize its own presuppositions and interpret Scripture in ways that merely confirm its existing convictions. The extension of the interpreting community to global dimensions holds out exciting possibilities.
- The community of interpreters may include a theological college, mission agencies, and so forth, provided they operate with genuine accountability and opportunities to test interpretations.[53]

Again, the educational implications to be drawn from the Anabaptist model of community-based biblical interpretation appear to be significant and worth further exploration. Of particular interest is the intentional bringing together of tradition and experience in the context of community discernment. This convergence includes the communal intention to seek the guidance of the Holy Spirit to understand those texts which are deemed authoritative and to gain insight in how to live, how to practice truth in daily life.

Also of interest is the suggestion that certain traditional community ideals provide the framework that makes it possible to have a shared conversation about how to live. While some traditional expectations have proven to be problematic in practice, the ideal of congregational involvement in spiritual discernment continues to focus debates, renewal and sometimes to forge unity among individuals and communities. The value of the tradition then, is for preserving authoritative texts and ideals, for communicating root metaphors and images that provide the imaginative context in which to carry on a shared and mutually engaging conversation?

Also intriguing for educational purposes is the interaction between "a hermeneutic of obedience" and "a hermeneutic of suspicion." The desire to be both a faithful disciple and to continually discern anew what it means to be faithful is the sort of creative tension that can provide a constructive conversation between the tradition and current experience. Critical for the educational process is the consideration of how the tradition is allowed to shape the community's practice and which experiences and voices will be allowed to enter the process. Murray's suggestion that the community of interpreters should include persons from "diverse social, political, and cultural backgrounds," lest a congregation not recognize its own presuppositions and simply confirm its own conventional interpretations will be critical to a vital educational process.

Ecclesiology: Tradition for Transformation

While many descendants of the early Anabaptists (Mennonite and others) largely withdrew into sectarian enclaves following decades of severe persecution and had a progressively diminishing impact on the culture at large, I think it would be fair to say the early Anabaptists saw their mission as one intended to transform culture. Evident in their writings and reported activities is the passion they felt to restore true Christianity.

Although the earliest Anabaptists seem to have hoped a reformation of the state churches could be achieved, they were soon disillusioned. They soon came to realize that reforming the state church system was inadequate and that forming believers churches was essential. They rejected Constantinianism or establishment Christianity and its symbols. They rejected "two-tier Christianity with different standards and callings for different Christians," and chose to apply New Testament standards to all Christians.[54] The renewal of the church, for the Anabaptists, included a critique of and dissent from any form of "establishment" Christendom that didn't involve voluntary commitment in defining a visible community. The renewal of the church had sociological and ethical implications as well as doctrinal and ecclesiastical significance.[55]

These Radical Reformers set out to reform the church in faith and practice, suggests Miller, as well as in structure. They didn't intentionally seek to impose this transformation on the larger society but they sought to renew the Christian community in a way which implied broader social change and potentially contributed to social transformation beyond their immediate congregations.[56]

Miller suggests that while the religious and civil authorities of the time viewed all sixteenth-century Radical Reformers "as social revolutionaries," this doesn't mean that all the Radicals set out to overthrow the established order or that they aimed to create a social revolution in the entire society. With the exception of the Munsterites, he argues, this was not their explicit concern. "They were concerned rather to follow Jesus in all of life, in the social and political as well as in the religious spheres. Out of this concern they insisted on religious freedom, developed a new economics, refused to take the oath, and did not participate in warfare. In the context of the sixteenth century, these beliefs, protests, and alternative practices in effect made Anabaptists 'socially revolutionary' in some sense."[57]

The calling of the church, argues Yoder, is to be "the conscience and the servant within human society," a role that is possible only when the church community resists the world's seductive pressures to live on the basis of values other than those directly exemplified by Jesus.[58] Yoder insists that the church's task of maintaining the integrity of its own life and witness isn't to be construed as a withdrawal from the world or a retreat from social issues to focus on private piety. "What needs to be seen is rather that the primary social structure through which the gospel works to change other structures is that of the Christian community." The church, he says, is called to contribute to the creation of structures more worthy of humankind. The church is called to make known to the powers, as no other proclaimer can do, the fulfillment of the mysterious purposes of God by means of Christ.[59]

To help the church in making known the transformative purposes of the gospel of Jesus Christ, Yoder's perspective on the role of tradition is helpful. Through the continuing process of communal moral discernment over time, he suggests, the Christian community develops a tradition that shapes its distinctive character in contrast to the values and norms of the world. Worship, he notes, "is the communal cultivation of an alternative construction of society and of history. That alternative construction of history is celebrated by telling the stories of Abraham (and Sarah and Isaac and Ishmael), of Mary and Joseph and Jesus and Mary, of Cross and Resurrection and Peter and Paul, of Peter of Cheltchitz and his Brothers, of George Fox and his Friends." Interestingly, Yoder here moves from the biblical stories to the stories of other reformers without marking a distinction. While he affirms the primacy of Scripture, he maintains the legitimacy and necessity of the church's response to changing historical situations in ways that are continuous with the New Testament.[60]

In his essay "The Authority of Tradition" Yoder writes,

> The clash is not tradition versus Scripture but faithful tradition versus irresponsible tradition. Only if we can with Jesus and Paul (and Francis, Savonarola, Milton, and others) denounce wrong traditioning, can we validly affirm the rest. Scripture comes on the scene not as a receptacle of all possible inspired truths, but rather as a witness to the historical baseline of the communities' origins and thereby as a link to the historicity of their Lord's past presence.

In other words, tradition will inevitably play a role in our moral deliberations, but it must meet the test of consistency with the historical roots of the community as definitively preserved in the New Testament.[61]

A community shaped by these principles will be engaged in a "modeling mission," embodying an "alternative order that anticipates God's will for the reconciliation of the world" and exercising influence disproportionate to its size or visible power:

Although immersed in this world, the church by her way of being represents the promise of another world, which is not somewhere else but is to come here. That promissory quality of the church's present distinctiveness is the making of peace, as the refusal to make war is her indispensable negative transcendence. . . . The church cultivates an alternative consciousness. Another view of what the world is like is kept alive by narration and celebration which fly in the face of some of the "apparent" lessons of "realism."[62]

Other noteworthy scholars, who are not explicitly Anabaptist, appear to affirm an Anabaptist understanding of church. The church, Richard Hays asserts, is a countercultural community of discipleship, and it is this community that is the primary addressee of God's imperatives. The community in its corporate life is called to embody an alternative order that stands as a sign of God's redemptive purposes in the world. And the coherence of the New Testament's ethical mandate will come into focus only when we understand that mandate in churchly terms, when we seek God's will not by asking first, "What should *I* do," but "What should *we* do?"[63]

Hays insists that without the embodiment of the Word, none of our other deliberations matters. We can do an excellent job of exegeting Scripture, looking for coherent themes that unify diverse New Testament Scriptures, and interpreting what relevance those Scriptures, from a world much different from our own, have for us. And yet the value of our exegesis, our interpretation, our theological and philosophical deliberations, will be tested by our capacity to produce persons and communities whose character is commensurate with Jesus Christ, and thereby pleasing to God.[64] It is the church, in the fullness of its life practices—not primarily its arguments—that draws others to consider the Christian faith.[65]

There are foundational implications for tradition-based education to be drawn from this discussion of Anabaptist understandings of church. I hear a persuasive case being made to affirm the value of a distinctive community that provides a context for cultivating transformative narratives, language and practices; a church that teaches people the language and practices that enable them to know Jesus as Lord.

Educational Implications

Many scholars, pastors and lay persons have lamented the increasing biblical illiteracy evident among church members and the population at large. There are many reasons for the loss of familiarity with biblical language, metaphors, and practices. One reason often suggested is the widespread assumption that only the academic expert is capable of deciphering the Scripture's complexities and apparent contradictions. In an intriguing way, there appears to be a resemblance between the clergy/ecclesial captivity of the Bible before the Protestant Reformation and the present situation in which we assume the Bible can only really be understood by scholars. We would do well to look again at the Anabaptist confidence that every believer is called to be an interpreter and within the Spirit led discerning community can come to understand the Scriptures as powerful and enlightening for faith and practice.

To rephrase an Anabaptist approach to Scripture, one could suggest that true understanding will only be given as persons enter into the world of the Scriptures through an act of imagination and love and live creatively and practically into the life they portray. As the Scriptures become "world-creating," their stories shape the primary world of believers—our practice, worship, and thought. And in turn, we come to understand the Scriptures and to know the truth of the gospel by practicing the gospel.

The Anabaptists provide us with a tradition whose educational commitment embodied an approach to knowing that was centered in the practices of the faith community. As a community of disciples, a community of interpreters, a counter cultural community, they have sought to cultivate formative practices that shape culture and character in the ways of Jesus.

What do we mean educationally when we talk about formative practices? Craig Dykstra and Dorothy Bass provide a helpful description of practices. Practices, they suggest, are shared activities through which persons come to know and through which perspectives on reality are formed. Practices are sites of learning that join ethical and epistemological dimensions.[66]

Practices, when woven together, provide a coherent and sustained way of life. They are concrete, physical and down-to-earth. They make ethical resources available and become the place where humans cooperate with God in caring for community. Practices are embodied thought.

They bear traditions which have taken shape over centuries as people respond to God's presence. They bear standards of excellence and are ancient and larger than we are. Practices are schools of virtue. We use them to express faith, but in turn they form us.[67]

The convergence of discipleship represented by the "following of Jesus in life" joined with the question about how we come to know God will form the core content of a constructive educational theory. Such a theory will highlight the educational implications of patterning our lives on Jesus as his disciples, of discerning truth communally, and of modeling an alternative community life that stands as a sign of God's redemptive purposes for the world.

But there are more conversational partners we want to hear from before weaving our theory into a multi-textured fabric.

Chapter 3

CLASSICAL *PAIDEIA* AND ANABAPTIST DISTINCTIVES

*H*ow might a classical *paideia* approach to education provide historical depth to an Anabaptist theory of tradition-based, critical education? In light of the current resurgence of interest in paideia, it appears that this ancient understanding may offer us wisdom that is ripe for re-appraisal and critical retrieval given our current educational challenges.

Paideia is an approach to education that is contextual, wholistic, culturally defined, and informed by the traditional narratives and practices of the community. A paideia approach focuses attention on communal shaping of character. It values the wisdom inherent within classical traditions and highlights "living ideals" which serve as guides for molding character.

Classical paideia provides an organic conception of society that emphasizes the social and historical fabric of human life, paying attention to the character of the community as a whole and the narratives and practices that shape the persons in that community. A paideia approach also anticipates that persons will be "in-formed" by virtue, which means that it takes the practices, the "habitus" of a way of life very seriously. Thus examining a paideia approach to education will be helpful for looking at the relationship between knowledge and character or, as the ancient Greeks would call it, the relationship between intellectual and moral virtues. For a brief overview of classical paideia, I largely rely on insights from Plato and early Christian thinkers, as summarized by Werner Jaeger, and expanded on by Edward Farley and David Kelsey.[1]

Classical Greek Notions of Paideia

Modern expressions like civilization, culture, tradition, literature or education don't really cover what the Greeks meant by paideia, writes Jaeger. Each is confined to one aspect of it. Paideia is understood to refer to the shaping of the Greek character and it describes the interaction between the historical process by which character is formed and the intellectual process by which an ideal of human personality is constructed.[2]

The word *paideia* at its first appearance meant "childrearing," but its meaning shifted gradually over the centuries until in the fourth century B.C. it came to be connected with the highest *areté* possible to humankind, with *areté* being used to denote the sum total of all ideal perfections of mind and body. The Greeks in and after the fourth century when the concept finally crystallized, used the word paideia to describe all the artistic forms and the intellectual and aesthetic achievements of their race, in fact the whole content of their tradition.[3]

Education in any human community (family, social class, profession, race, or state) is the direct expression of its "active awareness of a 'standard.'" The ancient Greeks were the first to recognize that education means deliberately molding human character in accordance with an ideal. The ideal of human character toward which they wished to educate each individual was not an empty abstract pattern existing outside time and space but the living ideal which had grown up in the soil of Greece and changed with the changing fortunes of the race. And literature was the expression of the process by which the Greek ideal shaped itself.[4]

The Greek creative genius conceived and attained a lofty educational ideal which Jaeger acclaims as superior to the more superficial artistic and intellectual brilliance of our own individualistic civilization. For them the shape and purpose of knowledge was compellingly social. Despite an increasing emphasis on individual personality (in the fifth century B.C.) it would have been unthinkable that education should be founded on anything but membership of the political community and training to serve the polis.[5]

While building on the old Greek paideia, Plato introduced new ways of relating to the traditional paideia even as he actively reshaped the paideia of his day.[6] The Greek educational ideals were always dominated by poetry, music, and rhythm. Plato declared education should begin with the education of the soul—namely, with "music." Music, in the comprehensive Greek sense is not simply a matter of sound and rhythm but also of the spoken word, the "logos." In Greek culture, poetry and music, "blest pair of sirens," were inseparable sisters. The same Greek word for music designates them both.[7] Poetry had an authoritative educational meaning and prestige natural to the Greek mind.

Poetry and music had always been the foundations of the education of the mind, and involved religious and moral education too. Jaeger notes that while we tend to feel certain that the enjoyment of a work of "art" has nothing to do with morality, the Greeks made a moral connection. If rational grounds for an argument were lacking, a line of Homer was always the best substitute. The authority of poetry in the ancient Greek world can only be compared with that of the Bible and the church fathers in certain particularly religious Christian centuries.[8]

The words for "education" and "child-rearing," originally almost identical in meaning, always remained closely akin. The main difference is that paideia came more and more to mean intellectual education, and child-rearing the pre-rational stage of a child's development. But Plato brought the two ideas together on a higher plane. He was the first to recognize that for intellectual education to succeed there are certain necessary preconditions related to climate and to growth. Despite its lofty intellectualism, Plato's idea of education or paideia was that it was like a slow vegetable growth, not in isolation, but in an environment appropriate to one's nature and disposition.[9] The state is necessary, he argued, not only as a legislative authority, but as the social atmosphere surrounding the individual. From his earliest infancy, every citizen must "drink in healthy air from these surroundings." There must be a state or a polis to assume the health of the social atmosphere if there is to be any education. And the culmination of the slow process of growth was the emergence of philosophers who were able to apprehend the truth and then in turn, to reshape the reigning paideia if necessary.[10]

The best way to sharpen the eye of the mind, Plato argued, is to train the character –a process in which the pupil unconsciously has his nature so changed by the highest spiritual forces—poetry, harmony, and rhythm—that he can finally grasp the nature of the Good by being educated into it.[11] It is only after learning to recognize in all words and combinations the A's, B's, and C's which are the simplest elements of everything written that we can really be said to know how to read. So we are not "musically" educated until we have learned to cherish wherever we find them imprinted, the "forms" of self-control and temperance, courage, generosity, nobility, and all qualities akin to them.

The highest aim of paideia, according to Plato, is the knowledge of Good, the supreme measure, the measure of all measures. And the Idea of Good is "the greatest subject of study." Pointing to the end of the journey—the steep pinnacle we have to climb—is nothing more or less than the Idea of Good.[12]

The essence of philosophical education, believes Plato, culminates in "conversion," which literally means "turning round." It means the wheeling round of the "whole soul" toward the light of the Good, the divine origin of the universe.[13]

For Plato it appears doubtful whether it is possible to apprehend the Good through any intellectual definition. He explains it by quoting its "analogon" in the visible world, the Sun.[14] As the sun is the source of light, making the visible world visible, so the Idea of Good is the source of truth and meaning, and makes the thinkable world thinkable. By making the Good monarch of the intelligible world, like the sun in the world of sight, Plato appears to give it the same divinity as the God of other thinkers, even though he doesn't actually call it God.[15]

So what noteworthy features of classical paideia may be helpful to our reflection? Paideia, particularly as developed by Plato, involved the interplay between the cultural fund of wisdom, described as music and poetry, and the philosophers who, with their knowledge of the good, were able to reflect on the life of the community. Paideia included direct expression of and reflection on a "living ideal" toward which education sought to deliberately mold human character. The purpose of the molding of human character was to equip persons to serve the community, or polis as it was described. The purpose of knowledge was social, to prepare persons to function as responsible citizens of the state.

The ideals of Greek culture for shaping human character were embodied in their literature, primarily. Poetry, music and rhythm, which were intrinsically religious and moral in character, were thought to provide the most potent resource for forming the mind. They provided the content for the pre-rational stage of development, preparing the way for more advanced intellectual development.

The community as a whole was responsible to provide the social atmosphere for wholesome development. To be able to eventually comprehend intellectually what is meant by the Good, persons must first gradually assimilate the good into their behaviors in the form of self-control, temperance, courage, generosity, and so on. These basic "forms" must be in place before the Good can be understood consciously or philosophically. So the best way to sharpen the mind is to first train a person's character through poetry, harmony, and rhythm. Formation in basic character virtues opens the way for "conversion" and the ability to grasp the supreme reality of beauty, symmetry, truth, or the Good. The ultimate goal of apprehending knowledge of the Good serves overall to give direction to education.

EARLY CHRISTIAN NOTIONS OF PAIDEIA

Early church leaders adapted the Greek understanding of paideia toward a Christian paideia involving the imitation of Christ.[16] Several features of that process can also inform a contemporary tradition-based, critical education. It was early Christian mission that forced missionaries or apostles to use Greek forms of literature and speech in addressing the Hellenized Jews to whom they first turned when entering the great cities of the Mediterranean world.[17] The Greek cultural ideals and Christian faith increasingly mixed. There was on both sides a powerful desire for mutual penetration. After many years of uneasy coexistence, both sides came to recognize that beneath them was a common humanistic core of ideas. The merging of the Christian religion with the Greek intellectual heritage made people realize both traditions had much in common when viewed from the vantage point of the Greek idea of paideia or education—which offered a unique general denominator.[18]

A critical question for many early Christian thinkers and writers was the question of how the Greek classical heritage ought to be incorporated into the structure of Christian thought. The evolution of the Greek mind revealed a growing tendency toward rationalization of all forms of human activity and thought. This evolution was supremely manifest in philosophy, the most characteristic and unique form of the Greek genius. This philosophy fulfilled a religious function, providing a set of dogmas which were primarily aimed at guiding human life and giving it an inner security no longer found in the outside world.[19]

Christians vacillated between flatly rejecting the religious value of the older pagan philosophy and culture and their appreciation of its historical merits. The Christian kerygma spoke of the ignorance of humanity and promised to give them a better knowledge than was offered by pagan philosophies and, like other philosophies, it referred to a master and teacher who possessed and revealed the truth.[20]

Clement of Alexandria, drawing from the Hellenic paideia, portrays Christ as "the divine educator who transcends anything of this kind that has appeared before in human history." He doesn't deny the value of Greek tradition, but claims that Christian faith fulfills this paideutic mission to a higher degree than had been achieved before.[21] True paideia is the divine paideia of the Christian religion itself, he suggests. Christianity was the new paideia that had as its source the divine Logos itself, the Word that had created the world.

There is evidence of the ever increasing influence of Greek literary and artistic form and the reception of the Greek ideal of paideia in the Christian writers of the third and fourth centuries. Origin expands and accelerates the integration. For Plato, philosophy had become the ultimate paideia, the education of humankind. And that was how Origen understood Christianity.[22] Christ, for Origen, was the great teacher, and in this respect Origin's view of Christianity as the paideia of humankind permitted him to stay close to the Scriptures and the picture the Gospels give of Jesus. The great difference of Christianity from Plato's philosophical approach is that it represents the coming of the Logos to humanity, not only as a human effort but as proceeding from a divine initiative. Origen finds evidence of this Logos and of Providence in the history of humanity and builds a picture of history that brings together both the facts of biblical history and the history of the Greek mind. Paideia is thus the gradual fulfillment of the divine providence.

The Cappadocian fathers, Basil of Caesarea, Gregory of Nazianzus, and Gregory of Nyssa freely used the Greek tradition. When they were criticized by their contemporaries for doing so they gave as their defense in part, the illustration of how Moses learned and used the wisdom of the Egyptians. Basil gave what became a famous oration on the study of Greek literature and poetry and its value for the education of Christian youth. Jaeger points out that in their appreciation and use of Greek literature these fathers didn't show a blind and uncritical enthusiasm for everything Greek.[23] They rejected the moral and religious content of ancient Greek poetry but they praised its form.

Gregory of Nyssa focused in particular on the development of the human personality envisioned in Greek paideia. He understood the primary purpose of Greek paideia to be the formation of the human personality and he returns again and again to the a priori ideal of all Greek reflection on this problem: the concept of "morphosis." The Christian educational ideal must be realized by a return to this philosophical insight, he contends. The metaphor of the gradual growth of the human personality and its spiritual nature implies the analogy of a person's physical nature but is different—and the nourishment of the soul must be regarded differently from the material food we consume. The spiritual process called education isn't spontaneous in nature but requires constant care. The virtues, whether moral or intellectual, are the fruit of both a person's nature and training.[24]

Christian virtue described by Gregory appears practically unattainable without divine help. He stressed the idea of divine assistance. Here divine grace could be introduced into classical paideia. He teaches that the assistance of the divine power increases in proportion to a person's own effort. With Plato, Gregory thinks that all human will and striving by nature aims at "the good."[25]

According to Gregory, if paideia was the will of God and if Christianity was for the Christian what philosophy was for the philosopher—assimilation to God—the true fulfillment of the Christian ideal was one continuous and lifelong effort to achieve that end. For Gregory Christianity was not a mere set of dogmas but the perfect life based on the theoria or contemplation of God and on ever more perfect union with Him. It is deificatio, and paideia is the path.

As the Greek paideia consisted of the entire corpus of Greek literature, so the mold of the Christian paideia was the Bible. Literature was paideia, in that it contained the highest norms of human life. In literature these norms took on their lasting and most impressive form. Literature provided the ideal picture of humankind, the great paradigm. Gregory didn't read the Bible as literature, as is the current tendency, writes Jaeger. Rather the formation of Christian persons, their "morphosis," was the effect of unceasing Bible study. The form was Christ. The paideia of the Christian was "imatatio Christi," Christ taking shape in a person. Instead of uttering "the prophet says" or "Christ says," Gregory often writes, "the prophet Isaiah educates us" or "the apostle educates us" implying that what the Bible teaches must be accepted as the Christian paideia. He conceived of the Spirit as the divine educational power ever present in the world who speaks through persons as instruments.

It wasn't enough to proclaim Christ the new pedagogue of humanity and Christianity as the only true paideia however, contends Jaeger. Christians had to show the formative power of their spirit in works of superior intellectual and artistic caliber and to carry the contemporary mind along in their enthusiasm. They had to build up a Christian paideia which wasn't possible without profound thought about the relationship of Christianity and the Greek heritage.[26]

In summary, it is worth noting that early Christian thinkers sought to adapt particular strengths of a Greek educational approach to their new Christian priorities. In an effort to reach their Hellenized world, they used concepts and approaches familiar to their listeners while filling those concepts and approaches with new content. In some respects they tried to build on the good they perceived in the Greek tradition but move it to a new level of understanding. They understood Christ as the greatest teacher, the Logos come to earth. They built on the Greek approach of shaping human character toward an ideal by teaching that we will achieve the human ideal through imitating Christ. They also took the opportunity to highlight the dimension of paideia that involved divine initiative, giving it a new focus. Christ not only represented a living ideal who grew out of the soil of Palestine—a historical person; he also represented an initiative by God to come near to humanity.

Gregory of Nyssa makes the notion of "morphosis" central to his understanding of paideia, drawing out the spiritual aspects of paideia at length. He shows the need for divine help in attaining the virtuous fruits of paideia, introducing divine grace into classical paideia.

Early Christian writers replaced the corpus of Greek literature with the Bible as the primary formative mold by which a person is shaped. The Bible provided the ideal norms of human life, the paradigms for forming our behaviors and imaginations. The imitation of Christ, with the Spirit's tutorial assistance, was the goal of the Christian paideia. Out of this emerged a "Christian culture" which was meant to rival the intellectual and artistic works generated by Hellenist culture.

Paideia and Theological Education

Edward Farley and David Kelsey have recently brought the discussion of paideia to the forefront of theological education. Farley suggests that the ancient Greek ideal of culture (paideia) in which education is the "culturing" of a human being in *areté* or virtue is absent in the perception that education means dealing primarily in the cognitive universe, a perception which has dominated theological and other education in recent centuries.[27]

Farley observes that "theologia" used to mean being formed in wisdom as one faithfully sought after the understanding of God. Theology in its original and most authentic sense referred to knowledge that is personal and wise. We've lost that meaning in theological education, he contends. Theology instead has come to be understood as a scientific discipline for examining the things of faith. Education as mere scholarly learning is not a process affecting and shaping the human being under an ideal, but a grasping of the methods and contents of regions of scholarship.[28]

The study of theology must once again involve personal formation in godliness, he suggests. Basic personal integrity must be at the heart of teaching methodology, an integrity that flows out of a unitary commitment to serve God and neighbor with all of one's heart, strength, and mind.

Farley also argues that proper pedagogy as it relates to learning to know God be defined neither by demands of clergy functions nor by the demands of scholarship but as a "habitus," a paideia that involves symbols, doctrines and practices, not unlike the paideia of classical Greece.[29]

Kelsey contrasts theological education in North America as being characterized either by "Athens" or "Berlin," suggesting that any course of theological study rests on some sort of negotiated truce between these two models of schooling.

Kelsey described the "Athens" model as paideia education. Paideia according to Kelsey, meant a process of "culturing" the soul with schooling understood to be "character formation."[30] It is the oldest picture of education to be found in Christianity, a model that was long prevalent in understandings of both Christianity and education.

The "Berlin" model, in contrast, originated in the newly founded University of Berlin in 1810 as a new type of excellent theological education which stressed the interconnected importance of orderly, disciplined critical research and "professional" education for ministry.[31]

A paideia model of education tends to focus on the student Kelsey argues, on helping the student undergo a deep kind of formation. The student's study focuses on various subject matters but more basically on the student's own appropriation of wisdom about God and themselves in relation to God. The teacher serves as a midwife in that process providing indirect assistance and disciplines that will capacitate the student for his/her own "moment of insight."[32]

The paideia approach is a powerful model in terms of its overarching goal or purpose, claims Kelsey. The purpose of such education isn't understood to be conveying information but to help students become formed (or in-formed) by certain dispositions and to act in certain ways (including actions associated with thought and speech).

Education in a paideia model proceeds indirectly by way of the examination of texts and practices whose study is believed to lead to understanding God and all else in relation to God. The "Berlin" model, by way of contrast, involves a movement from data to theory to application of theory to practice.[33]

At the core of the view of the human being underlying paideia and the "Athens" model is the view that *the* characteristic defining a human being is the capacity of reason in intuitive, cognitive judgment to apprehend the ultimate principle of being and of value—God. This intuitive act is the very heart of rationality; the act of knowing that provides the foundation for all other knowing. In the "Berlin" model the underlying view of a human being is the view that the characteristic defining human being is reason's capacity to test and if necessary correct any and all "intuitions" with disciplined and orderly critical inquiry.[34]

Kelsey acknowledges in conclusion that both the Athens and the Berlin approach to education leave something to be wanted. The Athens approach is insufficiently capable of critique of its own idolatries and susceptibility to ideological distortions. It needs the critical thinking characteristic of the Berlin model. The Berlin type on the other hand, is too open to individualistic and functionalist corruptions and needs the social and collegial character of the Athens type. No faith oriented education can abandon either type he argues, but tensions between them are unavoidable. The best that can be hoped for is an unstable truce between the two.[35]

CRITICAL RETRIEVAL OF PAIDEIA

An Alternative Paideia

Paideia in the classical Greek sense was associated with education toward citizenship in the state. The early Christians began to speak of the "paideia of Christ," which they offered as an alternative to the dominant Hellenist paideia. This Christian paideia offered an alternative approach to education until it was increasingly adopted by the dominant culture and ultimately made the official paideia at the initiative of Emperor Constantine. Constantinian Christendom with its "establishment" paideia has been with us in one guise or another ever since. There have been many reformations of the dominant educational paideia that have come and gone, leaving vestiges of their innovations. There have also been many attempts to offer an alternative paideia.

My intention is not to trace out a history of developments in education that come closer or deviate farther from classical notions of paideia. I simply want to explore the possibility of appropriating certain aspects of a classical paideia that will give historical depth to what I suggest as a counter-cultural, tradition-based ecclesial paideia.

Lawrence Cremin suggests that education fundamentally deals with the way a culture mediates its substance and character and that its form consists of an ecology of interrelated institutions. The substance and character of a culture, which constitutes the content of education Cremin calls the "paideia."[36] Cremin focuses on the fact that each culture has a dynamic "vision of life itself as a deliberate cultural and ethical aspiration." It is this vision, drawn from the traditions and experiences of a people that is the essential content of education. Education is not only a technical issue of transferring skills from one generation to another, but the dynamic process of defining what is crucial to a people's life together.

Every educator or educational institution struggles to discover what paideia will best serve the society given our current economic realities, ethnic pluralism, and social organization. What knowledge should "we the people" hold in common? What values? What skills?[37] And what is the role of religion in the paideia could also be asked.

The strategy by which paideia is mediated is defined by Cremin as a configuration or ecology of educational institutions. The task is to think comprehensively about the institutions that seek to mediate culture and how these fit into an educational matrix.[38] For education to be defined, the range of institutions and their interrelationships need to be discerned.

In discussing the church's role in the education of the public, Jack Seymour makes this observation about an earlier era in the United States: "In the national period, a distinctive stance on education was born 'to advance a popular paideia compounded of democratic hopes, evangelical pieties, and millennial expectations.'"[39] He further suggests that we are now at a "critical juncture in the history of both church education and public education." A new paideia is emerging and the configuration of educational institutions is being reformed. He encourages the church to play a significant role in this reformulation. Education must be seen in its variety of cultural manifestations, he argues, and must serve to infuse an appreciation for the transcendent into cultural life.

Given the ecclesiology of Anabaptist-Mennonites, where the church as the body of Christ is understood to be defined by the life and teachings of Jesus, distinct from the world and yet salt and light in the world, the notion of paideia as "education toward citizenship in a dominant culture" is not a helpful concept. However, in light of postmodernity and the new opportunity it presents for tradition-based rationality, morality, and education (described further by Nancey Murphy in chapter 4), the notion of a paideia for a counter-society appears suddenly very relevant. The church can play a significant role in the reformulation of the dominant paideia but do so by offering an alternative paideia that resources the dominant paideia as "salt and light."

Speaking of Mennonite college education, Rodney Sawatsky writes that because the church is the visible community of the redeemed distinct from the world, a primary task of the church college is to nurture loyalty to this alternative community. The public schools, he says, are mandated to socialize the next generation into the values and mores of the dominant society. Loyal citizenship is their purpose. Similarly the church, if it is to be a nonconformed community, must socialize its young into its ethic and ethos. Mennonite educators thus are called upon to nurture citizens of God's kingdom rather than of the nation.[40]

While the notion of paideia isn't referred to in Sawatsky's chapter on Mennonite education, I find his argument about nurturing loyalty to citizenship in the kingdom rather than the nation very applicable to my sense that paideia can be a helpful concept for theorizing about Anabaptist education and education in other distinct, counter-culture communities. At its best, he argues, the ethos propelling the church as a distinctive sociological entity and its educational enterprise is an ethic—the ethic of Jesus.[41]

Such an ethic gives rise to a particular paideia, I would argue, that has its formative texts and characteristic practices. The practices he highlights include: nurturing loyalty to the kingdom rather than to the nation, emphasizing the ethical life and Christian discipleship, encouraging an internationalist perspective, teaching the Bible as the authoritative text of the church, enjoying choral music as a means to build and express faith and community and instilling a communitarian ethos, all of which are premised on Jesus the Christ, the Incarnate Word.

An alternative paideia, based in a tradition-formed, particular community, can be focused on preparing persons to become citizens of the kingdom of God, as described by Jesus. While being formed according to the particular ideals, texts and practices of a distinct, local community, the focus of their anticipated service will be for the larger society in which they live and the international kingdom of God.

Paideia and the Ideal of the Good

We've observed that in a paideia approach the goal of the knowledge of the Good gives direction to education. As Jaeger notes, the Greeks were the first to recognize that education means deliberately molding human character in accordance with an ideal. The ideal wasn't an abstraction but a living ideal that had grown up in the soil of Greece and changed with the changing times. Inasmuch as for them the purpose of knowledge was compellingly social, the active and energetic cultivation of a common ideal enhanced the quality and character of their communal practice and discourse.

With clarity about the ultimate goal, an educational endeavor that seeks to deliberately mold human character in accordance with an ideal allows the community to work together toward a common and explicit purpose. The shared ideal enhances harmony in shaping the social atmosphere and working together in customary and traditional ways to maintain the pre-conditions for growth in the virtues valued by the community. In cultivating the awareness of an ideal, a community makes explicit what it most values and seeks to preserve what it most values in its texts and practices.

Dwayne Huebner suggests that in the past two decades in North America, questions of value have resurfaced in discussion about how we know and how we talk about priorities in education. In earlier years, when the emphasis was on individual intellectual achievement, the social and historical fabric of human life was an easily forgotten and often neglected background.[42] Throughout human history, however, individuals and groups have experienced transforming and transcending moments and these moments have been stored within the various traditions of these peoples.

The fact that these stored traces assume the status of religious classics speaks to the importance of these records. They provide a language and a symbolic world within which one can project and understand one's own possibilities. He also suggests that spiritual, religious traditions celebrate openness, love, and hope—values which were hidden from view when enlightenment modes of knowing held sway. He argues for a renewed appreciation of religious traditions that keep us open collectively and individually to the spiritual qualities of openness, love, and hope and that it is these qualities which enliven our knowing.

When working from a tradition-based rationality and morality, there is a new freedom and responsibility to listen to the wisdom inherent in the religious classics. As we collectively examine what is of value to our life together and what ideals will motivate us, we are compelled to consciously reflect on who we are and who we hope to become. Who we are as a community becomes a primary question which is largely answered by what we choose to value most highly and shape our lives in accordance with.

Over the course of the last twenty years or so the question of community has replaced the question of how we come to know as foundational for all other inquiries, argues Mark Schwehn, in his treatise on education. The answers to basic human questions, such as, What can we know? or How should we live? or In what or whom shall we place our hope? have come to depend, for a large number of intellectuals, upon the answer to a prior question, Who are we?[43]

The educational ideals of Greece were dominated by poetry, music, and rhythm. It was assumed that the spiritual and moral traditions they carried provided the optimal conditions out of which one could grow toward knowledge of the Good. The community wide affirmation of these ideals allowed for the maintenance of a social environment that frequently and consistently reinforced these elements. Who we are was defined by the ideals in the traditions which the community sought to embody.

A paideia model of education makes the embodiment of an ideal central to its approach. Such an approach is compatible with the Anabaptist conviction that our lives are to be shaped by Christ's life and teaching. The paideia model which extols the vital, formative role of poetry, music and rhythm suggests that an immersion in the poetry, narratives and music of Scripture as well as regularly patterned habitus or practices that embody the values inherent within Scripture will provide the basic formation required for healthy personal development. If the traditions of the community are truly life-giving and efficacious, it is the embodiment of the ideals they keep alive that will lead to ongoing "conversion" and renewed knowledge of the Good in each succeeding generation.

Paideia and Intellectual and Moral Virtues

Custom and tradition provided the simplest and most fundamental elements for Plato's paideia. These provided the basic A, B, C's which, when combined, allowed persons to move on to more complex reasoning and intuitive insight. But unless persons had been imprinted with the basic "forms" of self-control, temperance, courage, generosity, and so forth, as well as the harmony and right rhythm they provide, they could not hope to achieve the ultimate goal of intuitive insight and the knowledge of the Good. In other words, when custom and tradition are employed to achieve right harmony and rhythm, these provide the preconditions for developing the philosophical capacity to critically reflect on why that type of harmony and rhythm is good or could be improved. When the pre-conditions are met, one can learn to use philosophical reasoning to consciously reflect on the formative customs and traditions and change them if necessary. And one is also equipped with the moral and spiritual character required for "conversion" and intuitive insight into the source of truth and meaning, the supreme reality. The best way to sharpen the mind is to train the character by poetry, harmony and rhythm, suggested Plato.

Plato wrote almost all of his philosophical works in dialogue form principally for the purpose of a demonstration of the interdependence of moral and intellectual virtues, argues Schwehn.[44] *The Meno*, Plato's dialogue on the subject of education, features a title character whose failures to learn are more frequently the results of flaws in his character than of lapses in his logic. Meno needs to change if he is to come to know the truth, suggests Schwehn. Insofar as the truth comes to Meno, he does change—he becomes less arrogant, more self-disciplined, more courageous—not just in his ideas but in his way of living.

The questions that govern *The Meno* are, Can virtue be taught? What is the relationship between knowledge and virtue? Is virtue a form of knowledge, or is it a gift from the gods? These, observes Schwehn, are among the oldest questions in Western philosophy. So long as the activities of teaching and learning involve communal questioning in search of the truth, the exercise of virtues such as humility, faith, self-denial, and charity will be indispensable to education.[45] The link between our knowledge and character is crucial, he contends.

Schwehn argues for a historical connection between religious beliefs and these virtues (humility, faith, self-sacrifice, and charity). He contends that it is our spiritual traditions which are responsible for cultivating and sustaining the very virtues that make productive study of and conversation among rival conceptions of the good possible. To the extent that this is true, the risks of weakening the great religious traditions are very great.[46]

Schwehn believes that the most promising argument for an integral relationship between religion and higher education can be made through a demonstration that the practice of certain spiritual virtues is and has always been essential to the process of learning, even within the secular academy. He regrets that over the last century, the modern university has neglected to attend to character formation, or it has imagined that such attention has little or nothing to do with knowledge. From this perspective, he suggests, the current resurgence of a community focus to knowledge construction may be Western culture's way of awakening from a comparatively brief slumber induced by "enlightened" secular rationalism.[47]

Schwehn argues from the premise of one major assumption, namely that our assumptions about how we come to know have ethical implications and that ways of knowing are not morally neutral but morally directive.[48] If this assertion is true, it has enormous implications for a theory of education, highlighting the importance of reviewing classical, community-based approaches to paideia.

What "poetry, harmony and rhythms" are allowed to take shape in a child, becoming the basic forms out of which he or she shapes all other knowledge? An Anabaptist emphasis on immersion in Scripture and faithfully practicing the way of Jesus as they understood it, provided the pre-conditions for their on-going communal quest of knowledge and truth. While those were the pre-conditions however, the transformation of their lives involved the work of the Holy Spirit. While the quality of life and one's ability to understand and communicate depended on the pre-conditioning of scriptural tradition and ethical practices, the Holy Spirit's presence was the grace, light and love that powered the transformed lives of those who joined the communities of the radical reformation.

It was in reading the tradition's formative texts and engaging in new practices with the insight and power provided by the Holy Spirit that the Anabaptists were able to look with new eyes on the customs and traditions that had earlier formed them. They were able, in light of enhanced insight and recovered practices, to reformulate the tradition in ways that both kept faith with it but provided a new paideia to shape virtues that would further enlighten understanding.

Paideia and Critical Inquiry

Plato bases his educational plan on a paideia that includes "music" and "gymnastics." But the athletic and "musical" training is really only the foundation of a paideia that would lead to philosophical understanding by those responsible to supervise and construct a balanced paideia. It is these persons who are capacitated to reflect critically on what is customary and traditional and suggest refinements.

The discussion of paideia throughout this chapter has largely focused on its customary and traditional formation of basic dispositions and character. As Kelsey warned us however, such an approach to education is insufficiently capable of critiquing its own idolatries and is very susceptible to ideological distortions. It may become trapped in its own conventions and prejudices.

Furthermore, communities that become entrenched in their own versions of the truth must find ways to examine the quality of their own traditions. Their ability to do this will depend in part on whether they assume they are participating in a reality larger than their own life-forms and whether the language they speak is capable of referring to realities beyond the language itself.[49] And their ability to maintain an internal critique will also depend on the community's capacity for critical thinking.

David Tracy reminds us that commitment and action not open to critical inquiry are blind and that critical inquiry not open to commitment and action are empty. Critical inquiry and action rise or fall together.[50] He observes that the community of inquiry in the West lives through the power of the great Socratic ideal for true education, which is classically expressed in the saying, "The unreflective life is not worth living." Communities of faith add to that classic Socratic ideal the equally important thought that "the unlived life is not worth reflecting upon."

A paideia informed by the Anabaptist tradition will include the habitus, the dispositions and practices modeled on Jesus life and teaching. It will also incorporate critical reflection within the context of the discerning, interpreting community on how best to embody the way of Jesus in our daily lives.

Chapter 4

OTHER VOICES: A "KNOWING" CONVERSATION WITH THE ANABAPTISTS

What does it mean "to know" and how do the ways we come to know relate to our educational priorities? Without attention to underlying assumptions about how we come to know, it becomes very difficult to converse about the meaning of education. Inasmuch as education is concerned about what we can know, how we came to know it, and who it is that is doing the knowing, there are dimensions of epistemology that it would be helpful to examine as we develop a tradition-based, critical theory of education.

Overview of Our Ways of Knowing

Epistemology has tried to answer many questions about "knowing" over the centuries. Does knowledge come to us from the exterior world through the senses and write itself on our mind slates or do we instead have interior structures and innate ideas within our minds that we employ to make sense of the exterior world? Or perhaps both work together, with the interior structures interacting with data from outside in such a way that over time our knowledge increases not only quantitatively but qualitatively. Does knowing mean receiving knowledge like passive chunks of a substance that we swallow or is knowing an interactive, relational process that involves imagination, symbolization and practices? Do I know primarily in my head or does knowing have bodily roots?

Furthermore, what is the relationship of our present experiential learning to the tradition of the ancestors? What is the relationship of objective knowledge to subjective knowledge? Can knowledge be separated from the knower? Is all knowledge contextually defined or is there some universal knowledge in which we all share alike? Do we seek to know so we can answer questions of ultimate truth, or is knowledge merely functional, for our own use? Do we only truly know what we can verify by experimentation or are there other ways to know? Is knowledge communally based or individually ascertained?

The questions could go on, but I name these to make the point that discussions about *how we come to know* and *what we can know* reflect many questions and have also produced many answers. An effort to construct a theory of education will do well to examine aspects of our knowing as a central component to the theory.

Many scholars are describing ways of knowing more encompassing of the fullness of reality than the quantitative and instrumental ways of knowing which dominated discussions of epistemology in the modern era.[1] More and more thoughtful people are acknowledging that the roads to knowledge are many and can't be defined by any single system of thought and that relying on a single rationalist paradigm has distorted our conception of knowledge. Now there are many discussions about practical, spiritual, bodily, imaginal, and communal ways of knowing? And flowing out of these discussions are reappraisals of what implications these multiple ways for knowing have on educational endeavors.

When knowledge of the non-sensory, qualitative dimensions of life is not valued much, the capacity for experiencing and understanding the "noumenal, immaterial realities that are the wellsprings of all life and meaning, and that constitute the heart and essence of all the great religious traditions, dries up."[2] What is needed is a fundamental transformation in our ways of knowing. We must develop qualitative ways of knowing on par with our quantitative. We must develop ways of knowing the "non-sensory, supersensible realities in which the sensible world has its origin, being, and becoming." We must presuppose "a minimum intuition of non-sensory realities as the irreducible possibility of even our ordinary, sense-bound knowing itself." The task then becomes one of developing imaginative and intuitive capacities into full-fledged faculties of perception and cognition involving the whole person in the work of knowing (thought, feeling, will, and character).[3]

Voices Invited to the Table

I've invited three persons to the table to discuss various aspects of how we come to know, what we can know, and who it is that is doing the knowing. I've found these three persons particularly helpful as I reflect on possible affinities between an Anabaptist approach to knowing and recent conversations about knowing that lead us toward a fresh appraisal of religious ways of knowing in particular. They are Michael Polanyi, a scientist and philosopher; Rebecca Chopp, a feminist theologian; and Nancey Murphy, a philosopher of science and a theologian.

To my knowledge, none of these persons has interacted with the others invited to the table. They are each working on different projects and addressing different audiences. The language they use to address their concerns and the perspectives they write out of are in some ways very dissimilar. It isn't immediately apparent why these three persons should be sitting at the same table discussing knowing and its implications for education. Yet my sense is that their voices do, in many ways, resonate with each other. Their presence at the table is largely due to my own discernment that they represent somewhat compatible and yet critically complementary views. I also believe their perspectives can interact in a helpful way with the distinctives I've identified from an Anabaptist theological perspective and with what we've learned from a paideia approach.

I hope the intermingling of their voices will weave a rich texture of resonance and that, in allowing each to be heard in relation to the other, the conversation will model the sort of conversation vital to communal discernment. Knowledge making is a dynamic process of construction involving many voices from various social locations and expressing a variety of cultural and political interests.[4] Our knowledge is deepened by interacting with a relational matrix of theories, symbols, doctrines, and communal practices.

My emphasis will not be on a comprehensive analysis of each person's approach to knowing or an evaluation overall of each person's contribution to their particular field. Rather, this will be an opportunity to listen to three voices functioning as a community of interpreters. I hope the process of conversation among these three persons, representing somewhat different social and political interests will lead toward deeper understanding, more informed critical judgment, and a vibrant resonance from which to compose an educational theory.

Introducing Michael Polanyi

Michael Polanyi was born March 11, 1891, in Budapest, Hungary, and lived until 1976. To more and more people he is one of "the very great minds of our time," yet he has been "strangely ignored by much of the academic world and is largely unknown to the public," writes Drusilla Scott.[5] Polanyi was not trained as a philosopher. His actual professional careers included four areas: medicine, physical chemistry, social science, and philosophy. "His intellectual competence, his breadth of knowledge, and his intimate experience with intellectual and social issues have given him a vantage point for producing an original and penetrating view of our situation," writes Richard Gelwick.[6]

Polanyi became a distinguished scientist in physical chemistry. During the course of his life he moved from Budapest to Berlin, then to Manchester University in England, taking the Chair of Physical Chemistry. He established a world-famous school of physical chemistry there. He later increasingly turned to philosophy. Growing up around the turn of the century, Polanyi saw a brilliant European civilization torn apart and destroyed in two world wars, in revolution and terrorism and in the totalitarian tyrannies of Bolshevism and Fascism.

He began increasingly to move from his scientific study to reflect on the way science relates to the rest of life, reflecting on how a free society and a true practice of science depend on each other, and on the immense evils that spring from a false scientific outlook. What seemed new to him in the enormous upheavals of this century were the combination of a ruthless *contempt* for moral values such as truth, compassion and justice with an unbounded *moral passion* for utopian perfection. How could these two great streams of reason and of moral ideals that flowed from Socrates and from Christ and had nourished European civilization for so long, have produced by some strange modern fusion, a new and deadly poison? he asked.[7]

Polanyi saw the threat entailed for Western culture as a whole when personal responsibility in the work of the scientist is not recognized. A kind of knowing from which the knowing subject (shaped by historical, cultural and psychological factors) is ignored leads to a false "objectivity," he observed. As a working scientist, he knew the personal factors which shape all scientific work and "the necessary apprenticeship to a long tradition of scientific work, the learning of skills, and the personal gifts of intuition, imagination, judgment, courage and patience without which scientific advance would never happen."[8]

In his major philosophic work *Personal Knowledge,* published in 1958, Polanyi describes the prevalent distorting assumptions about the impersonality and certainty of scientific knowledge and the belief that anything outside of scientific "objectivity" is unreal. These assumptions devalue our moral values, spiritual powers, affections, responsibilities, and judgments, he claims.[9] All knowing of any kind, he asserted, involves personal commitment and the acceptance of personal responsibility for one's beliefs.

Polanyi's work is difficult and demanding, notes Gelwick. Any truly original and innovative thought couldn't be otherwise. His philosophical work undertakes "the most thorough and profound analysis of all the main epistemological issues raised by science and produces an alternative proposal. No other thinker since World War II has produced such a comprehensive study of the epistemological questions, Gelwick claims.[10] And yet, because Polanyi recognized the bodily, intuitive and traditional roots of our knowledge and the moral and aesthetic elements in all our understanding, he made himself suspect to the philosophic establishment.[11]

Polanyi's work begins as an inquiry into knowledge but soon expands into the widest dimensions of that subject and becomes also a philosophy with implications for ontology and ethics. His thought is highly interdisciplinary, drawing as it does on data from nearly every major department of knowledge. Political theorists, sociologists, lawyers, theologians, philosophers, engineers, educators, and scientists have found large areas of his work relevant to their tasks. Theologians were among Polanyi's earliest supporters and allies, in part because of the "fiduciary component in tacit knowing" and the recognition that it has a fascinating kinship with the Augustinian principle that to know one must first believe.[12]

Polanyi contends that a false objectivity prevails in the modern mindset and is expressed in what is called "the scientific outlook." He describes it like this, "The declared aim of modern science is to establish a strictly detached, objective knowledge," which he thoroughly denounces as a false ideal.[13]

Polanyi often spoke of the parallel between the old authoritarian control of thought by the churches and the present domination of scientism. Scientism he felt has limited thought as cruelly as the churches had previously done and he set about the task of re-equipping persons with the faculties that centuries of critical thought had taught them to mistrust.[14] There are examples everywhere, notes Scott, of the use of "science" to undermine confidence in any other way of knowing. Any judgment of value, any intuitive wisdom is banished to the realm of fantasy or whim, while any statistical or scientific type statement gets automatic endorsement. The devaluing of personal judgment becomes a self-fulfilling principle, since any faculty that is unused tends to decay. We have less and less opportunity to use personal judgment and when we're consistently told its unreliable and irrelevant it becomes so.[15]

The contribution of Polanyi, suggests Gelwick, is "not in his recounting and systematizing the philosophers of this period but in his recognizing the chain of influence through the central figures of this period that demolished our reliance upon tradition and impersonalized our ideal of knowledge." It seemed at the beginning that the Enlightenment ideals promised a moral and rational approach to problems. Instead "they set in motion the moral passion in the guise of the objective ideal that would nearly consume us in the twentieth century."[16]

The significance of Polanyi's philosophy, suggests Gelwick, can best be described as a new paradigm. Inasmuch as it articulates a comprehensive and alternative ideal, it needs a name that describes its decisive characteristic and suggests the range of its implications. Gelwick suggests the new paradigm be referred to as "a heuristic philosophy." Heuristic derives from the Greek, meaning to find or discover. The *nature of discovery*, suggests Polanyi, is the root idea that illuminates and motivates his philosophy. It is a new vision that beckons us toward a responsible "society of explorers." And Gelwick suggests that, "As much as Copernicus changed the former world view by making the earth revolve around the sun, Polanyi is changing it by making all knowledge revolve around the responsible person. The old paradigm was based upon a separation of logic and psychology. It tried to understand the nature of inference and reasoning without including the central role of the whole person."[17]

Key Polanyi insights relevant to
a tradition-based, critical educational theory

1. Personal knowledge. Polanyi worked for years at the frontiers of science among others who were pioneering new understandings of the universe. Scott notes that Einstein recognized the special character of discovery and that scientific laws can only be reached by "intuition, based upon something like an intellectual love," but he didn't follow up on this insight. Polanyi took up the challenge. He made this "mysterious intellectual love his starting point."[18]

Originality must be passionate, Polanyi wrote:

> Theories of the scientific method which try to explain the establishment of scientific truth by any purely objective formal procedure are doomed to failure. Any process of inquiry unguided by intellectual passions would inevitably spread out into a desert of trivialities. Our vision of reality, to which our sense of scientific beauty responds, must suggest to us the kind of questions that it should be reasonable and interesting to explore.[19]

Anyone who has solved problems, writes Scott, knows the feeling of the stage when you know and yet don't know—have a hunch, sense a connection but can't quite grasp it. Perhaps you sleep on it and then wake up knowing the answer. Many discoveries have been made like this, with a flash of illumination. Archimedes leapt out of the bath, rushed into the street shouting, "Heureka! I've found it!" Ideas connected with discovery are called heuristic; it is a heuristic passion when you are hot on the trail of discovery. Polanyi argues that this personal process of original discovery, with the emotions that care about what is involved, is the central core of science, the place to seek the essence of the scientific method.[20] "Everywhere, at all mental levels," he says, "it is not the functions of the articulate logical operations but the tacit powers of the mind that are decisive."[21]

The significance of this new conception of knowledge, he declares, is "the *personal participation* of the knower in all acts of understanding." He clarifies,

> But this does not make our understanding *subjective*. Comprehension is neither an arbitrary act nor a passive experience, but a responsible act claiming universal validity. Such knowing is indeed *objective* in the sense of establishing contact with a hidden

reality; a contact that is defined as the condition for anticipating an indeterminate range of yet unknown (and perhaps yet inconceivable) true implications. It seems reasonable to describe this fusion of the personal and the objective as Personal Knowledge.[22]

Polanyi contends that every act of knowing involves a passionate contribution of the person knowing what is being known, and that this dimension of knowing is a vital component of his knowledge.[23]

He quotes St. Augustine who observed that "Unless you believe, you shall not understand." Augustine's ordering, showing faith before reason, rang true for Polanyi. The "science" of measurement, experiment and doubt to which other knowledge was made to conform actually rests on a foundation of faith in what cannot be proved, in skills and imaginative powers that can't be formalized and in tradition by which alone such skills can be passed on. This change, notes Scott, opens the way to accept the validity of truths that can only be explored in myth, poetry and ritual. In fact, Polanyi had the courage to say that the truth of poetry and art, of morality, philosophy and law is more vital than the truths of science.[24]

2. Bodily roots of tacit knowing. Polanyi's most basic assertion is that we must reconsider human knowledge by starting from the fact that "we can know more than we can tell."[25] He observes that our bodily processes participate in the perceptions we make and notes that all thought has bodily roots, including our highest creative powers.[26] Polanyi suggested that understanding the way our bodily processes participate in our perceptions will throw light on the bodily roots of all thought, including our highest creative powers. Polanyi asserts that our body is "the ultimate instrument of all our external knowledge, whether intellectual or practical. In all our waking moments we are *relying* on our awareness of contacts of our body with things outside for *attending* to these things."[27]

Our own body, says Polanyi, is "the only assembly of things known almost exclusively by relying on our awareness of them for attending to something else."[28] We don't normally experience our body as an object, but use it to make sense of the outside world. The "body" that we dwell in, writes Scott, is not just the body that a medical student would see if he were dissecting us after death; "it is the whole complex of habits, aptitudes, skills and awareness that we have built up . . . ever since our first days of life. . . . Dwelling in it is my only means of knowing the world."[29]

Polanyi uses many illustrations to describe what he means by tacit knowing. Think of using a tool as a carpenter, he suggests. A novice will be very conscious of the feel of the tool handle in his hand, but a experienced carpenter's focus won't be on the tool but on what the tool is doing to the wood. So it is when you learn to drive a car, attending carefully to certain skills like changing the gears which later recede into the background as you focus increasingly on the road and traffic. In all these kinds of knowing and know-how there are two levels of objects; the parts, details, particulars *from* which you attend, and the whole or meaning *to* which you attend. This is the characteristic structure of tacit knowing. The way we get from one to the other, he contends, is not formal reasoning; it is skilled imaginative integration.[30] And to use a formula or a concept, a sign or a symbol is like using a tool. We have to indwell it and allow it to become a part of us in our subsidiary awareness to attend focally to the task at hand.[31]

Polanyi stressed the important role of the bodily roots of our intuitive capacities. He contended that knowledge is personal in that its creative or intuitive side is animated by bodily and passional vitality. In so doing he avoids the image of a disembodied intelligence that accompanies the common perception of a mind and body dualism.[32]

Descarte's methodological doubt developed an ethos in which mathematical rigor became paradigmatic for all thought. The consequence for our perceptions of the intellect is that it was uprooted from its previous grounding in our bodies. The further consequence of the Cartesian method was the notorious "bifurcation of nature" which carried with it the insistence on the utterly detached character of rational thinking.[33]

Tacit knowledge is Polanyi's most revolutionary idea, Scott believes. It allows us to give a truer picture of the process of scientific discovery. The power to sense the direction in which a solution may be found lies in a reservoir of tacit skills, aptitudes and awareness which underlie all conscious search. The old dualism of mind and body dissolve in the light of tacit knowing. And when we consider other than scientific kinds of knowledge, reached through art, poetry, myth and religion, the structure of tacit knowing supplies the link which allows all these kinds of knowledge to be part of one great range of understanding.[34]

3. Indwelling. Polanyi suggested that knowing involves the commitment to indwell the particulars of our own subliminal knowledge or the particulars of a given tradition before we can move on to new understanding and action. An act of knowing based on indwelling relies on "interiorizing particulars to which we are not attending and which, therefore, we may not be able to specify, and relies further on our attending from these unspecifiable particulars to a comprehensive entity connecting them in a way we cannot define, so that we will be able to pursue new discoveries."[35]

What does Polanyi mean by commitment to indwelling? Commitment, as it's often been used, means commitment to one particular view—the opposite of open-mindedness. It has often implied persons closing themselves off from consideration of other positions. The pioneers of modern science saw commitment to traditional beliefs as obstinate blindness and the enemy of truth.

But Polanyi repudiated this impersonal, dogmatic, and rule-bound approach which closes itself off from new discovery. The sense in which commitment has often been used is almost opposite to Polanyi's sense. Those fanatically dedicated to an ideology may appear committed, but Polanyi would assert that, rather than being committed, they are chickening out by hiding behind their rigid positions. They are avoiding responsibility. True commitment doesn't allow us to hand over our choice of beliefs to an authority or a rule or a formula—though these can be useful tools. The commitment is of *ourselves* to indwell *reality*, and as we can never know reality completely, such a commitment is always risky.[36]

Polanyi's idea of indwelling suggests that we dwell in our entire cultural heritage—the language, moral values, artistic standards, ways of behaving, dressing and looking at the world. It is this particular inheritance that equips us for handling and understanding the world. It would be futile to think we could get to any understanding of the world except by starting from the particular inheritance in which we were brought up, any more than we can learn language without learning a particular language, or a child can get a religious sense except through being nurtured in a particular religion.

One might ask whether this doesn't impose limitations on our power of knowing the real world? Yes, argues Scott, but from Polanyi's perspective, being a "particular person or belonging to a particular culture does limit our vision, but without these limitations there is no vision. Only by using the senses that we have, only by dwelling in the culture in which we are, can we come to transcend these limitations."[37]

Polanyi also clarifies that commitment is the link between the personal aspect of knowledge in which it is my knowledge, and the universal aspect in which it is knowledge of reality, valid for anyone. My commitment is from where I am, what I am, to a reality beyond myself. This is the difference between personal knowledge and subjective knowledge.[38]

What might be some of the implications of Polanyi's commitment to indwell which could lead to a truer understanding of religious practices? In commenting on how indwelling relates to the religious practice of worship Polanyi observes that, "Religion, considered as an act of worship, is an indwelling rather than an affirmation. God cannot be observed, any more than truth, beauty or justice can be observed. He exists only in the sense that he is to be worshipped and obeyed, but not otherwise—any more than truth, beauty or justice exist as facts. All these, like God, are things which can be apprehended only in serving them."[39]

4. Society of Explorers. The sureness of tests and rules for scientific verification has to be replaced by what Polanyi calls a "Society of Explorers" where the committed person in "an organically functioning community learns his skills from its traditions to make his own contact with reality. Within this society a person's commitment stretches him between the knowledge already held in tradition and the new shape of reality he discerns." Polanyi abandoned "all efforts to find strict criteria of truth and strict procedures for arriving at the truth." Instead, he contends, the scientist as a person "committed to reality, using his responsible judgment, is the criterion of valid knowledge." But then the question arises, How do we know a particular scientist *is* committed and responsible?[40]

At the beginning of the era of modern science, scientists battled against authority. Aristotle and the church were perceived to be enemies of truth. Polanyi knew science must be free from *external* authority, but he also concluded that both authority and tradition are vital elements of the free community of science. In rejecting the interference of political or religious authorities with the pursuit of truth, he argued that scientists "must do it in the name of the established scientific authority which safeguards the pursuit of science."[41]

The structure of authority exercised over a Society of Explorers, however, is different from a dogmatic authority to which a given society may submit. He speaks instead of a mutual control through which each scientist independently plays a part in maintaining scientific traditions. The authority Polanyi speaks of is a mutually imposed authority. It is a society where coherence is spontaneously established by "self-coordination" and authority is exercised by equals over each other.[42]

Every scientist, he contended, is under authority to the professional standards of science. "This internal tension is essential in guiding and motivating scientific work. The professional standards of science must impose a framework of discipline and at the same time encourage rebellion against it. . . . Thus the authority of scientific opinion enforces the teachings of science in general for the very purpose of fostering their subversion in particular."[43]

He further observes that "the standards of scientific merit are seen to be transmitted from generation to generation . . . in the same way as artistic, moral or legal traditions are transmitted. . . . The authority of science is essentially traditional. *But this tradition upholds an authority which cultivates originality.*"[44] Polanyi shows that science cannot live except in the traditions of a community united by trust and by love of truth and acceptance of authority.

Describing Polanyi's stance Scott contends that "If new insights in science arise by indwelling our tacit knowledge and sensing new coherence in it, and if this is a skill which cannot be exactly specified but has to be learnt from a master, then without tradition and authority there will be no new discovery." Polanyi shows that freedom must be rooted in tradition, but that tradition is the only real basis for radical change.[45]

Polanyi further contends that, "Science is constantly revolutionised and perfected by its pioneers, while remaining firmly rooted in its traditions."[46] And, he suggests, as in the community of science, the moral community must also impose its traditions and at the same time encourage dissent from them. "Such processes of creative renewal always imply an appeal from a tradition as it is to a tradition as it ought to be. That is a spiritual reality embodied in tradition and transcending it."[47] Furthermore, a community where persons conform to the traditions and yet are encouraged in creative dissent may come to see more deeply the truths that the tradition only partly embodies. Polanyi suggests that "a man who has learnt to respect the truth will feel entitled to uphold the truth against the very society which has taught him to respect it."[48] Such a community must rely for the transformation of tradition on the intuitive impulses of individual adherents of the community and it assumes that individual members are able to make "genuine contact with the reality underlying the existing tradition and of adding new and authentic interpretations to it."[49]

Polanyi's image of a Society of Explorers leads to a view of history as a drama of moral purpose. Such a society needs a "purpose which bears on eternity."[50] All knowers are personally involved beings. And science can have discipline and originality only if its explorers believe that the facts and values of science bear on "a still unrevealed reality."[51]

5. Tradition and religion. Polanyi contends that a great tradition provides the grounds for both its being maintained and its being changed. His structure of tacit knowing shows the relation between traditional frameworks which form the background of our subsidiary awareness, and the acquisition of new knowledge that arises as we pursue solutions to the problems we are currently focused on.[52]

At the end of *The Tacit Dimension*, as mentioned above, Polanyi wrote of humans needing "a purpose that bears on eternity."[53] For so long, religion has represented the dogmatism that stands in the way of free inquiry, observes Scott. Now the authority of religion is feared no longer and instead, science has the unquestioned authority that used to belong to religion. In claiming that religion and science are talking about the same world, and that knowledge has essentially the same meaning for both, Polanyi opens them up to each other in ways that demand a change of outlook in both. He appeals from science and religion as they *are* to both as they *ought* to be.[54]

He reassures those who are concerned about his stance on traditionalism that he's not reasserting it for the purpose of supporting dogma. To argue that confidence in authority is indispensable for the transmission of any human culture is not to demand submission to religious authority. While acknowledging that the priority of faith imposed by Augustine had impaired scientific progress in earlier eras, he shows how when that was overthrown, the opposite imbalance took its place. Polanyi, who believed in the necessity for faith and reason in science and in all knowledge, wanted to restore the balance.[55]

"The Christian inquiry is worship," Polanyi wrote. "The words of prayer and confession, the actions of the ritual, the lesson, the sermon, the church itself, are the clues of the worshipper's striving toward God. They guide [his] feelings of contrition and gratitude and [his] craving for the divine presence. . . ."[56] Furthermore, he contends, only a Christian who stands in the service of his/her faith can understand Christian theology and enter into the religious meaning of the Bible.

Polanyi believes it impossible for each succeeding generation, let alone each member of it, to critically test all the teachings in which it is brought up. He concludes then that "the idea of knowledge based on wholly identifiable grounds collapses, and we must conclude that the transmission of knowledge from one generation to the other must be predominantly tacit." Furthermore, he suggests that to more fully understand what is being taught a "pupil must presume that a teaching which appears meaningless to start with has in fact a meaning which can be discovered by hitting on the same kind of indwelling as the teacher is practicing. Such an effort is based on accepting the teacher's authority."

And he continues, suggesting that traditionalism, "which requires us to believe before we know, and in order that we may know, is based on a deeper insight into the nature of knowledge and of the communication of knowledge than is scientific rationalism that would permit us to believe only explicit statements based on tangible data . . . I believe," he confesses, "that the new self-determination of man can be saved from destroying itself only by recognizing its own limits in an authoritative traditional framework which upholds it."[57]

Polanyi concludes that "existence precedes essence," in that we must enter a situation or an exploration and commit to it before we can discover fully what it is. We give ourselves to it and in so doing come to understand its essence. As scientific explorers, he says, a person "is placed amid potential discoveries" with a purpose that "bears on eternity."[58]

As we noted before, theologians were among Polanyi's earliest supporters, in part because of the "fiduciary component" in tacit knowing and the recognition of its kinship with the Augustinian principle that to know one must first believe. Yet theologians and Polanyi have not been entirely comfortable with each other. Polanyi's belief in the centrality of discovery in all knowing implies that theology, like all fields of knowing, is obligated to an openness to growth and discovery that is fundamental to being human. Summarizing the import of Polanyi's thinking Gelwick suggests that, "Theology cannot be true to the nature of tacit knowing without a dynamic growth in its own field."[59]

Scott, in summarizing Polanyi says that just as in science we learn by dwelling in a tradition, learning from it so we can go beyond it, so we learn religious understanding by being brought up in it among people for whom it is meaningful and whom we trust. By dwelling in the "forms and rituals of one religion we can thus learn meanings which reach a more universal truth." In a note of irony, perhaps, Polanyi appears to be suggesting that the religious community ought to become more like the scientific community where respect for tradition and authority are maintained with the purpose of encouraging creative dissent that will change the tradition—"a Society of Explorers, rather than rule and dogma, to safeguard the search for truth."[60]

Scott says that Polanyi has shown how our "faith, imagination and personal judgment, so long paralyzed by the poison of skeptical doubt, in fact run right through all our knowledge. Without faith in a real universe and in our own powers of getting hold of some direction and sense in it, there is no knowledge at all. Science relies on these same powers and stands or falls with them. . . ." Furthermore, she asserts, the judgment needed in moral and religious questions is like that of science but more personal, more involving of the whole persons:

> We have to believe in our own powers, but we have to train them, use them and discipline them as the scientist does his faculties. The truth of feeling, of moral sense, and of art need as much skill and dedication as the truth of science. It is not our every emotional whim that is to be trusted . . . but the best judgment and discrimination that we can attain through self-discipline and through apprenticeship to the masters of our art, who speak to us with authority because we recognize in our hearts that they speak the truth.[61]

<u>Concluding thoughts on Polanyi</u>

There are many far-ranging and fascinating connections that can be made between Polanyi's epistemology and an Anabaptist perspective on tradition-based, critical education. Polanyi's concept of "personal knowledge" in which all knowledge revolves around the responsible person resonates on a profound level with the Anabaptist emphasis on discipleship. Each individual is responsible to make a personal, conscious choice to follow Jesus Christ as Lord and Savior. In addition, every believer is considered to be a minister and is expected to give witness to his/her faith as well as engage in an ongoing process of communal moral discernment, offering his/her own personal interpretation to be tested by the community.

The concept of tacit knowledge and the bodily roots of all knowledge relates in many ways to the practical, ethical dimensions of Anabaptist faith and life. The Anabaptists formed their thinking, language, and practices from the Scriptures. They steeped themselves in the Scriptures and sought in every way possible to conform their lives to the Scriptures so that one could say the text lived in them and they lived in the text. In Polanyi's language we could say that they committed themselves to bodily indwell the particulars of their faith heritage as shown in the New Testament and in so doing, found themselves radically transformed and able to transcend the conventions and limitations of the establishment tradition around them. In their "radical reformation" they demonstrated that a great tradition provides the grounds both for its being maintained and its being changed, reformulated, and revitalized.

When Polanyi speaks of the need to participate in the same kind of indwelling as the teacher is practicing to more fully understand, he strikes an anchoring vital chord with the Jesus-centered Anabaptist movement. Perhaps more than anything, the Anabaptists emphasized committing oneself to follow Jesus' teaching and example. Neither church structures nor doctrines were considered as centrally important as modeling one's life on Jesus and the early church.

Polanyi's contention that there cannot be a detached, impersonal way of knowing that excludes the personal, passional involvement of the knower and that knowing must involve apprenticeship to a tradition and a teacher finds an enormous amount of resonance with Anabaptist distinctives. The Anabaptists were committed to careful study of the Scriptures by all believers and of Scripture's authority and relevance in all matters of faith and daily life. Their desire to faithfully embody the practices of servanthood, love of enemy, sharing material resources, truthfulness and so on, allowed them to participate in the same kind of indwelling as their teacher had practiced.

Polanyi's concept of "indwelling" as necessary to understand the nature of reality and God appears to affirm the Anabaptist perception that no one can truly know Christ except by following him in life. And there is also that intuitive love or hunch that moves one to commit oneself to indwell in such a way that new discoveries will be forthcoming which resonates with the accompanying affirmation that no one may follow Christ unless he/she has first known him. For both Polanyi and the Anabaptists, knowing and doing appear to be inseparably intertwined.

In addition, Polanyi's concept of the "Society of Explorers" has many fascinating possibilities for interaction with the Anabaptist approach to communal discernment in the interpreting community. The heuristic character of discovery enriches understandings of the process of discernment which expects the participation of each member of the community and the presence and guidance of the Holy Spirit. The community of explorers guided by rules of accountability and yet open to new intuitive, imaginative insights appears similar to the Anabaptist approach to discerning truth in many respects. For the Anabaptists, consistency with the Scriptures and the agreement of the community were key criteria for discerning whether an interpretation or practice was of the Holy Spirit. The dynamic of discernment involves both an authoritative traditional framework that placed limits on each individual's self-determination and an openness to the inbreaking of new insights brought by the Holy Spirit through individuals and confirmed by the community.

Polanyi's contention that there will be no new discovery or basis for radical change without first indwelling an authoritative tradition has profound implications for a tradition-based educational theory. In addition, his suggestion that a community must rely on the intuitive impulses of its individual adherents for the transformation of the community and his assumption that individuals can make contact with a reality separate from the community which draws the community into truer and more desirable ways to live, are highly significant. His suggestion that there is a spiritual reality embodied in tradition that both sustains the tradition and transcends it invites both a rootedness in tradition and a critical, creative dissent from it which calls the tradition to become more of what it ought to be.

Polanyi's recognition of the bodily, intuitive, and traditional roots of knowledge as well as the moral and aesthetic elements in all understanding will undergird our theory in multiple and deeply significant ways, the implications of which will become clearer as we proceed.

Introducing Rebecca Chopp

Rebecca S. Chopp is president of Colgate University in Hamilton, New York, and former dean of Yale Divinity School. She has published widely in the areas of theology and culture, feminist theory, liberation theology, and theological education. Her research also focuses on political theologies and theories of rhetoric, pragmatism, and poststructuralism. Her publications include *The Praxis of Suffering: An Interpretation of Liberation and Political Theologies* (1986), *The Power to Speak: Feminism, Language, and God* (1991), and *Saving Work: Feminist Practices of Theological Education* (1995).

For our purposes here, we will draw most heavily on Chopp's reflection on theological education in her book, *Saving Work*. She has attempted in her book to develop a new method of reflection on theological education that pays attention to issues of particularity, to contextuality, and attends to cultural movements and actual practices in theological education, based on the current subjects of theological education who are increasingly women.[62] Chopp notes that the book was written out of her own journey, with the hope that what she proposes will be transformative for Christianity and for theological education. She suggests that if we can begin to name the possibilities for transformation that already exist in movements such as feminism, "We will aid in continuing Christianity as a living presence, appropriate to the promise of its traditions and compatible with many of the rich textures of contemporary experience."

Chopp is convinced that feminist practices of theological education hold great promise for the future of theological education in general but also acknowledges that feminism doesn't have all the answers and that in the pluralism of many movements currently enriching contemporary theological education there is promise of transformation. The presence of larger numbers of women in theological education has enabled the "uncovering of new voices and faces in history," as well as defining new areas of research, providing new resources and new models for understanding God and the church, developing a spirituality that is more earthly (bodily), and advocating for more inclusive language.[63]

Chopp notes that a variety of people have lamented the current crisis in theological education. She suggests that the problems of theological education arise in the concreteness of reality and the way to address them is not to reformulate an abstract ideal but to return to a level of concreteness that attempts to discern "the historical, cultural, and symbolic factors at work in present theological education." It is in using this more contextual approach that feminists can contribute new perspectives on theological education. It is by focusing on the actual persons involved in theological education and on the concrete practices they engage in that the transformative potential of theological education will be enhanced. Of our current practices in theological education we need to ask the following: What symbols do they invoke, what virtues do they create, what ways of naming God do they entail?[64]

Chopp's approach to theology reflects an overall trend in North America in the past twenty years that involves "doing" theology as a self-consciously contextual enterprise while attempting to reflect more and more the rich racial, gender and cultural diversity of the world-wide Christian movement. In her work overall, Chopp appears to work with the concept of a "critical theory" that is historically and socially contextual. She doesn't attempt to make universal arguments or constructs that will hold for all times and places. Rather, she prefers to examine issues and practices that arise in specific situations, and to use symbols, images and concepts involved in that situation to move "against distortion and dysfunction" and shape "new forms of flourishing." She presupposes that the normative ideas used to critique a society must be rooted in experience and reflection on that society rather than coming from anywhere else.[65]

There are four areas in particular that I want to highlight and examine from Chopp's writing, drawing most heavily on her work as it relates to theological education. These areas are the person or subject-centered approach to education; ekklesia (the feminist construction of church); her emphasis on "practices" which function as sites of learning; and her concern for theology as "saving work."

<u>Key Chopp insights relevant to
a tradition-based, critical educational theory</u>

1. Person-centered education. Feminists, says Chopp, are developing their own forms of theological education. An important consideration in this process must be the question of who the subjects of theological education are and what they are experiencing. Clearly, the subjects of theological education include many more women than they did a decade or two ago, so one is led to ponder what the implications are for theological education. Education isn't simply about correct ideas or handing down tradition or training in technical expertise, Chopp contends. It is about human change and transformation. What does that mean when increasing numbers of women are involved?[66]

For feminists, she suggests, the crisis of church, culture, and personal life can be spoken of in part as the crisis of symbols and of meaning that produces transformation. What symbols and narratives can best construct habitus, the practice of reflective learning in which wisdom and knowledge are integrated? Chopp suggests that education is a process of spiritual and ecclesial formation that is focused in and through theological wisdom. Feminists, in developing their own forms of theological education can provide resources for personal and communal transformation.[67]

Chopp identifies three basic practices which are vital to revisioning theological education from a feminist perspective: narrativity, ekklesiality and theology. Narrativity involves women working to rewrite their lives in theological education. Ekklesiality involves participating in new forms and shapes of Christian community and the practice of theology is best described as a habitus, as ways of naming God.[68]

The practice of narrativity in theological education, Chopp observes, will give women the space and resources for writing their lives in new ways. Narrativity, she contends, is the "active agency of writing one's own life: the ongoing construction of one's own life in the context of human and planetary relations." The dominant stories of what it means to be a woman are changing, she continues and asserts that, "The power to write one's life as an active agent is the power to participate, potentially and actually, in the determination of cultural and institutional conditions." The traditional narratives, the rules and roles no longer fit contemporary cultural and political realities, she contends, so "the act of creating oneself amid social and interpersonal relations requires new meanings, symbols, characters, images, and plots." Across race, class, and sexual orientation lines, almost everyone must compose their lives in new ways, she says.[69]

The narrativity of one's life becomes the occasion to free one's self from definitions imposed on one by others, she writes.[70] Narrativity is a practice that allows us to consider the intersection of education, theology, and the agency of women in constructing their lives.

In her book *The Power to Speak*, Chopp shows how language is the site where our subjectivity is formed. We think and feel and experience the world according to the categories given to us by language. What a woman or man is varies in different cultures, but these definitions are before the individual. Feminist consciousness raising occurs when women discover a new discourse that transforms the meaning of women's experience.[71]

Education is often discussed as the formation of the individual, observes Chopp. Almost every view of education includes some notion of the formation of the self. Greek paideia sought to cultivate in a subject the wisdom and virtues necessary for the polis. Modern educational structures seek to form the subject into an autonomous subject who can make universal, objective judgments. Professional education seeks to provide professional skills, forming the student into an expert. Each of these views, she says, gives rise to particular educational structures and emphases. The feminist practice of narrativity provokes persons to define themselves and she cites three themes that appear necessary to nurture education as a space for narrativity: imagination, justice, and dialogue. Imagination includes the possibility for subjects to place themselves in new roles, stories, and patterns and to think differently about the past, the present, and the future. Dialogue includes the possibility to listen and to speak, to hear and to be heard. Justice means that everyone gets a voice in self-determination.[72]

2. Ekklesia. Feminist practices of ekklesia provide new understandings of what counts as church, suggests Chopp. "Women-church" or "ekklesia" which Chopp prefers to call it, is a term broadly used to mean that women's reality—experiences, relationships, practices—is and has been and will be church.[73]

The theological space of church in feminism will parallel two important aspects of the "classical" Christian tradition. The first similarity is that an ecclesiology of church is formulated through the notions of sin and grace. It isn't defined through individual piety or the handing down of tradition but through the antithesis of sin and grace and the communal appropriation of that grace. Feminist churchly theology also parallels the "classical" understanding of church in that feminists see the model of church as a sign to the world. The church is that which manifests God's salvific activity by existing for others. It is a visible sign of God's invisible grace.[74]

Differences show up though in other aspects of ecclesiology. Feminist theology most specifically identifies sin with patriarchy. The ekklesia denounces sin as that which breaks relationships with God, with others, with ourselves and with the earth. The ekklesia announces grace as new ways of human and planetary flourishing.[75] It sees itself as a "counter-public sphere" in that it stresses justice as a normative process of ekklesia and it stresses justice as the defining mission of ekklesia.

Chopp suggests that "as a counter-public of justice, the ekklesia works to create larger relations of justice in the broader social order." In doing so it relies on biblical, theological, and critical-theoretical resources to become a just community.[76]

Much of Chopp's reflection on ekklesia, particularly as it relates to stressing justice as a normative process, appears related to her earlier extensive work in liberation theology. In her first book, *The Praxis of Suffering*, she speaks of liberation theology as representing a huge paradigm shift in theological education and makes an insistent case that true religion demands that we turn our attention to those who are suffering. In contrast to modern theology's preoccupation with the solitary individual, liberation theology emphasizes the transformation of human social existence through praxis. She suggests that we think of Christ neither as separate from culture or identical with it, but as the *liberator* of culture.

There are those who took issue with Chopp's emphasis related to liberation theology suggesting that Chopp collapses religion into politics to the extent that little if any distinction remains.[77] In her more recent writings, however, Chopp appears to be working out some of the implications of liberation theology for a theology of church in a more nuanced approach that acknowledges both personal and structural dimensions. She speaks of the deep commitment many women have to the church as a space of justice and community and as a force of real political presence.[78]

Ekklesia stands as a critique of oppressive practices concerning women and offers an alternative to them. It exists where the Spirit is present, and where the Spirit works through men and women for "the realization of new life for all, including the earth." Ekklesia is "that place of God's redemptive presence where women and men can be emancipated from sin and transformed into freedom. In this sense, the ekklesia is defined by the presence of the Spirit."[79]

And the ekklesia denounces sin but it also announces grace, providing a space and practices for experiencing and creating new forms of relationships with God, self, others, and the world. These relations may be personal, interpersonal, or structural. The ekklesia as "a counter-public sphere of justice," provides a space in which each participant has a right to have a voice in self-determination and community determination.[80]

3. Practices as sites of learning. What I find most fascinating about Chopp's overall approach in her book *Saving Work* is the way in which she combines ethics as an integral part of her "knowing." Truth, she says, is derived from "saving work" or "emancipatory praxis."[81] Truth is not a disembodied concept or proposition but is derived out of the concrete practices of daily life together, practices that include bodily manifestations of care, liberation, and justice.

What does Chopp mean by practices? She defines "practice" as "socially shared forms of behavior that mediate between what are often called subjective and objective dimensions. A practice is a pattern of meaning and action that is both culturally constructed and individually instantiated. The notion of practice draws us to inquire into the shared activities of groups of persons that provide meaning and orientation to the world, and that guide action."[82]

Chopp cites others who are also finding the concept of practices helpful in discussing theological education. David Kelsey has suggested that theological education be organized around the study of concrete practices in congregations. Relying on MacIntyre, he suggests that practices are shared, that they require interaction and mutual participation, and that they are guided by norms or implicit rules. Craig Dykstra also uses practices in relation to theological education suggesting that they are not individual techniques but shared activities through which knowledge—in its fullest sense—occurs.[83]

Practices involve full embodied actions. They hold inner intention and outer behavior together denying any systematic distinction between the spiritual/intellectual and the physical/material. If we examine the practice of worship, for example, we observe that it involves the movements of bodies—the sensory engagement of sight, hearing, taste, smell, and feeling—and it engages the affective, ethical, and cognitive dimensions of attentiveness. Viewing theology as a practice, suggests Chopp, may allow us to interpret its communal nature including attention to where and how theology is done and by whom, and to note that the "bodiliness of practice allows a fuller sense of what goes on in the physical and temporal space of theological education."[84]

Feminist spirituality emphasizes embodiment, notes Chopp. Care for bodies, including the body of the earth, is a deep and vital aspect of feminist spirituality. A spirituality of embodiment stresses an attentiveness to the body, attending to all bodies in their differences and attending to our own embodiment as "loci of God." There is a strong sense that a spirituality of connectedness and embodiment is necessary to counter the patriarchal spirituality of detachment and separation. Detachment from the body, the earth, and others has traditionally been understood as some of Christian spirituality's highest attainments. But a feminist spirituality of connectedness hopes to heal and resist the spirituality of detachment and separation.[85]

Many women have experienced the day-to-day living out of reproductive systems, caring for the wounded, the birthing of children, the feeding of souls and bodies. The religious experiences of many women include practices in the daily connections of life. The "nexus of religious experiences," is for many in and through relationships, friends, families and memories of the dead. Chopp asks, could the vision of God today—in a day desperate for care, sustenance, relationality, and physicality, come from a woman's day-to-day walk with her God?[86]

Moral theology has been dominated by an active body/mind dualism, Chopp contends, so feminists must construct embodiment as a moral value. There must be recognition that all of our knowledge is body-mediated knowledge.[87] Concentration on the bodiliness of practices allows us to think about education in new ways. To identify practices as the sites of learning is to avoid common divisions in thinking about education and to require new language to name the process of education, suggests Chopp. We gain new ways of thinking about education as a process and not simply a product. Teaching methodologies have been focused on conveying information and helping the student master and express such information. Constructive questions about education are usually limited to how to order cognitive learning. The advantage of focusing on practices within theological education is that it both requires and allows a fuller range of forms of knowing.[88]

4. Theology as "saving work." Chopp describes the practice of theology as like the communal process of quilting, weaving, and constructing, of bringing "scraps" of materials used elsewhere and joining them in new ways. She suggests that feminist theology be imaged as a quilt, or as weaving or reconstructing, and that it be understood to be a work of "emancipatory praxis."[89]

Theology, she writes, is "a socially shared behavior that provides meaning and orientation to the world and guides action." Often in the past, theology has been about formal and/or existential "knowledge" and has had only secondary implications for orientation and action. Yet for many women and men, she contends, theology is about "saving work," the emancipatory praxis of God and of the Christian community in the world. Students immersed in faith communities of saving work engage in denouncing sin and announcing grace—working toward radical transformation. "This participation in God's saving activity includes 'work' that ranges from creating spaces of lamentations, to analyzing systems of distortion, to becoming friends with those in need, to experimenting with new concepts and forms of justice. Women and men engaged in feminist practices of theological education participate in the socially shared behavior of saving work," Chopp contends.[90]

Chopp notes that feminist theology understands the "Christian thing" not primarily as a written tradition through which the past reveals the truth to us, but as the activity of emancipatory praxis in the present and future as much as in the past. Truth in other words, has to do with saving work. Feminist theologians tend to view the "tradition" in terms of how texts have functioned in harmful ways. They recognize that the past is represented too often through the texts of those in power, with almost total silence from women and those who are deemed "others." This is not to discount the use of the "tradition" within feminist theology, Chopp acknowledges, but rather to dispute that the tradition has ethical or epistemological priority over present and future survival and flourishing.[91]

Feminist theology, Chopp contends, strives to transform the faith or the tradition away from its "patriarchal distortions." The grammar or the symbolic logic of Christian faith is constructed in feminist theology through the understanding of "emancipatory praxis" and not through assuming a unified textual narrative that provides a kind of timeless grammar of faith.[92]

In a recent book Chopp edited, *Horizons in Feminist Theology*, which includes thirteen women reflecting on feminist theory and theology, there is virtually unanimous rejection of the past as the site of normative criteria. The present is the locus of feminist normative judgments, most say, and feminist theorists are responsible for the content and character of their criteria. The adequacy of claims must be evaluated, not by whether they cohere with an authoritative past, but by how they contribute to or constrain the creation of more viable cultures, societies, and communities. The articles in the book stress that religious beliefs, practices, and theological claims are formed for practical purposes and evaluative criteria are pragmatic in character.[93]

Feminist theology, as Chopp describes it, places ethics as central to the nature of theological "knowing." As "saving work," feminist theology is itself a type of ethical and moral practice aimed at survival and flourishing.[94]

Theology as saving work, asserts Chopp, brings together ethics and knowing within both its communal and personal dimensions. Persons engaged in theology must be shaped in virtues and must learn to know from action even as they learn to act. Such a theology will be contextual, helping people to interpret, analyze and transform their world but also speaking in and through such situations to broader global realities.[95]

Concluding thoughts on Chopp

While it may not seem readily apparent what feminism and Anabaptism have in common, a closer examination will show that there is significant affinity between Chopp's feminist approach and an Anabaptist understanding of how we come to know. There are also very significant points of difference.

Areas of resonance that can helpfully inform an educational theory include primarily the understanding that theology arises from reflection on daily practice and is understood as saving work. Truth isn't understood to be a disembodied concept but rather is derived out of communal discernment about how we are to live and about what our present and future activity should entail. Rather than priority being given to establishing an infallible interpretation of the Scriptures or a comprehensive and systematic theology, the stress in both cases is on reflection about how we are to practice our faith. There is also much affinity in relation to the desire to see Scriptures interpreted contextually, to reflect on what the Scriptures and the Spirit are saying in light of the problems and decisions that must be addressed right now, and to act on them regardless of the social consequences.

In Chopp's joining of the ethical with our knowing, she resonates with the Anabaptist concern to reflect continually on the practical consequences of a particular teaching or reading of the text. Practices that are understood to provide the most potent sites of learning serve both Chopp's and the Anabaptist's concern to avoid artificial dualisms whether between belief and practice, faith and life, body and mind, or spiritual and physical aspects of life. With their mutual awareness of the bodily and concrete character of practices, they also share an emphasis on embodiment in daily life of a community's central commitments.

There appears to be some resonance in the concept of church as a "counter-public sphere," and the model of church as a sign to the world committed to embodying just and caring relationships. Tension arises however, when the feminist agenda expects the role of the church in the world to become politicized along ideological lines. An Anabaptist critique would caution that such a stance begins to resemble the Constantinian fusion of church and state. For the Anabaptists, the church community will be comprised not on the basis of gender, ideology, or shared stories of oppression, but of baptized believers committed to following Jesus Christ and experiencing the regenerating activity of the Holy Spirit.

The role of the tradition in both approaches is one concerning which further discussion is needed. A first impression is that the two approaches are widely divergent on this question, yet some of the difference is more in emphasis than substance. The Anabaptists highly esteemed the tradition of the New Testament church and sought to emulate its practices and language in all that they did. They lived into that tradition because they deemed it authoritative, and also perhaps, because they had great confidence that it provided the best resource for flourishing in the present.[96] If I can use Chopp's terminology, it could be argued that the Anabaptists re-envisioned the New Testament tradition and gave it concrete shape in their everyday practices largely because they perceived it would lead to their "emancipation" from the oppressive practices of Constantinian Christendom. They appropriated a revitalized tradition for "emancipatory transformation."

Having said that, however, it remains important to emphasize that the Anabaptists drew the source of their inspiration from the Gospels and from Jesus, and were suspicious of any ideological, political, or ethical agenda imposed as a grid on the Scriptures. And the new freedom they experienced didn't include enhanced political clout or individual rights but a transformation of love and will that compelled them to freely give up their lives for the sake of Christ and his kingdom. The Gospels and the ethic of Jesus provided authoritative norms for them and it was in living into that which they deemed authoritative for guiding their daily life that they experienced a transformation they were willing to die for.

The feminist refusal to authorize the past as providing normative criteria for the present is, in my view, the most significant point of tension between the two approaches. Chopp suggests that adequacy is not evaluated by coherence to the past but by how the past is used to contribute to the creation of viable structures now. The Anabaptists' determination to give priority to the scriptural tradition as authoritative, while incorporating practices of discernment that assured its interpretation would be relevant to their present practice of discipleship and mission, meant that while norms were rooted in the past, they were always brought into dialogue with the present and proved to be powerfully transformative.

Chopp also emphasizes self-determination and the freedom that comes from narrating one's own life as well as the right to define one's own life. Her approach appears to emulate the modern individualist approach to self determination far more than the Anabaptists would have been comfortable with. In their own way, however, they "narrated" their own lives, proclaiming and living radically new ways of embodying the gospel as Christ-centered communities of disciples.

Chopp roots her norms in present experience without clarity about criteria for determining what constitutes "emancipatory praxis" other than an individual or communal determination that a practice is just and promotes survival and flourishing. The danger in Chopp's approach it seems to me, is that an individual or group can readily come to identify their own preferences with justice, or their own culture with the will of God. An ideology of emancipatory praxis dictates what may or may not be appropriate and only the Scriptures that are deemed emancipatory are taken seriously. It isn't clear to me why rejecting past religious tradition as authoritative for providing normative criteria and naming the present as the locus of normative judgments solves the dilemma of how to provide criteria for what comprises justice and flourishing. Rather than suggesting one as preferred over the other, as if one can function independently of the other, it would seem the part of wisdom to identify an approach that demonstrates their interdependence. For a resolution to this tension we turn to Nancey Murphy.

Introducing Nancey Murphy

Nancey Murphy holds doctorates in the philosophy of science as well as in theology. Most of her professional work has involved study of the relationship between theology and science. She is currently Professor of Christian Philosophy at Fuller Theological Seminary and member of the long-range planning committee for conferences on science and theology sponsored by the Vatican Observatory. Murphy is the author of six books, including *Reconciling Theology and Science: A Radical Reformation Perspective* (1997), *Beyond Liberalism and Fundamentalism* (1996), *Anglo-American Postmodernity* (1997), and with George F. R. Ellis, *On the Moral Nature of the Universe* (1996). Her book *Theology in the Age of Scientific Reasoning* (1990) received the American Academy of Religion Award for Excellence and a Templeton Award for books in theology and science.

Murphy observes that her career in theological academia has been rather varied. She received her philosophy of science degree from the University of California at Berkeley and her theological education at an institution identified with the liberal side of American Christianity (The Graduate Theological Union also in Berkeley), yet she has taught for a number of years at what is thought of as a conservative seminary. She calls herself "an explorer" of varied theological landscapes. She contends that the misunderstandings and disagreements among various theological perspectives are "comparable to the disagreements and communication failures that Thomas Kuhn recognized in the history of science," and that this is the case in theology and in science because persons tend to adhere to competing paradigms and so talk past one another. The current shift in philosophical assumptions in what she calls "Anglo-American postmodernity" is creating even deeper levels of misunderstanding among some constituencies, yet she argues that this "revolution" may offer hope for a rapprochement between Christians of the left and right. It is her desire to contribute to this movement.[97]

Murphy calls herself a convert to the kind of Christianity that descends from the Anabaptist or Radical Reformation heritage. The moment she knew she had to make a change, she writes, came in reading the life of Michael Sattler, who had been a Catholic (like Murphy). Later he became one of the most significant leaders of the little group of Swiss Brethren who began the Radical Reformation and played a leadership role in the Schleitheim gathering which gave rise to the first Anabaptist confession of faith. Soon after that conference Sattler was imprisoned, charged with heresy, brutally tortured, and killed. His final words were, "Almighty eternal God, Thou who art the way and the truth, since I have not been taught otherwise by anyone, so by Thy help I will testify this day to the truth and seal it with my blood."[98] Murphy has joined one of the groups who descend from the Anabaptist movement, the Church of the Brethren. She is ordained to the set-apart ministry in that denomination.

Murphy has written extensively about the problems of foundationalism in philosophy. She interacts on many levels with non-foundationalist philosophers of science and theologians.[99] She sees W. V. O. Quine's picture of knowledge as a web as pivotal in the history of philosophy. For a handy date to mark the beginning of the end of the modern period Murphy suggests 1951, which was the date of the publication of Quine's "Two Dogmas of Empiricism," which called the foundationalist account of knowledge into question.[100]

Quine's picture of knowledge as a web or a net, which Murphy describes as a holist theory of knowledge, differs in important respects from foundationalsim. First, she says, "there *need* be no intrinsically indubitable (unrevisable) beliefs; nor are there any sharp distinctions among types of belief, only degrees of differences in how far a belief is from the experiential boundary." Second, for foundationalists reasoning goes only in one direction—up from the foundation. For holists, there is no preferred direction of reasoning, and the kinds of connections among beliefs in the web are many: "strict logical implication, weaker probabilistic arguments, arguments 'forward' to further conclusions; arguments 'backward' to presuppositions." This, she says, allows holists to take account of the fact that data (scientific facts, interpretations of texts, or whatever) are theory-laden and partly dependent on theoretical knowledge. In general, "holism" relies on coherence of the web, in which each belief is supported by its ties to its neighboring beliefs, and ultimately to the whole.[101]

Murphy acknowledges a problem with Quine's image by asking what ought to be done when there are competing webs of equally consistent beliefs. In philosophy of science she observes an important line of development from Karl Popper to Thomas Kuhn and Imre Lakatos for addressing this problem. For theological purposes, she finds the epistemological work of MacIntyre's work in moral philosophy most helpful. Lakatos and MacIntyre have made important amendments to Quinean and Kuhnian holism, she argues, and she chooses to label their theories "historicist-holism."[102]

A reviewer of Murphy's book, *Theology in the Age of Scientific Reasoning*, observes that it is an impressive effort which shows how the philosophy of science of the late Lakatos can be used to develop a persuasive case for the argument that theological reasoning is similar to scientific reasoning. The book demonstrates Murphy's informed interest in the value of interdisciplinary research in the history and philosophy of science, theology and the philosophy of religion. She argues that assertions of theology provide knowledge in much the same way as do those of the natural sciences.[103]

Key Murphy insights relevant to
a tradition-based, critical educational theory

1. Relationship between science and theology. Murphy presents a hierarchical model—a schematic representation—to depict the relationship between theology and the sciences. Physics, the study of the simplest building blocks of reality, goes at the bottom. The rest of the basic sciences (chemistry, the various levels of biology) are located in order above physics to represent the fact that they study increasingly complex, comprehensive systems. Above biology the hierarchy branches. One branch includes the physical sciences that study increasingly comprehensive systems. Cosmology is at the top of this branch, since it studies the most encompassing system in the natural world—the entire universe. The second branch off of biology includes psychology and the social sciences. Murphy argues that theology can be thought of as the science at the top of the entire diagram, where both branches come together again, since it studies the most comprehensive and complex system of all—God in relation to both the natural world and human society.[104]

The relation between theology and the sciences is much like that between one science and another, Murphy contends. Each science has its own language and concepts and provides a relatively autonomous description of reality. Yet each can learn from its neighbors.[105] Murphy argues that theology is in fact much like a science, with its own proper data from history, revelation, and the cumulative experience of the church. Doctrines are comparable to theories in the sciences, rationally justified by their ongoing ability to explain the data. Christian doctrines are like scientific theories, in that they explain the *experiences* of Christians. For example the claims about the existence and action of the Holy Spirit are one important part of Christian teaching. We *need* the hypothesis of the Holy Spirit to *explain* what happens in the Christian life, just as a scientist needs a hypothesis to explain an observed phenomenon in the natural world.[106]

In science, while we never claim absolute certainty, she says, there are varying degrees of confidence. Theologians recognize the same sort of variation in Christian teaching. There are the basics we can't imagine being given up. But there are a variety of more speculative theories.

Murphy's lengthy analysis explains "theories of instrumentation" in science which she compares to theories of *interpretation* in theology. To illustrate her point, she turns to a case in astronomy. When a telescope was first introduced, a theory was needed to explain why appearances through the eye piece of this strange new instrument could be trusted to yield information about the nature of the heavenly bodies. In theology we need a theological hypothesis to explain how we can be confident about Christian teaching. She calls what is needed "the theory of Christian discernment." This theory asserts that the Christian community, because of the presence of the Holy Spirit, has the ability to judge whether or not practices, teachings, and prophecies are reliable. Christians possess an *inner witness* regarding what is or is not of God, as well as *public criteria* to test these judgments. In the New Testament this was often referred to as testing or discerning the spirits.[107]

Although the theory of discernment has received less attention than its due in recent years Murphy observes, it hasn't disappeared from the Christian scene. The sixteenth-century Anabaptists, as well as some of their contemporary descendants, put great emphasis on communal judgment. Their criteria, she says, include "consistency with Scripture and consensus of the community, on the assumption that the teachings and directions of the Holy Spirit cannot be self-contradictory."[108] We'll examine this Christian epistemic practice in more detail later.

2. *Role of tradition and formative texts.* Murphy, who relies extensively on MacIntyre's tradition-based approach to epistemology and ethics, notes that in his perspective a tradition always begins with some "contingent historical starting point—an authority of some sort, usually a text or set of texts." A tradition as he depicts it, Murphy contends, "is a historically extended, socially embodied argument about how best to interpret and apply the formative text(s)." All traditions tend to go through similar states, when inadequacies are identified in the face of theoretical or practical problems or due to challenge from other traditions. Over time, a tradition is reformulated and elaborated to meet such inadequacies. "The new version is obviously justified over its predecessor because it solves the problem its predecessor could not solve."[109]

A tradition then develops through successive attempts to interpret and apply the texts in new contexts Murphy continues. Application is essential. Traditions are socially embodied "in the life stories of the individuals and communities who share them, in institutions and social practices."[110] Inasmuch as traditions are embodied in social practices, we *live* in our traditions and can only think and perceive by using the categories, images, and stories they provide, Murphy contends.[111] And, she argues, taking up the *practices* of the early church is as important for entering the world of the Bible as is entering it through textual interpretation. Historical critical interpretation helps us recover the practices of the early church in their own setting and attempting to live out those practices in our setting will sensitize us to new meanings in the texts.[112]

Murphy also suggests that while the above definition of a tradition guarantees an authoritative role for Scripture, it guarantees as well a role for experience. The emphasis on social embodiment and application of the texts is another consequence of the postmodern recognition that "language and knowledge are not over against the world, and therefore needing to be compared or related to it, but rather that language and knowledge are part of the social world." Following from this emphasis on social embodiment must follow the acknowledgment that there can be no theology that doesn't in one way or another take account of contemporary experience. The process of *applying* a text requires knowledge of the situation *to which* it is applied. And if a tradition is by definition socially embodied, this application won't be an ivory-tower exercise, she asserts. Consequently experience is just as necessary a contributor to theology as are the formative texts, dissolving any perceived opposition between Scripture and experience as sources of theology.[113]

Murphy reverts to Quinean terminology when she suggests that the theologian can "be imagined to be contributing to the reweaving of the doctrinal web . . . whether this means minor repairs or a radical reformulation to meet an epistemological crisis in her tradition. In this reweaving she will be responsible to the formative texts, understood in light of the long development of communal practices of interpretation, but also responsible to that to which the texts are applied—the boundary conditions provided by current experience, in the broad sense . . . the life of the church in the world.[114]

3. The priority of the ethical and theological to intellectual life. One of the purposes of Murphy's work on the relationship between theology and science, she suggests, is to show that theology has a significant role to play in the academy as well as in the church. She also makes the bold claim that theology has as much to contribute to science as it has to learn from science. In particular, she argues, the social sciences could learn a lot from the vision of social relationships taught by Jesus and modeled imperfectly by believers churches.[115]

Murphy asserts that the question of what the ultimate goods are for human societies to pursue is an ethical question. The social sciences can't decide this for themselves. They need the discipline of ethics to answer this question which, she says, is a boundary question arising at one level on the hierarchy of sciences but calling for an answer from a higher level (see note 105). Murphy depicts how the social sciences have argued that they must be "value-free," and only describe what reality is. She cites ample evidence however, that demonstrates how they are not value free and how ethical positions have been incorporated without acknowledgment into the social sciences, particularly with their assumption about the necessity of violence to control human behaviors.[116]

Murphy argues that theology should have a top-down influence on both ethics and the social sciences, and she makes the bold claim that the teachings of Jesus, especially as Mennonites, Brethren and Quakers have understood it, provide a radically different view of the possibilities for human good than what is generally communicated in the social sciences. These teachings, particularly the Sermon on the Mount, she contends, should serve as an interpretive norm through which all the rest of Scripture should be understood.[117]

In their book *On the Moral Nature of the Universe*, Murphy and George Ellis show how a particular moral vision—a "kenotic" ethic—is supported "from below" by the social sciences and "from above" by theology. They argue that contemporary cosmology points ultimately to an ethic that centers on self-sacrifice and nonviolence and they develop a concept of self-sacrificial love that is applicable both to God's relation to the world and to human relations.

Murphy argues in that book and elsewhere that an ethic of self-sacrifice and nonviolence, drawn from radical reformation theology, can be made consistent with the social sciences. She refers to the social-Darwinist account which emphasizes competition for survival and nature "red in tooth and claw." When biologists emphasize a picture of nature as a scene of competition for survival, how are we to reconcile this with a picture of a self-sacrificing God who reaches out to save the weak, the lost, and even the enemy she wonders and suggests that what is needed is a change of perspective.[118] She suggests an approach that reconciles the "morality" of evolutionary biology with a Christian ethic of self-sacrifice, as well as with the self-sacrificial character of God by teaching us to see the work of God not in the predator but in the prey.[119]

Such an interpretation of suffering she contends, is consistent with Anabaptist thought in which "the suffering of Christians is not generally seen as a punishment for sins but rather as redemptive participation with Christ in the expected consequences of obedience to God amid a sinful world." Murphy is suggesting that a different theological perspective, along with a different moral formation, can predispose us to see reality differently than do those in other traditions.

A Radical Reformation perspective leads to a "hermeneutic of suspicion" directed toward the standard histories of science. If we learn "to live in the world without power—from the perspective of the prey rather than the predator, from the perspective of those living in solidarity with the weak and the outcast," then reality in all its aspects looks somewhat different. When we identify with the prey rather than the predator, we see "prefigured there the Lamb of God."[120]

Why, Murphy asks, did the radicals emphasize the separation of the church from the world? Because, she says,

> It is the church's job not merely to theorize about alternative social structures, but to provide empirical evidence that an alternate society is possible. A society based on reconciliation, a society that uses no violence, a society whose ultimate form of punishment is nothing harsher than the request to leave the fellowship—such a society can actually exist. By showing this possibility, Christians are light to the world.

To illustrate her point she describes a restorative justice approach as an alternative to the retributive justice system of an eye for an eye, a tooth for a tooth currently predominant in the United States. Jesus' teaching stimulates us to envision alternatives, she suggests.[121]

Murphy makes a strong case for the priority of the ethical and theological to the rest of the intellectual life. Rather than right understanding preceding right action, she says, "moral formation aimed at subduing the will-to-power is a necessary *prerequisite* for seeing reality aright."

We can't expect right living to follow a good education; moral formation in our educational contexts must be a first priority.[122]

4. Practices characteristic of the Radical Reformation heritage. Murphy has begun to detail some of the characteristic practices that grow out of the Radical Reformation represented by the Anabaptists. While agreeing with MacIntyre's assertion that outside of all tradition one is morally and intellectually destitute and that it is our traditions that give us the resources for justifying our actions as well as our truth claims, she suggests that his account of traditions embodied in social practices has two major weaknesses. One is that he gives an overly optimistic evaluation of social practices and thus of the capacities of the (socially embodied) intellect. Secondly, she suggests, he ought to acknowledge Nietzsche's account of the epistemic distortions caused by the will to power and provide a more nuanced account of social practices.[123]

Jesus recognized the corrupted power of institutionalized religion of his day. So we too must recognize the power of institutionalized religion. Yet this need not deter us, she argues, from witnessing to the powers of the world by forming communities in which social structure and practices can more closely approximate God's will for the ordering of human life. As a powerful antidote to modern individualism, she argues, the church must be a new counter-society.[124]

Murphy suggests, with remarkable relevance to this conversation, that a set of social practices characteristic of the Radical Reformation heritage provides just exactly the remedy needed to tame the will-to-power. The role of these power-renouncing practices and the virtues it takes to participate in them leads her to claim, as shown above, a priority for the ethical and theological over the rest of the intellectual life.

Furthermore, Murphy believes that the Radical Reformation emphasis on power-renouncing practices provides resources that demonstrate the possibility of human knowing even while responding to the widespread recognition of the distortions caused by the will-to-power. From the perspective of those who have learned to live in solidarity with the weak and outcast, reality looks somewhat different. This perspective needs to be reflected throughout our educational curriculum, she suggests.[125]

The power-renouncing practices Murphy cites are as follows: nonviolence and its refusal to use physical force against another; "revolutionary subordination," a strategy John Howard Yoder describes for righting injustices without the use of any power other than that of the imagination;[126] the separation of church and state as the rejection of institutional longing for alliance with the power of the state; and learning to live simply, which reduces the need for power to defend one's economic privileges.

The critical core practice within a faith community, however, will be that of discernment, she asserts. Murphy calls "discernment" as it is practiced within Radical Reformation churches a "Christian epistemic practice"—a communal practice aimed at the pursuit of truth. In general, this practice involves criteria for judging teaching, prophecy, and decisions as being or not being of the Spirit of Christ.[127] She suggests in particular the practices of nonviolence, simple living, and revolutionary subordination as necessary to produce people with the virtues needed for the practice of discernment (for her the central and critical practice of community life) to succeed.[128]

Murphy explores the concept of a "Christian epistemic practice" at great length in her book *Theology in the Age of Scientific Reasoning*. She argues that Christians are able, because of the indwelling of the Holy Spirit, to recognize what is or is not a genuine work of the Holy Spirit, and she claims to have found a great deal of agreement on criteria for making such judgments among Christians.[129]

Murphy argues that on the basis of the practice of communal discernment, participants in a wide assortment of Christian communities select certain observable events in ordinary church life and designate them as acts (or words) of God. Furthermore, they believe they are entitled to say they *know* that they are acts of God and explain how they know it by referring to identified criteria and practices. If these claims to know about God's involvement in certain events appeared only occasionally or in fringe groups, she said, one might be inclined to dismiss them. But against the background of the episodes in Christian history, the claims have some warrant to be taken seriously. Judgment practices aimed at detecting the work of the Holy Spirit in human life certainly don't go beyond what the New Testament says Christian communities are able to do.[130]

Murphy cites several influential Christian leaders who developed criteria by which a community can discern whether or not an interpretation, decision or practice was of the Holy Spirit. She shows in Jonathan Edwards's work why the criteria he developed seem to be the appropriate ones for such judgments. Edwards shows us a plausible theoretical connection between the nature of God (love), God's manner of operation (indwelling of the Holy Spirit), and the effects (making the person like Jesus) so that we understand why appearance of the "fruits of the Spirit" is a defining criterion for the action of God in a person's or a community's life.

She also illustrates the approach developed by Ignatius of Loyola, observing that according to Ignatius, the spiritual director and retreatant have identifiable ways to discern the presence of the Holy Spirit to determine whether a vocational decision was made in accordance with the call of God.[131]

The Anabaptist community also had ways to evaluate teachings that pertain to doctrine, morality, and discipline. Consistency with the Scriptures served as the *criterion* for decision-making among the radicals, yet the *practical test* of consistency was the agreement of the entire community, and the *means* of reaching agreement was open discussion within the context of prayer.[132]

In comparing the Anabaptists to Ignatius and Edwards, Murphy remarks that among the Anabaptists we see even more dedication to "thinking with the word of God in the Scriptures" than we found in Edwards and Ignatius. We also see the emphasis on love as a sign of God's work and among the Anabaptists an even greater emphasis on reconciliation. "We have been brought to unity" rings through their documents, she claims. In general, the Anabaptists tend to be much more "practical" in their approach than the other approaches cited, and willingness to suffer for Christ takes a much more prominent place.[133]

Murphy argues that for the Anabaptists the Spirit's role in shaping the practices and doctrine of the community is more creative than it was for Edwards or Ignatius inasmuch as we see the development of practices new in their day such as believer's baptism, the ban, and rejection of the sword and oaths. The Anabaptists saw the role of the Spirit as being to help them *determine* what the Bible teaches. It is especially among the Anabaptists and their heirs, she suggests, that we find the belief in the Holy Spirit's primary relation to a community expressed in communitarian practices, and it is their emphasis on discernment as a communal practice that corrects for individual delusion and ignorance.[134]

Concluding thoughts on Murphy

Murphy's perspective will play a defining role in our development of a tradition-based, critical approach to education that is informed from an Anabaptist perspective. Her contribution is especially significant because she has already interacted extensively with Anabaptist distinctives and integrated them into her philosophy and theology.

The purpose of this summary then, will not be to show connections or distinctions between Murphy's approach and that of the Anabaptists, as was the case for Polanyi and Chopp. Rather, it will simply be to highlight central features and bring them into conversation with the other two voices at the table.

Murphy's interdisciplinary approach shows how science is more like theology and vice versa than many have assumed. She moves us gently but firmly away from foundational conceptions of knowing toward an energizing vision of the opportunities made possible for tradition-based thinking and practice by nonfoundational epistemology. Murphy demonstrates convincingly that theology has a significant role to play in both the academy and in the church and that it should have a top-down influence on ethics and the social sciences. She boldly asserts that the teachings of Jesus and the Anabaptist tradition provide the most potent resource for the social embodiment of the good. And she is convinced the social sciences could learn a lot from the vision of social relationships taught by Jesus and modeled imperfectly by believers churches.

In Murphy's daring advocacy of one tradition and its often misunderstood and disregarded resources for enriching public debate and practice, she demonstrates the new freedom for explorations about knowing made possible by a non-foundationalist approach. It is now an open season for testing and comparing the adequacy of rival traditions, for identifying weaknesses and addressing inadequacies, for providing resources from other traditions that suggest more adequate answers to epistemological crises.

Murphy is eager to demonstrate how one particular tradition has the resources to address the problems endemic to postmodernity. She invites us to enter the world of the Bible in much the same way as was done by the Anabaptists, who took up the practices of the early church and learned to think and speak the language and world view of the Scriptures. Murphy encourages us to recover traditional reading strategies that entice us to enter sympathetically into the world of the text with the intention of embodying the practices of the early church in our own setting.

Murphy contends that by living into the texts and practices of a particular community's tradition, we participate in an historically extended, socially embodied argument about how best to interpret and apply a given tradition's formative texts. By engaging both with formative texts and with their present embodiment and application, we are continually involved in a dynamic process of communal discernment about how to construct life together. The practice of discernment is for Murphy one of the points at which theology can be said to most resemble science, with its own criteria for judging claims about truth.

Murphy identifies several potent contributions to epistemology, theology, and ethics that originate in the New Testament but find social embodiment in the Anabaptist tradition. Among the primary contributions she sees the Anabaptist tradition making to the public debate about knowing is the practice of communal discernment with its identified criteria and process.

Related to the process of discernment is the Anabaptist recognition of the tendency for a will-to-power to impact relationships and to obscure the truth. She applauds the Anabaptists' sensitive appropriation of power-renouncing practices and the recognition that persons must be formed within the virtues of these practices to appropriately enter into the communal and Spirit-led discernment. In perhaps her boldest assertion yet, Murphy argues that these practices, characteristic of the Anabaptist heritage, provide resources that demonstrate the possibility of human knowing even while offering the remedy needed to ameliorate the distortions caused by the will-to-power.

With the Anabaptists as her exemplars of persons willing to suffer rather than inflict violence and suffering on others, Murphy builds an intricate worldview based on the image of a self-sacrificing God who reaches out to save the weak and even the enemy. Such a theological perspective predisposes us to see reality differently, from the perspective of the prey rather than the predator. The central and vital role of these power-renouncing practices and the important virtues that grow out of participation in them leads her to claim that ethical and theological concerns must have priority in the rest of the intellectual life and should be reflected throughout any educational curriculum. In a profoundly daring and insightful move, she has retrieved the Anabaptist tradition, shown its penetrating relevance to current debates about how we come to know and about tradition-based, critical educational practices.

In discussing the implications of her approach for the future of Mennonite higher education she draws three conclusions: 1) the tradition-dependent character of all inquiry provides a way ahead for academia in general and also offers a rationale for the particularity of a higher education thoroughly steeped in its own formative texts; 2) the priority of moral formation to the intellectual life which includes not only shared information but a specific form of life needs to be adopted and practiced in all aspects of campus life; and 3) an awareness of a different theology which emphasizes power-renouncing practices and originates from the perspective of those living in solidarity with the weak and the outcast will lead to a perspective on reality which ought to be reflected all across the curriculum.[135]

Chapter 5

AN EMERGING CONSENSUS ABOUT "KNOWING"

Michael Polanyi, Rebecca Chopp, and Nancey Murphy have demonstrated the possibility of ways of knowing that are more encompassing of the fullness of reality than the purely rational or quantitative modes which dominated the modern era. We have seen a variety of ways of knowing described—tacit, bodily, communal, intuitive-imaginative, practical, traditional, and spiritual ways of knowing, as well as efforts to maintain the best of clear thinking.

As we have listened to all persons at the table speak out of their own areas of passion and expertise, it has become evident that there are areas of resonance among them. There are also areas of dissonance; this helps highlight what issues need more discussion. It is not my intention or interest here to point out all areas of agreement or disagreement or to attend fully to the differing presuppositions or priorities. Rather, I hope to weave a web of interrelatedness that has enough integrity and is strong enough to bear the weight of an emerging theory of tradition-based, critical education from an Anabaptist perspective. The areas of resonance and dissonance will be explored in the following discussion, then will be woven into a more comprehensive whole in the final chapter.

Exploring New Paradigms

Our concepts of knowledge have been dominated by a paradigm which suggests that unless knowledge can be constructed on infallible, provable foundations and shown to be true by formal verification procedures and empirical proof, it will not be deemed worthy of serious consideration nor become a viable structure. The distortions that have resulted from this truncated view of how we come to know have been described at length in the work of Polanyi, Chopp, and Murphy, as well as many other authors cited earlier, including Edward Farley, Douglas Sloan, Alisdair MacIntyre, and more. One dominant paradigm of knowledge, while serving to describe imperfectly one mode of cognitive functioning, has failed to capture the rich ways that we come to know.

Our conversation partners have suggested other paradigms. Polanyi's includes the concept of "personal knowledge," knowledge which revolves around the responsible person, a person who brings bodily, intuitive, and traditional components to knowing. Any individual, by indwelling the tacit knowledge subliminal to personal awareness, is in a position to reach beyond what is known to make new connections and discover new aspects of reality.

Gelwick described Polanyi's paradigm as a "heuristic philosophy," a paradigm that depicts the discovery possible when one is well rooted and immersed in a great tradition, yet has an intimation of a reality that beckons one to transcend the limits of that tradition. Polanyi's paradigm embraces both the dimensions of traditional, accumulated wisdom based on the experiences of the past and the present intuitive explorations into the unknown. A responsible person within the "society of explorers" is encouraged toward original discovery from within the context of a disciplined community.

The paradigm suggested by Chopp, though she refers to it as a metaphor, is that of a quilt. Theology no longer attempts to uncover unchanging foundations or build its edifice purely on cognitive truths but rather involves "quilting, weaving, and constructing" as a communal process of bringing "scraps" of materials used elsewhere and joining them in new ways.[1] Theology as "saving work" joins ethics and epistemology in a partnership of knowing that makes ethics the central and defining component. It is "emancipatory praxis" that brings harmony to the quilt, not by providing a new metatheoretical framework but by providing the ethical guide that will bring harmony to the various theories stitched into the quilt. Emancipatory praxis that promotes personal and social flourishing provides the ultimate aim of doing theology communally. Emancipatory praxis involves composing narratives, imaging new meanings for symbols, and engaging in practices of justice as communities of discourse and practice who together stitch a warm and beautiful theological quilt.

For Murphy, the image of knowledge as a web provided by Quine appears to serve as the defining paradigm. She describes the "web" paradigm as a wholistic theory of knowledge, and that unlike foundationalism, it needs no absolutely certain knowledge on which to build a reliable structure. All knowledge is connected to other knowledge in ways that support it and tie in into the whole. The connections between kinds of knowledge are stronger or weaker, based on what supportive evidence can be shown to reinforce confidence in the truthfulness of what is perceived. There are no sharp distinctions among types of belief. Rather, there are degrees of difference in how far a belief is from the experiential boundary. Every belief is supported by its ties to neighboring beliefs and can be justified by being closely tied to beliefs we have no good reason to call into question. When, because of conflicts in the web or because of new experience, the web becomes weak or tears in one place or another, there are ways to revise and reweave it that restore greater consistency and coherency with the whole.[2]

Murphy appears to suggest that webs are constructed within traditions and that traditions and their webs, when confronted with an epistemological crisis, either succeed or fail depending on whether they find the resources to deal with the crisis. Each of us contributes to weaving the web as we offer new insights that arise out of our own individual or communal discoveries. It is individuals, within the context of communal discernment, who add to the viability and beauty of the web of knowledge that undergirds our life together.

Each of these paradigms in its own way emphasizes the personal responsibility of its participants to enter into a communal process of knowledge construction. Polanyi highlights the tacit knowledge out of which knowledge is constructed. Chopp emphasizes the ethical mandate that must be central to that construction even as Murphy underscores the interconnectedness of all knowledge both with traditionally established sources of knowledge and with present experience. Each in his or her own way provides a helpful alternative both to foundationalism and to relativism, describing "strategies of truth" informed by tacit traditional knowledge, present practices, imagination and communal discernment. The paradigms and strategies they offer open up an exciting new space for shaping fresh images and efforts to reconceptualize education.

KNOWING AND TRADITION

It is fascinating to observe the broad resonance between Polanyi and Murphy in their approach to tradition. They each make a case for traditional frames of reference. Polanyi's suggestion that traditionalism is based on a deeper insight into the nature of knowledge than is scientific rationalism resembles the notion of tradition-dependent rationality that Murphy expounds. They both seem to suggest that one can't achieve understanding except by starting from a particular cultural inheritance through which we learn language, moral values, and any number of socially embodied practices. What Polanyi describes as tacit knowledge (the background subsidiary awareness we've learned by apprenticeship to the tradition) resembles Murphy's acknowledgment that we live in our traditions as socially embodied arguments about how best to apply the formative texts. In fact, it is largely by apprenticeship to a particular tradition that we not only understand it but transcend its limitations.[3]

Polanyi makes the explicit assertion that it is by dwelling in the forms and rituals of one religion that we can learn meanings which reach a more universal truth. Murphy's various discussions about traditions engaging each other to provide both resources and correctives to each other seem to be reaching in similar fashion for a more universal rapport and mutual engagement around the question of what is true and good.

Polanyi suggests that a great tradition provides the grounds for both its being maintained and its being changed—and that the religious community ought to become more like the scientific community where respect for tradition and authority are maintained *with the purpose* of encouraging creative dissent that will change the tradition. Murphy suggests in similar fashion that traditions are continually responding to epistemological crises and, depending on how rich and strong the tradition, will either find the means to reformulate and renew the tradition or experience disintegration. And it is the tradition itself that authorizes ongoing discernment about how we should live in light of the new data and new problems that present themselves. The tradition itself encourages prophetic voices and expects the inbreaking Holy Spirit which may shatter comfortable conventions. Polanyi and Murphy don't see traditions primarily as stultifying and rigid but rather as dynamic, adapting organisms that maintain continuity primarily in the interests of ongoing discovery and growth.

Traditions also provide authoritative frameworks that limit any individual's self determination, both Polanyi and Murphy suggest in their own way. Traditions protect communities from being manipulated and dominated by an ideology or autocrat. There is safety within the ancient and generational accumulation of communal wisdom. By being rooted in the tradition and the formative texts of the community, persons are less vulnerable to overpowering movements with political agendas that claim ultimate loyalties.

Chopp seems much more wary of the role of tradition. She doesn't want to assume a unified textual narrative that provides a timeless grammar of faith but finds commitment to the ethical mandate of "emancipatory praxis" far more reliable for judging present actions. She explicitly says there should be less emphasis on tradition than on the present activity of "emancipatory praxis" and that tradition ought not have ethical or epistemological priority over present/future survival and flourishing. It is the voices from the margins that remind us that the traditions haven't served us well which occasion Chopp's and other feminists' disavowal of the role of tradition. While Polanyi and Murphy illustrate the distortions that occur when we lose our rootedness in tradition, Chopp shows what distortions tradition itself has imposed on us. The adequacy of a practice ought not be evaluated by its coherence to a past tradition, she says, but by how it contributes to the creation of viable new structures.

To use Murphy's terminology, it would appear that in Chopp's view, the current epistemological crisis within the Christian tradition requires a revolutionary reformulation. But rather than electing to stay within a traditional framework and trust its capacity to flex and accommodate necessary change, Chopp chooses an ethical grid through which to evaluate all traditions. It's not clear where this ideological priority originates. It seems clearly to be an attempt to address a current crisis within the tradition but chooses to stand outside it to critique its oppressive inclinations. The Anabaptists, by comparison, stepped outside the church tradition to effect revolutionary change but did so by appealing to the formative texts of that same church tradition, calling their neighbors back to Jesus as the most trustworthy guide for correcting the tradition.

Chopp's ideological approach to solving the current epistemological crisis seems somewhat precarious. What is the grounding for her ethical mandate other than pragmatism and rhetorical theories? What will prevent the ideology of "emancipatory praxis" from being manipulated by those in power for their own ends, much as a tradition can be manipulated by those in power? What will limit its becoming arrogantly self-determinative in an oppressive way for those who take issue with its criteria? What is to keep feminists who flex power from becoming too confident about knowing best? What does it mean to follow the One who calls us to deny ourselves even as we come to find ourselves named and claimed by the One in whom we live and move and have our being? Is it possible to "write one's life as an active agent," freed from others' definitions even as one keeps a realistic appraisal of one's relationship to the Alpha and Omega?

In a fascinating chapter in *Horizons in Feminist Theology*, edited by Chopp, Kathryn Tanner argues that it may be important for feminist theology to remain traditional and that the influence of feminist theology is strengthened to the extent that it wrestles constructively with the theological claims that have traditionally been important in Christian theology. Tradition need not mean stultification but can become the material and context for innovation and change, she suggests. A politics of culture may be able to show that the recoverable past is wider and more diverse than any particular identification of it, and that the way it is construed in the present remains a matter of human responsibility.[4]

Chopp appears to assert that the authority of Scripture as a community's formative text is in principle subordinate to the authority of the critical insight of those who have been oppressed. My sense is that both Polanyi and Murphy, and certainly the Anabaptists, would say this: Yes, the experiences of oppression and marginalization must be brought into every context of spiritual discernment and discovery; however, a much stronger case can be made for redressing the problem from within the tradition itself than from a somewhat arbitrary ideological stance situated outside. There is nothing to keep someone standing within the tradition from drawing on resources from other traditions. There is great freedom to reformulate and revision but to do it from within a framework that is communally constructed over generations of those committed to conserving for the sake of encouraging creative dissent and exploration.

Knowing and Ethics

All three of our conversation partners have argued in their own way that ways of knowing are not morally neutral, as might have been supposed. They are morally directive, and there are ethical implications that grow out of our assumptions about how we come to know.[5]

Polanyi has discussed at great length the distortions and moral erosions that have arisen when we have assumed there is a kind of knowing within which the knowing subject must be ignored. He elaborates on the immense evils that have sprung up in this century from a false scientific outlook which led to the strange modern fusion of a passion for utopian perfection accompanied by a contempt for moral values such as truth, compassion, and justice. The notion of scientific detachment and impersonal objectivity that characterizes the modern mindset is a false notion and a false ideal.

Such a notion has destructively influenced other disciplines and been used to undermine confidence in any other way of knowing, suggesting that all other knowing is akin to fantasy or whim. The validity of the truths from poetry, art, morality, and philosophy is suspect. And when our own capacity to make reliable personal judgments based on tacit knowledge and imaginative powers is devalued, it tends to become a self-fulfilling prophecy in that our personal and communal powers to make reliable personal judgments become less and less reliable.

Chopp also agrees that our ways of knowing are morally directive and that ethical implications grow out of those assumptions. When truth was defined by the dominant, patriarchal authorities it tended to impose definitions on women and men rather than encouraging them to narrate and compose their own lives. She suggests that truth, rather than being a disembodied concept, must be derived through reflection on the daily practices of life together. When women are actively invited to name their own experiences, narrate their own stories, and engage in their own emancipatory practices, there are new dimensions of knowledge that become evident. In theological education it is the practices of narrativity, ekklesia, and theology as "saving work" that provide the context and the process through which we come to know. Inasmuch as we come to know through embodied practices and by reflecting on those practices, we can assume that ethics will play a central role in our "knowing" and that there will be multiple ethical implications that flow out of a commitment to keep knowing and doing inseparably related.

What Chopp suggests appears to be an active and creative response to Polanyi's lament about loss of confidence in our powers for making reliable personal judgments. When we hold women (or anyone) responsible to make their own moral judgments based on their interaction with the tradition, their practical experience, and their ethical vision for justice, we begin to restore the confidence that individuals and communities can reclaim their capacity to personally and truthfully discern what is true and loving and just.

For Murphy as well, ways of knowing are considered morally directive and have profound ethical implications. She makes a strong case for restoring the priority of moral formation to the intellectual life. Most striking is her notion that the Anabaptists' power-renouncing practices, particularly that of communal discernment, demonstrate the possibility of human knowing while ameliorating the distortions brought on by those who seek to dominate the production of knowledge.

Those nurtured in specific character-forming practices will have the personal capacity to discern what is true. Gathered in communities of faith nurtured by traditions and informed by present experience, persons will be empowered to make wise decisions about how to live together for the good of all. And inasmuch as the community's power-renouncing practices bring them into contact with the weak and disenfranchised, community members will see reality from that perspective rather than from the perspective of those who seek to rule over others.

Both Chopp and Murphy offer profound practical responses to Polanyi's appeal for a recovery of "personal knowledge." They illustrate how ethics is a vital and decisive component in "our knowing." Though they differ in the significance they attribute to a reliance on tradition, they seem in full resonance on the recognition that ethics must inform our ways of knowing and that our ways of knowing have far ranging ethical implications. Murphy is more sanguine, in my view, about the potential distortions of power and the need to build in practices that address that problem. Chopp is able to see the distortions of power caused by patriarchy but offers little to suggest that feminists too may be prone to abuse power.

Our three conversation partners remind us that ethics is not something that comes into play only after our ways of knowing have done their work. Rather the foundations of morality are already built into our ways of knowing.[6]

Knowing as Narrative in Action

Polanyi suggests that all thought has bodily roots and that there need be no more dualism between mind and body. All knowledge is grounded in our bodies. Even theoretical concepts may be thought of as tools. They may be regarded as extensions of our body, subsumed in our awareness for use in the pursuit of our focused intentions. Polanyi's tacit knowledge is a personal and practical way to conceptualize knowledge. In contrast to purely cognitive depictions of knowledge, tacit knowledge makes room for knowledge emerging from personal narratives. Tacit knowledge derived from a person's narrative can be employed for the practical purpose of meeting the demands of a particular challenge. Knowing and doing then are inseparably intertwined. This approach to knowing, where theory and practice are unified in the actor through her "narrative unities of experience," has been described as "narrative in action"[7] composed of such experiential elements as images, rituals, habits, cycles, routines, and daily rhythms.

It strikes me that narrative in action can serve well to describe Polanyi's tacit knowledge and that describing it that way heightens its resemblance to Murphy's and Chopp's narrative and practical approaches to knowledge. Murphy's extensive discussion of traditions as socially embodied arguments appears (while not intentionally) to build directly on Polanyi's notion of tacit knowledge. Traditions are lived narratives, and knowledge is generated by explorations that grow out of practices and narratives embedded in the life of communities. We live in the stories and practices of our communities and can only think and perceive by the images and categories they provide. To truly understand the Scriptures for example, we must attempt to enter the world of the Bible by learning its language and taking up its practices. It isn't enough to know about the world of the Scriptures. Knowing that will approximate the intended meaning of the texts will require a bodily and imaginative investment of the knower.

Chopp also deals extensively with a concept of knowledge that focuses on practices and narratives, suggesting that such a focus allows for a fuller range of forms of knowing, "as intersubjective and embodied." Women bring more attention to the bodily aspects of knowing she suggests, demonstrating how an emphasis on bodiliness and practices as sites of learning avoids the common body/mind dualism, holding together the intellectual and material, the spiritual and physical.

The emphasis on knowledge that is derived from our personal experiential narratives and socially embodied practices by all three persons highlights the importance of a deep, tacit participatory knowing that must be nourished by tradition and communal experience.

Knowing and Intuitive Imagination

In addition to recognizing the traditional and bodily roots of our knowledge, Polanyi recognized the intuitive-imaginative roots as well. While describing the bodily roots of our intuitive capacities, he suggested that the way we get from the bodily roots of knowledge to the focus of our work is not formal reasoning but skilled imaginative integration. It follows then that intuitive imagination is required to grasp reality in its relationalities and complexities and to help us make the connections between what we know tacitly and bodily and the new insightful discoveries we intuitively grasp.

It is intuitive imagination that is by far the most important and most neglected of all the components of knowing, suggests Farley. All understanding depends on intuitive imagination. Imagination is not "mere fancy," but the capacity for experiencing and understanding the noumenal, immaterial realities that are the sources of inspiration and revelation.[8] Farley would agree with Polanyi that needed is a transformation of our ways of knowing which brings development of imagination in the fullest sense back into the center of our work in education. Polanyi argues that without the gifts of intuition, imagination, and personal judgment, scientific advancement will not happen.

In Polanyi's "personal knowledge," the non-sensory, qualitative dimensions of knowing are shown to play a vital role. Intuition and imagination are valued as sources of newness and discovery, since through them we come to sense the connections intrinsic to reality. Inasmuch as our knowing arises out of our tacit knowledge and reaches toward greater integration and connections with all of reality, it is intuition and imagination that help to provide the linkages between scientific and other kinds of knowing, whether art, poetry, myth, or religion.

All understanding, contends Polanyi, is an intimation of a reality which may yet reveal itself to our deepened understanding. We have an obligation to search for the truth through our own intimations of reality. The intuitive impulses of individuals within the community are what make possible genuine contact with the reality underlying the existing tradition. Such impulses transform the tradition and the community. Intuition, Polanyi suggests, is based on something like an intellectual love—a mysterious and passionate intellectual love that first senses a problem, becomes preoccupied with it, then makes a daring leap of imagination toward a new connection. Concept and intuition, rigor and imagination have to wrestle together; the total victory of either makes us lose touch with reality.

Chopp's discussion about the role of imagination in our knowing appears to affirm Polanyi's perspective. She also contends that to make imagination central in the educational process may well be one of the most crucial requirements of forming new ways of knowing and new ways of learning. Indeed feminist theology makes imagination central to the work of theology, since the "saving work" of theology requires reimaging and imaginative revisioning. It requires looking for unrealized possibilities in a situation, creating new meanings, symbols, characters, images and plots. The role of imagination must not be seen as some romantic turn in knowing but as the ability to think the new, which is so essential to addressing the current crisis in traditional theology.

Theology focuses on the symbols and symbolic patterns of Christianity and thus imagination and aesthetics play an important role. Imagination is essential for persons who, while resisting other's definitions, imagine themselves in new roles, stories, and patterns in the practice of narrating their own lives.

Murphy does not discuss the role of imagination in any specificity that I am aware of, but much of her discussion of the connectedness of knowledge and of what it means to live into a tradition and enter the world of the Scriptures, for example, appears to assume a significant role for the imagination. When Murphy speaks of entering the world of the Bible, I think she would agree, in light of her other affirmations, that it requires an act of imagination to journey into the strange and distant world of the Scripture and that such an approach is required if Scripture is to have the power to shape our present world of understanding and behavior. It will take imagination to perceive the relationship between the tradition or the experiences of truth of previous generations and our current reality.

Murphy also seems to assume a role for imagination when she speaks of the human species evolving to the point where it has the capacity to "image" God, to sense the subtlety of the design of the cosmos, and in so doing, to choose to follow the example of Jesus by imitating the moral, self-sacrificial character of God. We are able to image God, she suggests, when we imitate the life of Jesus.[9] It is imitation then, or to use Polanyi's words—apprenticeship—which deepens tacit knowledge and makes it possible to image God with any reliability.

Murphy also suggests that a typical Anabaptist stance or practice like nonviolence requires the cultivation of imagination and ingenuity—the ability to imagine peaceful solutions to intractable problems and the ingenuity to find creative ways to bring about those solutions.[10] Such imagination, I think she would agree, will arrive at a helpful solution only by arising from a deeply formed reservoir of bodily, intuitive and traditional knowledge.

Communal Knowing as Disciplined Discovery

Each of our three conversation partners articulates a community-centered approach to knowledge making and discernment.

Polanyi's notion of the Society of Explorers offers a model from the scientific community that can be more generally appropriated. Within such a society, each scientist committed to exploring reality and using responsible judgment is under authority of the professional standards of science. The authoritative framework of that society disciplines each person's own rights to self-determination, but it is a framework mutually imposed and controlled. In such a society, authority is exercised by equals over each other. And the framework of discipline is such that it encourages rebellion against its limitations, if good reason can be provided for why the framework no longer serves a helpful purpose.

Polanyi also suggests that this society needs a "purpose that bears on eternity," and that science can have discipline and originality only if its explorers believe that the facts and values of science bear on "a still unrevealed reality." He suggests that the religious community ought to become more like the scientific community by maintaining respect for tradition and authority, with the purpose of encouraging creative dissent that will change the tradition, and he proposes that members of the Society of Explorers are those responsible to safeguard the search for truth.

Polanyi appears to offer the mutually agreed on authority of the Society of Explorers as the authoritative traditional framework in which persons can find safety and freedom to exercise their powers of discovery. The safety is provided by the authoritative traditional framework that keeps one's own inclinations for self-determination from becoming self-destructive. But it also becomes a context in which we are encouraged by the group to come to believe in our own powers, and to train them, use them and discipline them as the scientist does his faculties. Not every whim can be trusted, he suggests, but we can pursue the best judgment and discrimination we can attain through self-discipline and apprenticeship to the "master of our art."

Murphy's discussion of the core practice of discernment as practiced in Radical Reformation churches bears a striking resemblance to Polanyi's description of the Society of Explorers. The "Christian epistemic practice," a practice aimed at the pursuit of truth, is a communal practice in which only believers who follow Christ and rely on the Holy Spirit's inspiration are expected to engage. There is a mutually agreed on authoritative frame of reference. It includes a variety of ways to judge whether or not an interpretation, prophecy, or practice is led by the Spirit of Christ. The criteria for making such judgments include ascertaining whether an item is consistent with the Scriptures and whether the community can come to consensus around it.

Interpretation is primarily a communal event, limiting the potential destructiveness of persons left to determine their own individualistic, privatized interpretation. And yet the discerning circle is made up of individual believers who, in their commitment to follow Christ and open themselves to new Spirit-led understanding and practices, bring their own experiences into dialogue with the Scriptures. The role of the Spirit in discernment is vital to the community's confidence that discernment will lead to new visions of reality that transcend a community's conventional wisdom and call them toward new dimensions of kingdom living.

Chopp's notion of how communal discernment and discovery occur is a little harder to conceptualize, although it also strongly resembles Polanyi's Society of Explorers. Chopp's concept involves neither the authority of the professional standards of science nor the authority of the formative texts of the community around which the society gathers, however. Rather, the authority appears to lie in Chopp's notion of a mutual commitment to justice and to "emancipatory praxis." Her vision of community or ekklesia is defined by the presence of the Spirit, as is Murphy's, but it stresses justice as a normative process and justice as its defining mission. Justice, for Chopp, means that everyone must have a voice in the deliberation and a right to have a voice in self-determination and community determination.

While Chopp's vision appears to include mutuality exercised by equals, as do Polanyi and Murphy's visions, her's exercises this mutuality for the sake of assuring that each person has a right to self-determination and community determination. Justice, imagination, and dialogue that include openness and respectful mutual critique will characterize the community discourse. Voices representing diversity of all sorts will be welcomed. There will be an emphasis on envisioning new forms of relating and community building. And there will continually be reflection on current practices while moving toward new practices of emancipatory transformation that grow out of that reflection.

Many of Chopp's emphases appear not only compatible with Polanyi and Murphy's communal approaches, but powerfully enriching. Her emphasis on hearing the truth of each other's lives assures that persons' present experience will provide the dynamic grist for discerning how we should live together. Diverse voices present in a circle will assure that various perspectives are represented and taken into consideration. Justice and imagination for envisioning new symbols and practices for transformative community life are welcome.

The differences of perspective however, are significant and need to be noted. While Chopp acknowledges relying on biblical, theological, and critical theoretical resources, she chooses not to function within any authoritative framework defined by the tacit wisdom of a tradition. She prefers to give primary freedom to individuals for self-determination rather than to value the freedom that emerges from rootedness in a tradition. Her approach, while designed as corrective to oppressive communal practices, focuses more on individual rights than on meaningful criteria for communal discipline and discernment. Polanyi, in my view, holds individual exploration and communal discipline in a dynamic and creative balance. And Murphy demonstrates how a community of Spirit-led believers can benefit from the accumulated wisdom of the tradition while dynamically interacting with the daily experiences of individual believers, so that tradition and experience become part of a seamless process of discovery about how to model our lives on Jesus, the founder and finisher of our faith.

Chapter 6

WEAVING A THEORY OF EDUCATION FROM THE CONVERSATIONAL STRANDS

Constructing a Theoretical Framework

The time has come to gather together the strands of conversation from around the table and weave them into a new and vibrant coherency. The voices have intermingled and engaged us with their multiple perspectives and concerns. They have modeled the sort of conversation that is vital to communal discernment and construction of knowledge.

Now the task is to design a beautiful and practical pattern for the host family's familial and communal educational efforts out of the wisdom shared around the table. What guidance can we discern for how Mennonites and other heirs of the Anabaptists should do education? And what guidance is there for any particular faith community that hopes to think strategically about education? This is the challenge.

As I review those qualities which most dynamically characterized the Anabaptist forebears of my faith community, I've become increasingly concerned that many practices essential to the educational and confessional priorities of our community are rapidly being discarded or simply neglected. I'm concerned that we're uncritically importing many activities that are taking the place of earlier faith forming practices. I'm concerned that we haven't paid enough attention to whether or not current everyday practices are embodying what we believe ought to characterize the lives of our families and our faith communities. And I am disquieted by the suspicion that we have largely underestimated the formative function of down-to-earth bodily practices, ritual behaviors, and the deep substratum of knowledge they provide. If that internalized substratum of knowledge out of which our language, behaviors, and imagination flow has been depleted of its faith content, what approach to education may contribute to the renewal of the wellspring of our communal life?

Constructing a theory is like designing a framework to bring order and direction to our educational endeavors. Such construction is an attempt to deal with the chaos of information and experience in a way that makes sense of our current situation and organizes various perspectives into a coherent and meaningful whole. A theory can help us in identifying and articulating a purpose for education. And it can suggest several strategies that may be useful for achieving the purposes of education.

While what follows is shaped by Anabaptist thought and practice, it can serve to model an approach for any community's tradition-based, critical approach to education.

Defining the Purpose

Earlier we identified several qualities particularly relevant to education which had been most characteristic and transformative in the early Anabaptist movement. These characteristics are discussed at some length in Chapter 2. We refer to them as "classic" distinctives which have endured and continue to inform the core ideals and the core commitments around which Mennonites and other heirs of the Anabaptists gather as a community of faith.[1]

Every interpreter of Anabaptism will offer a slightly different version of the features of the tradition that are most characteristic or significant. I venture to say, however, that the ones offered below would receive wide affirmation as qualities that characterized the early Anabaptists and have continued, at least confessionally, to be important to their heirs. These are the qualities which give shape to the purpose of education informed from an Anabaptist perspective.

Among the early Anabaptists there was an intense desire to know and do the will of God as they understood it through the life and teachings of Jesus. They emphasized that the Christian life is a voluntary life of discipleship. Discipleship was about a relationship with Jesus who was regarded as Savior and Lord. Those who knew Jesus as the one who called and sustained them by the regenerative power of the Holy Spirit were committed to following his self-giving example even to death. The life, teachings, and cross of Jesus Christ as conveyed in the Scriptures constituted the definitive, dynamic pattern for shaping the Christian's life in the world. By "abiding in Christ" and with the transformative power of the Holy Spirit, the early Anabaptists were able to renounce violence and to share material and spiritual resources in their exercise of mutual care and communal discipline. They believed that those who walked in Jesus' way by following his example and commands were the ones who came to know him more fully and intimately. Knowing and doing were inseparably intertwined.

The Anabaptists understood the Scriptures as the Word of God and as thus having a central, defining authority for their personal and community life. To understand God's will and to discern what God expected of them, they entered into the world of the Scriptures, immersing themselves in its narratives, practices, and teachings. Such scriptural ingredients were world-creating, making the biblical world as real for them as their own world (or more so). They learned many of the Scriptures by heart, reciting them when questioned about their faith. They understood themselves and their world through and by means of the Bible.

Their immersion in Scripture grew out of their desire to live faithful lives of discipleship. They believed God confronts us in and through the text of Scripture as it is read in the community of faith when that community is genuinely seeking guidance about how to be faithful to the way of Jesus. They were committed to reading the Word of God together, as a body of believers, with a sense of expectancy that the Holy Spirit would empower them to know and do the will of God.

The Anabaptists also believed the church is called to be a pioneering, model-building community of God's people in the larger society. As the faithful, called out disciples of Christ, they were convinced the church must be distinct from the world. However, they also believed that the church is called to be a conscience and servant within society, embodying Jesus' sacrificial love, including love of enemies. In their own worship and communal life, the Anabaptists cultivated an alternative construction of society through a supportive and disciplined congregational life, sharing the gospel in song and word and practicing communal moral discernment. They sought through witness, service and peacemaking to share the good news of Christ with their neighbors.

An educational theory that calls itself Anabaptist will keep these core and classic distinctives in mind. Its purpose will be to guide the formation of children, youth and adults by modeling personal and communal life on the way of Jesus. It will seek to enhance the communal experience and discernment of the Scriptures as world creating and life directing. And it will promote the cultivation of a particular visible community of disciples as distinct from the world and yet for the world.

A Formative Paradigm

We observed the paradigms that depict in imaginative ways each of our main theorists' approaches to knowing. For Polanyi, the paradigm was referred to as a "heuristic philosophy," a paradigm whose primary motif is personal knowledge that is well rooted and immersed in a great tradition and yet is drawn on to new discoveries because of "an intimation of a reality" that beckons one to transcend the limits of that tradition.

For Chopp, the paradigm was that of a quilt which, in a communal experience of theological knowledge construction, involves the bringing together of "scraps" of narratives, symbols, and practices of justice into a new harmony stitched around the central defining motif of "emancipatory praxis."

For Murphy, the paradigm of knowledge as a web depicts the wholistic character of knowledge which is integrally connected in many directions to supporting knowledge that reinforces one's confidence in the truthfulness of what is perceived. Murphy sets up her paradigm in sharp contrast to foundationalism, the reigning paradigm in modernism, which suggested that knowledge structures can only be built from a fully reliable foundation of certain and verifiable knowledge.

The Anabaptists have contended that there is no foundation other than Jesus Christ. They sought to base their life directly on biblical teachings and tended to use biblical categories and terms rather than relying on creedal affirmations or standardized doctrinal formulations. Over the years they reformulated confessions of faith to affirm central, defining motifs, echoing over and over again what was the key verse and theological motto for one of their founders, Menno Simons, "For no one can lay any foundation other than the one that has been laid; that foundation is Jesus Christ" (1 Cor. 3:11).

Jesus was foundational for the Anabaptists. They placed his teaching and example at the heart of their faith and practice. It was through identifying with him and "abiding in him" that they drew strength to live a radical life of discipleship. While they used the concept of foundation to describe the source of their confident knowledge, their foundation was not based in a rational, empirical attempt to ground all knowing. Rather, it was an historical person who continued to be alive for them through narratives, practices, and the regenerating presence of the Holy Spirit.

The Anabaptists chose to root their faith and life in Christ. I suggest that the paradigm that will best serve the purposes of an Anabaptist tradition-based, critical educational theory will be that of the grape vine. Jesus said, "I am the true vine, and my Father is the vinegrower. . . . Abide in me as I abide in you. Just as the branch cannot bear fruit unless it abides in the vine, neither can you unless you abide in me" (John 15: 1, 4-5).

The paradigm of a vine holds many possibilities for imaging the work of education. It is a biblical image which is in harmony with the Anabaptist immersion in Scripture. It is a scriptural motif which is Christ-centered. A vine is deeply rooted yet continually growing and reaching for the sunshine, suggesting an interplay between tradition and current experience. There are many branches on a vine which, while remaining connected to the main stem of the vine, reach out in supportive ways to other branches and provide a canopy of shade. A vine periodically goes through dormant phases and must be pruned to enhance its fruitfulness. Its health and fruitfulness is dependent on its being carefully and critically tended.

While the vine metaphor cannot illustrate every aspect of an Anabaptist educational theory, it provides a picture with rich possibilities for exploration. One particularly potent connection worth investigating as we reflect on the relationship between ethics and our knowing is the way Jesus links abiding in him to the inherent relationship between loving, obeying and knowing God. "If you keep my commandments, you will abide in my love, just as I have kept my Father's commandments and abide in his love" (John 15:10).

In a true Anabaptist biblically based fashion, I want to explore this connection further and so ground this theory more thoroughly in Jesus as the true vine with the scriptural acknowledgment that it is in abiding in Jesus that we come to know God and God's purposes for our lives.

For the writer of the gospel of John and of the Johannine epistles, knowing God and loving God are closely intertwined. And not only are knowing and loving bound up together, but each is inseparably related to behavioral expressions or practices. John writes, "Whoever does not love does not know God, for God is love" (1 John 4:8). He also writes, "Now by this we may be sure that we know him, if we obey his commandments" (1 John 2:3). Then he adds, "And this is love, that we walk according to his commandments" (2 John 6).

John is exploring the intimate link between loving and knowing that extends throughout the Judeo-Christian Scriptures. In the Old Testament, the word *know,* used to speak of lovemaking between a husband and wife, is the same word used for our knowledge of God. Even in Greek where the concepts are not likely to be mixed, the New Testament writers continue to link knowing and loving. The most common word for know used in the New Testament is also used for lovemaking.

Clearly the implication is that true knowing comes from the sort of personal and bodily investment in a relationship that resembles the covenanted intimacy of sexual embrace. Knowing God involves opening oneself to God with the transparency and vulnerability most closely paralleled in our trusting, passionate knowing of one another. On becoming naked to the depths of our souls in a spirit of repentance, we come to know the unimagined depths of God's forgiving love. And in the embrace of God's love, we are freed to know ourselves more truly and to live our lives in a lyrical harmony with our Maker.

John describes the strong relationship between knowing, loving, and obeying God's commandments. It jars the consciousness, somehow, to link obedience of the commandments with the wonderful intimacy of a loving relationship. Yet John shows again and again that if we are to know God and to enjoy a loving relationship with God, it comes by way of obedience in practical, behavioral actions. The love of which John speaks is not a nice love manufactured out of wishful thinking but a love that is woven out of the moral fiber of a just and righteous God. "Little children," writes John, "let us love, not in word or speech, but in truth and action" (1 John 3:18). The love John asks us to emulate is nothing less than the selfless love of Christ himself, who said "This is my commandment, that you love one another as I have loved you. No one has greater love than this, to lay down one's life for one's friends" (John 15:12).

The paradigm of the vine links knowing, loving and doing in a dynamic way which will enrich our ongoing theory construction.

How Do We Know?—Philosophical Assumptions

My intention in this section is to describe several underlying, philosophical assertions about how we come to know that can guide our further reflection on education. These have been discussed at some length in earlier chapters so here will be distilled with as much brevity and clarity as possible. Various approaches to knowing have been separated out below to highlight somewhat distinct features. In practice, however, the ways in which we know are a complex, organic matrix of rootedness.

Our underlying assumptions about how we come to know what we know and about what can be known have far-ranging influence on our communal discernment, our cultivation of practices, and the value we place on imagination, for example. Because of the effect these assumptions have on our behaviors, I assert yet again that one central educational task will be to transform our images and understandings about what it means "to know." An educational theory informed by an Anabaptist perspective will seek above all to come to know God, self, and others by daily practicing the way of Jesus.

The Traditional Roots of Knowledge

Knowledge making is rooted in culture and needs a narrative context to become intelligible. Each of us belongs to a particular culture or mix of cultures which places limits on our vision but also equips us to have vision. It is by dwelling in a particular cultural inheritance, a particular language, a particular religion that we gain the ability to glimpse a reality that extends beyond our particularity. It is largely by apprenticeship to a particular tradition that we gain capacity not only to understand the tradition that has formed us but to transcend it.

It is our traditions that give us resources for justifying our truth claims and our actions. All inquiry and exploration is tradition-constituted and tradition-dependent. We live in our traditions and think and perceive and make new discoveries by means of the categories, images, and stories they provide.

An understanding of tradition as an "historically extended, socially embodied argument about how best to interpret and apply the formative text(s)" suggests a dynamic interaction between an authoritative text(s) and the current experience of social embodiment. Tradition when understood in this way appears not to be primarily concerned with the perpetuation of conventions but rather cultivates continuity with the past to encourage new discoveries and creative dissent that may in turn revitalize the tradition. When aspects of a tradition are demonstrably stultifying or oppressive, its inadequacies can be named, confronted and reformulated to better serve the purpose of human flourishing.

For the Anabaptists the primary tradition was that of the Scriptures. They reclaimed that tradition in a day when other competing traditions had gained precedence over the narratives and practices of Jesus and the early church. The fundamental clash for them was not between tradition and Scripture but between irresponsible tradition and faithful tradition. The scriptural tradition, with the Holy Spirit's enlightenment, provided the link to their community's origins and to the historicity of the person, Jesus Christ, on whom they sought to model their lives. In conforming their lives to the Jesus they saw in the Scriptures and bodily indwelling the particulars of their faith tradition, they found themselves radically transformed and able to transcend the conventions and limitations of the establishment tradition around them. They demonstrated that a great tradition provides the grounds both for its being maintained and its being revitalized.

The Spiritual Roots of Knowledge

Religious and spiritual traditions claim that while we live in our traditions, we also participate in a reality larger than the limits of their conventional language and practices. Such traditions affirm that there is an external reality of which we are only partly aware but about which we receive intimations and revelations of a truth that extends beyond our own communal definitions and visions. Clues available to us point toward this hidden reality.

Throughout human history, individuals and groups have experienced transforming and revelatory moments which are stored in the spiritual traditions of these peoples and which serve to keep us open collectively and individually to spiritual qualities such as faith, hope, and love. Over time, persons have reflected on these moments or events and formed theologies that help groups collectively make sense of their experience of the transcendent. These theologies help to give direction to communal ethics, discernment and practice.

Religious and spiritual traditions have nurtured and sustained virtues such as humility, faith, self-denial, and love over hundreds of years in part by cultivating the religious affections that assure these qualities will be life-giving rather than turn into the dead letter of the law. Our traditions are themselves, in turn, sustained and strengthened by the relevant virtues needed to maintain life-giving narratives and practices.

The Anabaptists give evidence of transforming encounters with God that awakened in them a passionate love and desire to give themselves completely in service to their Lord. They were devoted to Jesus, encouraged by the Holy Spirit and sustained by prayers and songs. Many went to their deaths singing and praying and exhorting one another to be strong and of good cheer. Their joyful, dynamic discipleship illustrates what it means to "abide in Christ," just as a branch draws life from the vine.

The Communal Roots of Knowledge

Each major theorist we have heard from in this study articulated a community-centered approach to knowledge-making, stressing the formative power of language, symbols, and practices of a particular community. Knowledge is understood to be constructed by communities rather than being an abstract entity discovered outside the complexities of daily life.

The question of who we are as a community has in recent years, become foundational for all other inquiries. Who we are is, in part, defined by the ideals or standards upheld by a tradition the community deems authoritative and seeks to embody. A given community culture that is somewhat identifiable from mass culture will have a vision of life as a "deliberate cultural and ethical aspiration" and will seek to shape the character of its members and its communal life around that vision.

Acknowledged community ideals will contribute to human flourishing unless wielded with moralistic harshness. They will enhance communal practice and discourse by giving clarity about the ultimate goal or anticipated shared future of communal life. Communal construction of knowledge will involve making explicit what the community most values and seeks to preserve in its texts and practices. And the educational efforts of the community will involve deliberately molding the character of its members in accordance with its acknowledged ideals about what is considered to be a good culture. Who we are as a community, what we deem as authoritative and as true, and how the ideals of our traditions are socially embodied—these are questions that necessitate ongoing communal discernment, particularly by those in leadership who seek to promote a wholesome atmosphere or paideia for the formation of the community's children and youth.

Polanyi's concept of a Society of Explorers who exercise discipline for the sake of promoting originality is helpful in thinking about communally rooted knowledge and discernment. Each explorer is under the authority of mutually agreed on rules of accountability. The agreed on framework within which the community of explorers works encourages rebellion against the tradition's limitations provided good reason can be given for why it no longer serves a helpful purpose. The explorers, while guided by rules of accountability, are open to new intuitive, imaginative insights. The notion of a Society of Explorers offers a dynamic view of knowledge construction that involves both an authoritative, traditional framework that places limits on each individual's self-determination and an openness to the inbreaking of new insights brought by the intuitive, imaginative insights of its individual explorers.

For the early Christians and the Anabaptists, Christ, as an historical person personified a living ideal around whom they sought to mold their lives. But the way in which they discerned how this ideal was to be embodied was communally discerned. The manner in which they sought to conduct their communal discernment demonstrated the possibility of human knowing while ameliorating the distortions brought on by those who might seek to dominate the production of knowledge. Discernment was for them a Christian epistemic practice aimed at the pursuit of truth, a communal practice which was disciplined and yet open to the new inbreaking of insights from individuals inspired by the Holy Spirit. There were mutually agreed upon criteria for assuring a measure of reliability in the truth that was discerned involving consistency with Scripture and communal consensus.

The Bodily and Tacit Roots of Knowledge

In some ways it seems self evident that all knowledge has bodily roots, including our highest creative powers, yet we have lived with a body/mind dualism for so long that it feels somewhat daring to make such a claim. Bodily processes participate in the perceptions we make. The body we dwell in is the body itself as well as the whole complex of habits, aptitudes, skills, and awarenesses we have built up since our first days of life. Dwelling in it is our only means of knowing the world.

We have often underestimated the importance and persistence of the bodily aspects of social memory, but we do it to our own peril. Those who understand the Christian tradition as primarily the social embodiment of the narrative and ethic of Jesus rather than the exposition of an abstract doctrine will pay particular attention to the assertion that we preserve the past most memorably in our bodies. The values we are most anxious to conserve we will entrust to bodily automatisms because the past can be best kept alive by a habitual memory sedimented in the body.

The complex of bodily habits, aptitudes, skills, and awarenesses we indwell have been referred to as tacit knowledge, a knowledge which is a part of our subliminal awareness and provides the roots of our creative, intuitive, and critical thinking capacities. Interiorizing the particulars of what we have received from our early training and relying on them will enable us to reach toward a more comprehensive, interconnected awareness. Dwelling in our cultural heritage will equip us with the capacities to make new discoveries.

This means that a particular community will largely need to rely on custom, tradition, and early modeling to provide the A, B, C's of a child's formation. The best way to sharpen an individual's ability to think creatively and critically will be to assure strong bodily character development in self-control, courage, generosity, patience, trust, affection, and other virtues of the good life. The cultural fund of Scriptures, poetry, music, stories, and the habitual rhythms of practices that are intrinsically religious and moral in character will provide the most potent resources for forming advanced intellectual capacities and virtuous behavior.

All of our primary theorists highlighted the importance of a tacit participatory knowing that must be nourished by narratives and communal bodily practices. This knowing can be referred to as narratives in action. We bodily live in the stories and practices of our communities and can only think and perceive by the images and the categories they provide.

For the Anabaptists, immersion in Scripture and modeling one's life on the life of Jesus provided the communal preconditions for the early formation of their children and youth. The early Anabaptists demonstrated a strong sense of parental responsibility in the training of their children. Charged with gross neglect of children's well-being because of their refusal to baptize infants, they responded with increased diligence in their parental responsibilities. Menno Simons stressed to parents the significance of their own example, highlighting modeling as a key principle of parental responsibility. Since children were not automatically incorporated into the church, it became doubly important that adequate processes for nurturing their growth in discipleship be set in motion. The role of the family was central in that process.[2]

The Intuitive and Imaginal Roots of Knowledge

Intuitive imagination is required to grasp reality in its relationalities and its complexities. It assists us in making the connections between what we know tacitly and bodily and the new discoveries we intuitively grasp. The way we get from the internalized particulars of our awareness to the idea or thing on which our attention is presently focused is imaginative integration.

Intuitive imagination, it has been suggested, is the most important and most neglected of all aspects of knowing. All understanding depends on it. We need a transformation of our ways of knowing that brings the development of our intuitive powers and our imagination back to the center of our work in education. In fact, it has been observed that intuition is at the very heart of rationality and is an aspect of knowing that provides a foundation for all other knowing.

The authority of science is traditional, but this tradition upholds an authority which cultivates originality. Science is constantly revolutionized and perfected by the intuitive, imaginative discoveries of its explorers even while remaining firmly rooted in its traditions. So too a faith community must rely on authoritative traditional frameworks, but those frameworks function to provide the context which will capacitate individuals to explore beyond the limits of those frameworks. For a faith tradition to remain viable and life-giving, the community must rely on the intuitive impulses of individual adherents of the community who can make genuine contact with the reality underlying the tradition and add new and authentic interpretations of the tradition which may contribute to its ongoing transformative power.

It is intuition and imagination that help to provide the linkages between scientific knowledge, for example, and other kinds of knowledge such as art, poetry, and myth. Imagination assists us in looking for unrealized possibilities in a situation, and creating new meanings, symbols, characters, and images within our faith tradition.

For the Scriptures to be "world creating" required that the Anabaptists enter into them with imagination and an intuitive ability to make sense of the ancient narratives in their present context. It would have been impossible to live creatively and practically into the life the Scriptures portrayed without the intuitive and imaginative powers needed to grasp the relationalities between the life of Jesus and the early Christians and life in the sixteenth century and life now.

The Rational Roots of Knowledge

A few words must be said about the cognitive roots of knowledge lest we forget, in our desire to acknowledge other ways of knowing, what a significant role reason has played in providing disciplined and logical clarity to our knowing. Even as we resist the hegemonic influence it has exercised in modernity, its positive contributions to our consciousness must be preserved—namely the capacity for clear, orderly critical thinking disciplined by agreed upon rules of logic and rational consistency.

When there is widespread agreement about the rules of rational inquiry and what is required to verify or substantiate an argument, individuals are freed to engage in dialogue and debate with persons from other, somewhat dissimilar communities. When mutually agreed upon rules of reasonable, civilized discourse are established, meaningful conversation can occur across cultural and religious barriers.

In acknowledging and highlighting other ways of knowing, we do not want to return to premodern states of consciousness in which the self was submerged in the divine, in nature, or in the tribe and community. It is dangerous when communities and individuals become so entrenched in their own versions of the truth that they have no reasonable way to test the rationality and quality of their own traditions. Reason can help with critiquing a particular community's uncritical passions, idolatries, and susceptibility to ideological distortions. The health of a tradition will depend in part on a community's ability to maintain the capacity for internal, critical inquiry and its ability to engage in rational discourse with persons and communities representing other traditions.

Many of the early Anabaptists were highly educated and skilled in reasoned discourse and disputation. While they largely drew on the Scriptures as the source of their arguments, they did so with an alacrity and sharpness of reasoning skills that frequently amazed and dismayed those who interrogated them. As dialogues recorded in *The Martyrs Mirror* show, the Anabaptists were not timid about standing up to their accusers and attempting to provide sufficient evidence and persuasive reasoning to win the debate.[3]

It was not for want of reasonable, well-informed argumentation that they were struck down. Rather, it was because their persecutors failed to see that in the Anabaptists' passionate and reasonable critical retrieval of their common traditional formative texts, they were embodying the innovative, transforming power of those traditional texts.

The Ethical Roots of Knowledge

Having spoken of the value of reasoned thinking, it is important to remember that immense evils have arisen from the false scientific ideal of impersonal objectivity, or when the body and mind are regarded as separate entities, or when truth is defined by patriarchal authorities and imposed on women, for example, without regard for their experience.

Rather than right understanding preceding right action, moral formation which trains character virtues and is aimed at subduing a self-serving will-to-power is a necessary prerequisite for seeing reality aright. Ultimately the cultivation of virtuous behaviors is the best way to sharpen the mind, enhance critical and imaginal thinking, and enable constructive dialogue among different points of view.

For the Anabaptists, ethical commitment to follow Christ was necessary to understand the Scriptures and to understand God. The teachings of Jesus, particularly the Sermon on the Mount, served as an interpretive frame through which all the rest of Scripture could be understood. An ethic of Jesus centering on self-giving service and nonviolence brought them into solidarity with the weak and outcast, changing their perspective on reality.

The ethic of Jesus is what guided the Anabaptists toward becoming a distinctive sociological entity. Such an ethic gives rise to a particular paideia that has its own formative texts and characteristic practices which assume that knowing and doing are inseparably intertwined and that both find their proper relationship as we "abide in Christ."

The Practical Roots of Knowledge

Persons from a variety of disciplines are taking increased interest in the function of practices in our knowing. Practices are shared activities through which persons come to know and through which perspectives on reality are formed. They are sites of learning that join ethical and epistemological dimensions. They have been referred to as embodied thought.

Rather than truth being regarded as a disembodied concept, it is more helpful, particularly from an Anabaptist perspective, to think of truth as deriving from the concrete practices of daily life. We will know the truth only by following Jesus in the concrete practices of healing, liberation, and justice.

Engaging in the practices of the early church is important for entering and understanding the world of the Bible. Rather than first establishing the truthfulness of the Scriptures based on historical criticism or textual analysis, a practical approach to knowledge suggests that it is in practicing the gospel that we are capacitated to properly interpret it.

Pedagogy has often tended to focus on conveying information. Concentrating on the bodiliness of practices allows us to think about education in new ways. An educational approach that focuses on practices will allow a fuller range of forms of knowing.

Practical approaches to knowing will pay attention to such experiential elements as images, rituals, habits, cycles, routines, and daily rhythms. The critical retrieval of the Anabaptist tradition of power-renouncing practices and the significant virtues that grow out of participation in them offers a potent resource to current educational theory and practice.

EDUCATIONAL SETTINGS

In our theory construction we will briefly look at the community's primary educational settings. The educational strategies discussed in the next section will have a somewhat different character and function in the setting of the church, the family and the school. These institutions which have traditionally been the primary mediators of the community's culture or paideia can together form an ecology of institutions that strengthens and reinforces the tradition-based, critical education of its children, youth and adults. Any one of these institutions on its own will find it much harder to promote an alternative paideia. When all three work together, however, drawing their primary formative ideals, narratives and practices from common traditional sources, they can provide a much more viable context for withstanding the pressures of uncritical assimilation into the surrounding culture.

The Church

Central to this theory is the confidence that a church community who reclaims its cultural heritage as a peculiar people will offer not only an alternative way of life but will understand its mission to be that of the transformation of culture in general. By living into its formative narratives and socially embodying its ethical aspirations, the church will demonstrate the goodness of a wholesome culture and invite the world to reconsider the classic distinctives of its religious traditions. By encompassing people from every tribe and nation, the church serves as a sign of the presence of the kingdom of God among us. The church, by its life and witness, proclaims the reign of God.

When we think of educational strategies that invite us to revitalize core practices, it is the church, first of all, that carries primary responsibility for keeping the formative narratives and practices alive. It is the church that is our first family, the family of God. The church is the social agent that most significantly shapes and forms the character of Christians. While a front-line mission of the church will be to work for the renewal of family cultures and to generate the vision for tradition-based education, as the body of Christ it provides the moral energy to be faithful to the way of Jesus.

Stanley Hauerwas reminds us, for example, that marriage and family life are only possible if they are sustained by a community more significant than the marriage or family itself. If the church doesn't show us, through its narratives and practices, what it means to be faithful to self and others in the church, then we have precious little chance of learning it through marriage and the family. It is through learning to be faithful in relation to God's faithfulness that we develop the character capable for loving through thick and thin.[4]

It is the church, where we are knit together not by our common genes, but by a common loyalty to the kingdom, that provides us with an alternative story, alternative practices and an alternative place to stand so we can resist the powerful social forces of mass culture and build strong and healthy families and schools.[5]

The Family

The church provides the moral energy needed to be faithful disciples and cultivates an alternative construction of reality, but nothing can substitute for the uniquely formative home environment. The church has consistently held that education in faith and character begins in the home as children imitate parents and participate in family and community worship.[6] A child is an ever-attentive witness of grown-up morality. Children look for clues from the day they are born as to how to behave. They find them aplenty as parents go about our lives, making choices, showing in action our rock-bottom assumptions, desires and values, thereby telling them much more than we may realize.[7] To master the instincts, children have to find a reason to do so, a source of moral energy that enables them to do so. They want to be able to rely on the grown-ups in their lives and to find their values trustworthy and believable because those values emerge from the shared experience of a life together?

Much of modern liberal education, stemming from Rousseau, assumed that children flourish when given the freedom to select among many faith and value options in developing their own perspectives and faith responses. Parents have often been reluctant to "impose" their beliefs on their children. Why, I wonder, do we think of equipping our children with an orienting faith story and faith practices as an imposition when we don't have the same reluctance to teach a particular language, mathematical system, or driving skill?

The point is not to deny that faith practices have often been dogmatically and hurtfully imposed. But, to use a comparative illustration, we don't discard all good sex because rape unfortunately happens. Parents who genuinely want our children's responses to faith to be freely chosen will provide them with the basic A, B, C's of a deep and rich traditional frame of reference out of which they are equipped to make informed, discerning choices. Otherwise, they may become illiterate stutterers without a coherent cultural language and orientation with which to decipher meaning amid the overwhelming flood of information.

Good parents will counter the cultural flotsam with deep, rich stories and practices that equip their children to critically and appreciatively engage the wider world.

Home-based practices are absolutely crucial for establishing the essential pre-conditions for healthy spiritual, moral and cognitive development? So much depends on the A, B, C's learned or not learned at home. With that acknowledgment in mind, I want simply to highlight that any educational strategy in this day will work to recover the health and vitality of a family home-based culture.

Don Browning argues that it is theologically, politically, and strategically important for both church and society to make the creation of a new family ethic central to their agendas. With the growing evidence in society at large of the declining well-being of children, the increasing impoverishment of women, particularly single mothers, and the rise of male detachment from families, family issues are not private issues; they have quickly become the great public issues of our time. More than anything else, churches must retrieve their marriage and family traditions, even though they must do so critically. They must promote a "critical familism" and a "critical culture of marriage," which is sensitive to the power distortions. They must do this by constructing a theory of family love that makes equal regard or mutuality central and then makes self-sacrificial love an essential but subordinate component of love that is mainly in the service of equal regard.[8]

Each church must join with other churches and with the schools to create a new marriage and family culture that can simultaneously proclaim the New Testament ideals for covenantal marriage where Christians make unconditional promises and mean them, as well as handle shortcomings with grace and forgiveness.[9] Such a culture will include daily age-appropriate family worship, prayer, Scripture reading, acts of service, conversations about faith around the dinner table, before bed and on trips. The continuity between the gathered church and the church at home has been a constant theme throughout Christian history. Because the early church met in homes, sacred actions around rituals and common meals in the gathered church spilled into home life. Home became a little church.[10] And for our children to thrive it will be important to integrate authentic, loving practices of faith into the rhythms of our daily lives. There is perhaps no more important agenda for building healthy communities.

The School

The tradition-dependent character of all inquiry provides a way ahead for academia in general and a rationale for the particularity of an Anabaptist education. Such an education will be thoroughly steeped in its own formative texts and will steward the rich resources of its own tradition(s) even as it invites explorers toward new discoveries. Such a school will also keep in mind the priority of moral formation to the intellectual life which will include not only shared information but specific forms of life practices included in all aspects of school life. And the cultivation of spiritual virtues such as humility, faith, self-denial, and charity will be seen as essential to the process of learning.

Education that is informed by an Anabaptist perspective will cultivate an awareness of a theology which emphasizes power-renouncing practices and originates from the perspective of those living in solidarity with the weak and the outcast. This awareness will lead to a perspective on reality that ought to be reflected all across the curriculum.[11] All studies, including the sciences, humanities, and professions, will be guided by comprehensive theological perspectives on reality. Each discipline, using its own "proper data" and systematized approaches, will seek to answer the questions that arise from within that particular discipline. But each discipline will look for ultimate guidance to theology as the discipline able to provide the most comprehensive and complex system of all—knowledge about God in relation to both the natural world and to human society.

Seeing the tradition-dependent character of all education frees church-related educational institutions to gladly own and strengthen a clear sense of their own distinctive vocations. Such alternative institutions offer alternative perspectives on reality as well as the virtues and practices vital for our communal quest of knowledge and truth.

STRATEGIES AND METHODOLOGIES

The above deliberations about ways of knowing provide direction for educational strategies that enable particular communities of faith to "bear fruit." Jesus said, "Those who abide in me and I in them bear much fruit" (John 15:5). The test that finally proves the value of our theorizing will be the test of fruitfulness. What strategies for educating children, youth and adult members of our communities will be helpful in directing the tradition-based, critical educational task so that the fruits of our labor are fruits worthy of the Christ we seek to serve?

The strategies and methodologies suggested below grow directly out of the ways of knowing we've articulated above. In this study we can only begin to point the way toward their practical implications. Many other persons' imaginative and innovative efforts will be required to explore the multiple dimensions of practical application illuminated by these theoretical beacons in the different educational settings outlined above.

Reimaging Communal Ideals

Contemporary Anabaptists (and other faith groups) are heirs to a powerful resource. We have a history with tremendous dynamism and integrity. We have received a tradition that flows out of that history as a gift borne through the generations by the daily living and storytelling of our forebears. We are now the stewards of a legacy that contains within itself many elements that offer potent, life-giving resources to this generation.

The question, Who are we? continues, however, to dominate many discussions about what it means to do education from an Anabaptist perspective, or any particular perspective. How do we do tradition-based, community shaped education when the very definition of what it means to be a distinct people seems to be growing vaguer every day?

In many of the centuries since the early Anabaptist movement, "who we are" has been defined in part, by ethnicity and communal boundary maintenance with clearly identified inner and outward markers that distinguished "us" from "them." In more recent years, however, it is widely acknowledged that acculturation to the larger culture is the most prominent feature of the twenty-first-century Mennonite church and other Anabaptist groups as well.[12] There is still desire to maintain some semblance of boundaries to prevent the loss of whatever unique identity and practices Mennonites have but there are also powerful forces at work on all fronts to eliminate those boundaries.[13]

The metaphor of boundary maintenance that keeps some groups separate from "the world" has little appeal to many contemporary heirs of the Anabaptists. For many, it no longer works as a metaphor to describe the way in which we intend to be a distinct and yet resourceful community to the larger society. Earlier I offered the image of the vine and the branches for revisioning our educational efforts. What the vine image suggests as an alternative to boundary maintenance is a call to return to the source, and to the center. A spirituality informed by Anabaptist forebears which centers on love for Christ and the commitment to follow Christ in all of life must be at the core of communal life and again become the tap root of its vitality. It is out of abiding in Christ that ethical commitments and practices will be directed and energized.

An educational strategy suggested by current community efforts to strengthen our tradition-based educational endeavors is the dynamic process of defining what is crucial for life together as an alternative community of faith. That process will involve reimaging and celebrating core communal ideals and symbols. It will be around these core ideals that we can rally our educational efforts rather than around concern to maintain boundaries at the edges.

A community's corporate longings or ideals help to shape its paideia, the organic social, historical, spiritual, and ethical fabric of our somewhat distinct culture. A cultural paideia involves the narratives and practices that shape and embody our vision for a shared communal life and a shared future.

A variety of ideals can be articulated which would have integrity with the tradition-based, Christ-centered ethical spirituality of the early Anabaptists. They will play out somewhat differently in family, church and school settings. As the primary institutions that mediate culture, the family, church and school form an educational matrix or ecology that articulates and enacts a community-wide paideia.

As the spokesperson for this conversation, I will be so bold as to articulate a vision with ideals for shaping a community-wide paideia informed from an Anabaptist perspective. I do this by way of illustration rather than in an attempt to offer a definitive list. It will be important if this strategy is to energize educational efforts, for every gathered group of believers, whether in a family, church or school setting, to name and own their own articulation of visionary ideals around which to rally. Those mentioned below will coalesce around keeping faith with the Scriptures, a community's faith heritage and, in the case of my particular community, the contemporary 1995 *Confession of Faith in a Mennonite Perspective*.

The list of ideals I offer are largely inspired by the early Anabaptists but are clearly also informed by current educational challenges. I suggest these because I believe they have particular significance for educational endeavors today. More could be listed, but let me name just a few:

1. The Scriptures will become world-creating for our children and youth. With imagination and love we will show them on a daily basis how to live creatively and practically into the life embodied by Jesus so their basic characters will be formed in Christ-like virtues.

2. Family based culture will be acknowledged as the most basic unit of the church's mission to the world and as the foundational context of a child's character formation. Renewing families and teaching what it means to practice truth at home will become the church's most urgent, missional task.

3. Each believer, ordained by baptism, will join a "society of explorers" engaging in communal moral discernment with the assistance of the Holy Spirit, about the meaning of the Scriptures and their implications for daily life. *The Martyrs Mirror*, *The Confession of Faith in a Mennonite Perspective* and contemporary experience will be among the primary resources for communal reflection and discernment.

4. Each believer will regard discipleship as abiding in Christ and will be devoted to living a life of witness, service, and peacemaking. Ethical practice and servant activism will flow out of a deeply rooted, Christ-centered spirituality.

5. Each believer will be a "resident alien" giving primary loyalty to the kingdom of God rather than to the nation. While being anchored in a particular local community, each believer will become globally aware and will freely serve others throughout the world and for the transformation of the world, in the name of Christ.

Indwelling Narratives and Practices

For the Anabaptists, neither church structures nor doctrines were considered as centrally important as modeling one's life on Jesus and one's communal life on the early Christian church. Their emphasis on following the example of Jesus in personal discipleship resembles what has been described as "indwelling." Only by participating in the same kind of "indwelling" as their teacher and Lord would they come to understand God and God's will for their life.

The concept of indwelling suggests that we live and think out of the most deeply formed, bodily particulars of our internalized skills, habits, attitudes, and images.

What might an educational strategy that focuses on what it means to participate in the same kind of indwelling as our teacher and Lord include? Let me suggest these characteristics.

1. Indwelling will involve direct as well as indirect teaching. It is not primarily about conveying information. A parent or teacher will help a child by immersing him or her in formative texts and practices which will allow the child in a regular, disciplined, imaginative, and loving way to internalize their meaning. Immersion will include telling and reading stories, memorizing and singing poetry, drawing, and dramatizing images and events. This indirect exposure will prepare the child for his or her own moments of insight, and later for critical, reflective thinking.

2. Indwelling as a strategy will mean living into the story and ethic of Jesus to such an extent that I come to interpret and experience myself and my world on its terms. Indwelling the formative narratives of my faith community will mean that its language and metaphors become the primary shapers of my imagination and practices. To enhance the abilities of our children to understand their world primarily in light of the Scriptures, from the day they are born we will surround them with poetry, songs, images, symbols, and stories of the Scriptures and their faith tradition on a daily basis. Our best poets, artists, story-tellers, song-writers, and faith heroes will embody and enact our community's most formative literature.

3. The ability to indwell the way of Jesus will first mean engaging in regularly patterned, habitual behaviors that reflect that life. It will mean, from the day our children are born, we will surround them with the daily rhythm of biblically informed, bodily practices among which would be prayer, worship, hospitality, peacemaking, truth-telling, respect for elders, and service to neighbors.

4. Indwelling the tradition of one's teacher will provide a way of seeing and forming a particular perspective on reality. Indwelling the Jesus story bodily, for example, will mean practicing servanthood, love of enemy, sharing of material resources and in so doing coming to see reality from the perspective of those whose reality we come to share. By indwelling the forms and practices of the Jesus way, we are enabled to see reality from the perspective of the poor, the weak, the outcast.

5. Indwelling the world creating stories and practices of Jesus will root us in the vine, a loving, imaginative and vital identification with Jesus, rather than dutiful obligation to be good disciples or keep the law.

To employ the strategy of indwelling will mean that we pay far more attention to the bodily aspects of social memory by identifying bodily practices which convey virtues and values that we hope our children will learn. It will mean identifying a cultural fund of Scripture, poetry, music, stories, and daily, habitual practices which convey the spiritual and moral qualities deemed essential for forming basic character dispositions and the capacity for innovative, critical thinking.

Much work will need to be done to identify which narratives and which bodily behaviors most nearly embody the values we confessionally consider central to who we are as a distinctive community. Specific suggestions will emerge in the discussion of core practices and in proposals for family, church, and school life.

Communal Moral Discernment as a "Society of Explorers"

Through the long night of honoring those who engaged primarily in detached rational thinking, many of us have come to doubt our own powers for faithful, imaginative and personal judgment. We must develop confidence in our own personal powers of judgment once again. This won't mean that our every emotional whim can be trusted but that through self-discipline and apprenticeship to the masters of the art of moral discernment, we can learn once again to use our faculties of personal judgment for the good. All knowing, asserts Polanyi, must involve personal commitment and acceptance of responsibility for one's insights and beliefs. The passionate and intuitive contribution of each person doing the knowing is vital to every act of knowing.

A primary strategy of education will be to invite adults to engage their powers for faithful, imaginative and personal judgment. We must find ways in the family, at church and at school to provide opportunities for persons to use their personal judgment in communal moral discernment around the Scriptures and in conversation with present experience. Adults need to be reassured that they know more than they think they know and that even as relatively uneducated, ordinary church members, they are capable of listening to the Spirit and the Scriptures and assisting in communal discernment.

The Anabaptist tradition tells of congregations of believers meeting together around Scripture to learn how to live as disciples. It was assumed that Scripture was clear enough for ordinary Christians to understand and apply when read communally and under the inspiration of the

Holy Spirit. It was assumed that clarity about the meaning of the Scriptures was provided to those who approached them with a right attitude out of a commitment to faithful living rather than mere curiosity. Making the church body the locus for biblical interpretation nurtured a broadly based love of and familiarity with the Bible.

Modifications to the Anabaptist practice of discernment have been suggested so the discerning circle can benefit from scholarly input, from the wisdom of earlier generations and from persons who represent diverse social, political and cultural backgrounds lest a given circle of discerners not recognize its own presuppositions. In discerning the Scriptures it will be important to include the voices of those who tend to be disregarded and marginalized.

Commitment to reading the Bible in the context of the congregation of believers means readiness to have our theology and church life shaped by the biblical vision rather than adjusting the Bible to a theology and church life formed primarily by other sources. It also provides the opportunity for intentionally bringing together the wisdom of the tradition and the present experience of diverse individuals in the context of community discernment. And it allows for individuals to freely explore new interpretations and test fresh ways to apply the formative texts, within the framework and accountability of the communal circle.

Strategies for communally discerning how we should live and what we should do and be in light of the teachings of Scripture can be activated in the family, at church, and in the schools. By encouraging persons to exercise their own personal, critical, moral judgment in the context of communal discernment, our community of faith will experience renewed energy for a distinctive and Christ-centered life.

Revitalizing Core Practices

The educational strategy that has the most power for transforming our families, churches and schools is the revitalization of core faith-based practices. Our practices are shared activities through which we come to form perspectives on reality and to know the truth as embodied in Jesus Christ.

But it is also through our practices that we bear fruit. Our practices of making peace, telling the truth, opening our home to the stranger for example, when done in the name of Christ, suggest the sort of fruitfulness that comes from abiding in Christ.

So we have a fully formed circle, an inseparably intertwined cord of epistemological and ethical dynamics. Engaging in ethical practices modeled on Jesus is essential for coming to know the truth of the gospel and those same practices also embody the fruitful outworking of that truth—the gift of the gospel to the world.

An educational strategy that seeks to renew community life by identifying and revitalizing core practices which reenact the self-giving life of Jesus holds great promise for wide community interest and involvement. When people are invited to talk about practices in their childhood home or in their faith community, they are often eager to offer vivid memories and concrete, down-to-earth stories. Reflection on practices generates strong feelings both about the abuses and the creative possibilities of specific practices.

When asked to imagine what a good culture might look like, whether a family, school, or church-based culture, persons are energized to imagine what the concrete patterns and practices of a good and godly life together might look like. If we're not talking about a legalistic imposition of authoritarian dictates from the past but about a quality of life that promotes human flourishing, generosity, mutual respect, and the celebration of our faith stories, persons are energized to think about revitalizing core practices. They glimpse the intrinsic connection between down-to-earth practices and "the abundant life."

Imaginatively shaping concrete practices that give character to everyday life is distinct from talk about adopting new church programs for ministry to families. It is also distinct from a more psychological, therapeutic approach for working with families who presumably are dysfunctional, enmeshed, or whatever other label we so frequently impose. Inviting families and even schools and churches to reflect on the concrete practices that make up their everyday lives holds great promise for empowerment of parents and others to reclaim their freedom and ability to shape a life-giving culture at home and at work.

Practices provide shelter for families, shelter from the overbearing pressures of an invasive and consumer driven North American mass culture. Families can be shown how to disconnect from forces and systems that harm them and reconnect with people, places, and practices that sustain them. This is frontline missional agenda for faith communities.

Brian McLaren, a pastor, author and interpreter of postmodernity observes that the premodern Celtic era was one of the most vibrant eras in Christian history, lasting some 700 years and extending its influence throughout Europe. He notes that the Celts didn't have a written theology but rather encoded their theology in ritual, dance, song, and a sacramental approach to daily life. They invested their faith in shaping a way of life rather than in devising an elaborate, rational system of beliefs. Many persons in postmodernity are drawn, not toward adopting a system of beliefs but rather toward down-to-earth practices that construct a way of life; practices whose gestures are gifts that have taken shape over centuries as people respond to each other in community and to God's presence; practices that are ancient and larger than we are and yet can be newly shaped to fit our time and need.

Again, as the spokesperson for this discussion, and as a Mennonite, I will be bold and suggest core practices that are compatible with who contemporary Anabaptists confessionally claim to be but more broadly reflect the gifts of other Christian traditions. Every family, church, and school, however, will want to identify and name those practices which most nearly express the quality of life together that they long for and creatively choose to construct.

What practices are vital for sustaining ourselves and our communities of faith? I mention several briefly here. Each deserves much more imaginative elaboration in our homes and faith communities.

Keeping Sabbath

This is at the top of the list intentionally because our ability to revitalize life-giving practices is all about our relationship to time and the purported lack of time that is at the root of so many of our current ills. In the frenzy of our schedules, we often experience time as the enemy. Rest and renewal are expansive good gifts of our tradition. Sabbath keeping allows us to reclaim "time" as a gift and a friend. Sabbath keeping frees us to regain a healthy perspective on our world of work as we reflect on who we are, who God is; and most profoundly on who it is that we love so that our work is a work of love.

Sabbath keeping may include many life-giving practices: *assembling together for worship, giving and receiving forgiveness, celebrating the Lord's Supper, testifying to God's faithfulness in the past week, offering hospitality*—*with meals in each other's homes, visits with extended family, relaxed space for conversation, long walks for reveling in God's natural world, family games, afternoon naps, journaling. . . .*

<u>Cultivating sacred spaces</u>

Most of us can quickly identify our favorite places. If we review our store of childhood memories, there will be the deep couch in front of the fireplace where we read aloud, the tree house, the neighborhood ballpark, the meadow by the stream, the café on the corner . . . We tend to be powerfully attached to places where we've experienced security, intimacy, encouragement and friendship. Where are those places for our families? How can we better understand the significance of shaping places to nurture life at home and in school and church communities?

Thoughtful attention to our use of space may include identifying places that give shape to much that we hold dear and hallowing those places: *a prayer room or corner set aside for listening to God, a porch swing for watching the sunset, a marriage bed blessed by joy and fidelity, a favorite park for picnics, a basketball court for intergenerational camaraderie, a dining room table for real meals together, a den filled with great read aloud books, a favorite restaurant for celebrating birthdays . . .*

<u>Engendering a unique identity</u>

Remembering who we are, whether as families, churches or even schools, hugely impacts our freedom to function with grace and confidence. Each of us has a unique history, a history that is interwoven with many others, but also has its own story and character. It is in knowing that we are "somebody," somebody to be glad about, somebody with a place to belong and a purpose that "bears on eternity" which frees us to invest our lives in enhancing the life of those around us.

Engendering a unique identity will involve many practices that grow out of a family or faith community's own story, personality and context. The activities that both connect us with a web of identity larger than ourselves, but are also consciously incorporated as our own special way of being may include no end of possibilities—countercultural faith practices, recreational pursuits, hobbies, ethnic characteristics. Just by way of illustration, some of these practices might be *singing and making music together, turning off the TV, bird watching, making great pies, gardening, conscientious objection to war, delighting in international foods, serving at the local food kitchen, family meetings for corporate decision making, camping trips, special pets, poetry writing/reading, careful use of money, simple living, demonstrating radical love of enemy, keeping promises, truthtelling. . . .*

Cultivating rituals and celebrations

There are all sorts of wonderful ways to mark time lest it pass by us in a frenzied blur—*morning and evening rituals, weekly rhythms, rites of passage, commemoration of significant achievements and seasonal changes, baptism celebrations, church year festivities, milestones in the life of a marriage, family worship, Sabbath meals, bedtime prayers, good-bye hugs, healing prayers and rituals* . . . Rituals and celebrations surround us with a cloak of security, with rhyme and reason, with anticipation and fulfillment, over and over again.

Is it possible to celebrate too much? Perhaps. But most of us long for the fun, food, faith and companionship that we share in these events. We thrive on the simple pleasures that come from marking and enriching moments in time. On any ordinary day, there are far too few hallowed moments, too few gestures of old fashioned hospitality, too few expectations that healing can happen, too few festive activities to send our spirits soaring.

Weaving relational networks

We thrive on multi-generational relationships and have too often neglected those nearest—our extended families. Fragmentation of communities and enormous mobility of individuals makes urgent the cultivation of the ties that are important for sustaining our well-being. Practices that contribute to this reweaving might be *visiting grandparents often, giving priority to reunions, developing parent support groups, planning block parties, engaging with intergenerational service projects, planning vacations with other families, providing mutual care in the form of shared resources, writing old fashioned letters and making plenty of phone calls, joining an adult "society of explorers" discernment group, lingering over the table for long conversations about faith, respectfully addressing elders, keeping vigil with those who are ill and dying.* . . .

Writing and telling stories

Stories are a marvelous resource for giving flesh and color in a churchly/religious world that has been all too saturated with wordy abstractions and elaborate systems of belief. We can recover some of the stunning drama of "God with us" when we ennoble each other with the stories of those who have exemplified goodness, faithfulness, transforming love, kindness to enemies, endurance in suffering. Rather than conceding air time to the multi-national storytellers that saturate the airwaves, we can cultivate the practices of *reading out loud during every stage* of family life, inviting grandparents to tell their stories, keeping family/church albums and histories, "When I was your age" stories at birthdays, "indwelling" the Bible stories during family worship, telling hero stories of martyrs and peacebuilders and stories of "ordinary" triumphs during public worship, inviting the elderly to recount their life stories. . . . [14]

Reflecting on Practices

Many more practices could be identified for the contribution they make to constructing a good culture in which everyone can flourish. I've only begun to point the way and would simply encourage families, churches and schools to imaginatively identify those practices that most nearly embody their vision, their confession of faith. How might educational priorities be shaped around core practices? A school or church may well identify many practices different from or in addition to those named above. What might some of these practices be?

Eastern Mennonite Seminary, my school community, has identified core practices within its purpose statement:

> Eastern Mennonite Seminary equips men and women to grow as disciples of Jesus Christ, prepared to lead the church in mission with passion and integrity. As a community of disciples, we are humbled by God's call, formed in Christ, transformed by the Holy Spirit, and empowered to serve with knowledge and grace.
>
> As the graduate theological school of Eastern Mennonite University and a pastoral training center of the Mennonite Church, EMS seeks to embody this central purpose within the following core practices:
>
> HUMBLED BY GOD'S CALL
> - Discerning and humbly claiming a call to ministry
> - Cooperating with what God is doing among us and throughout the world
> - Becoming aware of personal and communal strengths and limitations
> - Cultivating understanding of and appreciation for our Anabaptist heritage
> - Extending hospitality to persons from diverse cultures and confessional traditions

Formed in Christ
- Acknowledging the lordship of Jesus Christ in life and study
- Devoting time to daily communal and personal spiritual disciplines
- Claiming the Christian Scriptures as authoritative for life and practice
- Expressing mutual care and respect for each other
- Promoting justice and compassion in all relationships
- Committing ourselves to holy living and peacemaking
- Witnessing to the good news of Jesus Christ in word and deed

Transformed by the Holy Spirit
- Practicing a prayerful disposition in all of life
- Celebrating the presence of God in ordinary things
- Worshipping together as communal discipline
- Singing our faith as a corporate body
- Modeling personal transparency in teaching and learning
- Ministering healing and hope with priestly courage

Empowered to Serve with Knowledge and Grace
- Interpreting the Scriptures for life through thoughtful and imaginative exposition
- Dialoguing across disciplines of study throughout the university
- Enhancing global and non-Western perspectives in the community of learning
- Engaging contemporary realities through critical reflection and scholarly research
- Linking academic rigor with Christian commitment
- Confessing sin, offering forgiveness and living with joyful freedom

Whether at home, at school or in church, an educational mission that focuses on revitalizing core practices will also want to include methods for reflecting on the meaning of those practices and the new knowledge that has emerged from them. Action/reflection models abound and can be thoughtfully incorporated into family settings or into other community educational planning.[15] In the activity of reflecting on the meaning of core faith practices we will be doing the work of theology—

saving work. What practices characterize our life together? Which are life-giving? What more may we want to incorporate to shape our life together in wholesome ways?

Many of the practices listed throughout this chapter can be described as power-renouncing practices because they seek to serve the kingdom of God rather than merely one's own self-centered interest. They provide the resources for coming to know and see reality from the perspective of the One who gave his life that we might have life. They shape us in the virtues necessary to enter into communal discernment about how to continually re-make and re-vitalize our guiding traditions. An educational mission that focuses on the continuous revitalization of communal practices and critical, Spirit-led discernment about their meaning in light of the Scriptures and current experience, will renew the well-spring of family and communal life.

Conclusion

The time has come to bring closure to the conversation at the table. Everyone present has contributed in small or large ways. Each voice has added color and texture to the design. While many other voices could have joined in, these that have spoken contributed substantially to our critical reflection on approaches to education informed from an Anabaptist perspective. More than that, they have modeled an approach that could be used by any distinctive community hoping to think together about tradition-based, critical educational endeavors.

As the host of this conversation, I have been challenged and energized by the interaction. I was surprised and delighted by discoveries along the way and the synergy that developed among the various perspectives shared. What the implications of this conversation are for education will be worth pondering for some time to come. I for one am grateful to have been the recipient of the wisdom shared here and to have had a hand in weaving it into a coherent design. I hope that this theory design can contribute to the revitalization of the educational vision and practice of my faith community and other faith communities as well.

GLOSSARY

Definitions of Key Concepts

Church

The church in Anabaptist-Mennonite thought is understood to be the body of Christ, defined by the life and teachings of Jesus, transformed by the death and resurrection of Jesus the Christ, and empowered by the Holy Spirit. As the church is one very significant vehicle through which God works his will in the world, it is called to be distinct from the world and yet to be an agent of God's reconciling love in the world.

The Mennonite church is made visible and recognizable by embracing persons who are baptized as adults upon confession of faith in Christ and who commit themselves to follow the way of Christ as interpreted in the *Confession of Faith in a Mennonite Perspective*.[1] The Mennonite church is made up of local congregations united by a common tradition, confession, and polity into a denomination. In turn, the Mennonite church is united to the worldwide Christian church by Mennonite regard for the authoritative character of the Scriptures and the historic creeds of the early church.

Community

A community is comprised of persons bound to others by a shared relationship to a center of value and power, a mythos, or a tradition. The shared relationship may consist of a shared loyalty to a particular tradition, a commitment to identify oneself with a particular tradition, and/or a common valuing of a particular tradition and its ongoing communal expression. A community, in contrast to a church, is more inclusive of persons who may value many aspects of a particular tradition but are not necessarily committed to follow the way of Christ as interpreted in a church's confession of faith.

Culture

Culture refers to an historically transmitted pattern of meanings embodied in symbols, artifacts, rituals, practices, languages, and laws that give form to daily life. It is a system of inherited forms by means of which persons communicate, perpetuate, and develop their knowledge and attitude toward life. Culture is the form and shape humans give to their inner longing for ultimate meaning. Culture embodies what is considered of value in given contexts.

Unless civilization manages to convey its cultural achievements from one generation to the next, its culture will cease to exist, thus requiring enormous educational effort to adequately teach that which gives life meaning and form beyond our natural processes. Because there is no such thing as human nature independent of culture, culture is not just an ornament of human existence but an essential condition for it.

Education

Education is the intentional transmission of a culture as well as the ongoing process of defining what is crucial now to a people's life together. Education is the deliberate, systematic and sustained way we mediate the substance and character of a culture and critically reflect on its relevance for our present life together. The essential content of education is drawn from the traditions and experiences of a people and their vision of life as a cultural and ethical aspiration.

Habitus

A "habitus" (a term common in the writings of sociologist Pierre Bourdieu and drawn on by a variety of writers treated in this book) is a "settled disposition" to act in a characteristic way or engage in a certain practice. While many habits dispose us to act automatically or without thought, habitus disposes us to act "intentionally, thoughtfully, self-critically, and inventively in light of the actual circumstances of the action."

Ideals

An ideal is a cultural or ethical aspiration that arises from within a community's experience and history. It is the historically constructed identification of those qualities which are considered good and most desirable by a particular culture.

Practices

Practices are "socially established" activities engaged in because the community recognizes their value. Practices involve "cooperative human activity" and include "goods internal to that form of activity," meaning moral, even spiritual goods. Elements of the good life are experienced in carrying out certain practices. And practices include "standards of excellence" suggesting that cooperative human effort can be done well or badly. By learning a practice well and making sure others learn to do it well, our own lives are enhanced.

Praxis

Praxis can be understood to mean "reflective action." Praxis refers to the intentional commitment to reflect theoretically on our current and past practices and to inform that theoretical reflection by the experience that grows out of our current and past practices. Praxis is an attempt to keep theory and practice together in a mutually enriching relationship.

Service

Service is a function not only of what we do but of who we are. Service involves an unselfish interest in the welfare of others and, for my purposes in this paper, can be defined as the commitment to make Jesus' style of self-giving the model for every profession and vocation. Jesus' model of servanthood has a social-political character which takes on concrete social meaning in Jesus willingness to die and in so doing demonstrate both his love for enemies and his willingness to absorb hostility by forgiving the perpetrators of violence.

Tradition

Tradition refers to especially valued practices, beliefs and narratives that are handed down from one generation to the next. Tradition applies to the transmission of some of the elements of culture, but not to all elements. It refers to those elements which are valued and considered especially worthy of attention and embodiment by a particular community. Specific traditions that continue to be chosen over time by a community become normative and serve to identify the center of value and power for a community and to intensify group consciousness and cohesion. A normative tradition will often be advanced as the source of legitimacy and authority in a particular community.

More specifically, for our purposes in this study, tradition refers to an "historically extended, socially embodied argument" about how best to interpret and apply the formative text(s) of one particular community. Tradition then refers not only to a deposit of normative texts and related practices that are passed on but to an ongoing living experiment that involves active engagement with the community's formative and normative texts/narratives to find their most life-giving interpretation and embodiment now.

Tradition-based, critical education

Tradition-based education is a deliberate, systematic, and sustained effort to ground educational purpose, theory, and practices in the tradition(s) a particular community considers normative for its life together. In as much as knowledge and truth are rooted in culture and need a narrative context to become intelligible, tradition-based education seeks to provide cultural practices and narrative contexts to communicate and embody the knowledge and affirmations of truth a particular community finds most life-giving.

Tradition-based education also cultivates continuity with the past to encourage new discoveries and the creative, critical dissent needed to revitalize the tradition. A great tradition provides the means both for maintaining itself and for the constructive, critical discernment needed to keep it vital.

Transformation

Transformation takes place when revelatory events and experience work on the image and motivational structures of a person, causing a lack of ease with the way things have been and a yearning to live in harmony with a new master-image of life and reality. Transformation is the work of the Holy Spirit bringing a person to repentance and faith and empowering an individual or community to envision a new image of self and reality. It involves a metamorphosis or new birth, involving a change in one's thinking, emotions, and behavior to conform more nearly with the Spirit and ethic of Jesus.

Virtue

Virtues are those character dispositions or behavioral qualities which are considered morally good because they enable persons to sustain practices considered necessary for achieving a good quality of life.

Notes

FOREWORD

1. Stephen Toulmin, *Cosmopolis: The Hidden Agenda of Modernity* (New York: Free Press, 1990), 167.

2. Jeffrey Stout, *The Flight from Authority: Religion, Morality, and the Quest for Autonomy* (Notre Dame: University of Notre Dame, 1981).

3. Alasdair MacIntyre, *Whose Justice? Which Rationality?* (Notre Dame: University of Notre Dame, 1988), 367.

4. See George Lakoff & Mark Johnson *Philosophy in the Flesh: The Embodied Mind and its Challenge to Western Thought* (New York: Basic Books, 1999).

INTRODUCTION

1. Nancey Murphy, "A Theology of Education" unpublished paper (presented at a consultation on Mennonite Higher Education, Winnipeg, Man., Canada, June 13-15, 1997), 3. For a discussion of the cultural climate that gave rise to the ideal of human knowledge focused on the general, the universal, the timeless, and the theoretical see Stephen Toulmin, *Cosmopolis* (New York: The Free Press, 1990). *Postmodernism* is a term usually associated with so-called post-structuralist thinkers such as Michel Foucault and Jacques Derrida who champion a strong non-objectivist strand of thought. They contend there are no objective criteria for determining the truth of a scientific claim, the validity of an interpretation, or the morality of a behavior. The world is an ever evolving construction of a contingent self that is not firmly rooted in history, tradition, or community. Summarized by H. A. Alexander in "Postmodern Themes in Religious Education," *Religious Education* 93, no. 1 (Winter 1998): 5.

2. Rodney Clapp, "How Firm a Foundation: Can Evangelicals Be Nonfoundationalists?" in Timothy Phillips & Dennis Okholm, eds., *The Nature of Confession: Evangelicals & Postliberals in Conversation* (Downers Grove, Ill.: InterVarsity Press, 1996), 84-89.

3. Douglas Sloan, *Faith and Knowledge: Mainline Protestantism and American*

Higher Education (Louisville, Ky.: Westminster John Knox Press, 1994), 223, 233. Here Sloan is referring to the work of Lindbeck, MacIntyre and Hauerwas.

4. Alasdair MacIntyre, *After Virtue* (Notre Dame, Ind.: University of Notre Dame Press, 1981), 208-10.

5. Ibid., 216.

6. Ibid., 221.

7. Murphy, "A Theology of Education," 4-10. Murphy refers extensively to these ideas in several of her other books which we will note later. MacIntyre describes "tradition" as a historically extended, socially embodied argument about how best to interpret and apply the formative text(s) of a tradition.

8. George A. Lindbeck, *The Nature of Doctrine: Religion and Theology in a Postliberal Age* (Philadelphia: The Westminster Press, 1984), 34, 128. Gregory C. Higgins in "The Significance of Postliberalism for Religious Education," *Theological Perspectives on Christian Formation*, Jeff Astley, Leslie Francis, and Colin Crowder, eds. (Grand Rapids, Mich.: Eerdmans, 1996), 135-45, makes several significant observations about how postliberalism has impacted educational methodologies. He briefly describes the three approaches to the study of religion Lindbeck discusses (propositional, experiential-expressive and cultural-linguistic) and the type of religious education that grows out of each approach. The propositionalist approach is best represented by a "catechism approach," in which religious education consists of the inculcation of certain orthodox beliefs. The experiential approach, on the other hand, begins with the experiences of the students and relates these to traditional affirmations of the faith. Tillich's method of correlation most ably demonstrates this approach. Correlation relates the questions of human existence with the answers given by Christianity. This methodology directly addresses itself to the deepest questions of the students, thus making an effort to keep Christianity relevant.

Lindbeck feels that the experiential-expressivist approach fails to recognize the formative influence of language. He insists that language is prior to experience. Instead of deriving external features of a religion from inner experience, it is the inner experiences which are derivative, he argues. Language shapes domains of human existence and action that are preexperiential.

Lindbeck also takes exception to the liberal commitment to apologetics as the best means of commending Christianity to the world, arguing that such an approach has been detrimental to Christianity. He writes, "In short, religions, like languages, can be understood only in their own terms, not by transposing them into an alien speech" (Lindbeck, *The Nature of Doctrine*, 129). He insists that the development of strong communities of Christian witness offers Christianity its best chance for relevance to the modern world.

While Lindbeck puts great emphasis on the argument that we are shaped by the language we have received, he acknowledges that the relationship between religions and experiences is reciprocal—that we in turn shape the language and vision of the church of tomorrow (Lindbeck, 33). He also does not entirely dismiss apologetics but insists that it must not stand at the center of theology (Lindbeck, 129).

9. Sloan, 223-24.

10. It is important to acknowledge, if one chooses a communitarian approach to make truth claims, the danger of tribalism and the violence that arises among rival

tribes when each is wedded to their respective versions of the truth. Mark Schwehn argues that objectivism arose primarily as a way of avoiding violence. Any alternative to foundationalism or objectivism will seem to open up the prospect of renewed violence among different communities who seem to have no rational foundation on which to adjudicate disagreements. The fear of tribalism and violence is likely the foremost difficulty that communitarian accounts of knowledge must face, argues Schwehn in *Exiles from Eden* (New York: Oxford University Press, 1993), 29-32.

11. For a fuller definition of the meaning I intend by "tradition-based, critical education" and "education" refer to the glossary. Along with Lawrence Cremin, I am suggesting that each culture (including a church culture) has a vision of life as a deliberate cultural and ethical aspiration. It is this vision, drawn from the traditions and experiences of a people, that is the essential content of education.

12. Thomas Finger, *Christian Theology: An Eschatological Approach*, vol. 1 (Scottdale, Pa.: Herald Press, 1985), 85. In some ways believers' church theology is similar to liberation theologies in that both are primarily concerned with matters of action. Theological reflection is in order to guide action and is evaluated by how well it does, being concerned with matters relevant to practice. While tending to reject natural theology, there is a heavy reliance on Scripture, which they insist cannot be understood and obeyed apart from God's Spirit.

13. Thomas Finger, "The Constructive Appropriation of Scripture and Anabaptist Tradition," unpublished paper presented at conference entitled, "Gordon Kaufman's Theology as Imaginative Construction" (North Newton, Kan.: Bethel College, November 3-4, 1996).

14. See Irwin B. Horst, Proposition V of Theses, appended to his doctoral dissertation for its defense, cited by Willard Swartley in "The Anabaptists Use of Scripture: Contemporary Applications and Prospects," *Anabaptist Currents: History in Conversation with the Present*, Carl F. Bowman and Stephen L. Longenecker, eds. (Bridgewater, Va.: Penobscot Press, 1995), 70.

15. An Anabaptist ecclesiology is a fundamental dynamic shaping a distinctively Mennonite post-secondary educational perspective suggests Rodney Sawatsky in "What Can the Mennonite Tradition Contribute to Christian Higher Education?" *Models for Christian Higher Education,* Richard Hughes and William Adrian, eds. (Grand Rapids, Mich.: Eerdmans, 1997), 194. The church in Anabaptist-Mennonite thought is

> the body of Christ defined by the life and teachings of Jesus, transformed by the death and resurrection of Jesus the Christ, and empowered by the Holy Spirit. As the primary vehicle through which God today works his will in the world, the church is to be separated from and nonconformed to the world, yet is also salt and light in the world and the agency of God's reconciling love in the world. The church, accordingly, is visible and tangible for it embraces all those who are baptized as adults upon confession of faith in Christ and who commit themselves to follow the way of Christ in fellowship.

16. Fayette Breaux Veverka, "Religious Identity and Community: Educational Strategies in a Postmodern World," unpublished manuscript and keynote address (New Orleans, La.: APRRE Annual Meeting, November 23-26, 1996).

Chapter 1

1. John S. Brubacher, *A History of the Problems of Education* (New York: McGraw-Hill Book Company, 1966), 105. Brubacher is citing Aristotle, *Politics*, book VII, chapter 13. Plato distinguished three components in human nature: appetite (referring to senses and bodily drives), spirit (referring to the will), and reason or intelligence. While appetite and spirit were classed as functions of the body, reason traced its lineage to some state of preexistence. The virtues associated with appetite and spirit were thought to be due first to habit and only later did the rational component manifest itself, 102-03.

2. Aristotle, *The Nicomachean Ethics*, trans. and introduction David Ross (Oxford: Oxford University Press, 1980).

3. Paul Connerton, *How Societies Remember* (Cambridge: Cambridge University Press, 1989).

4. Ibid. Connerton describes "incorporating practices" and "inscribing practices." Both may be the objects of our interpretive activity. Inscribing practices have always formed the privileged story, incorporating practices the neglected story in the history of hermeneutics. Incorporating practices have for long been backgrounded as objects of explicit interpretive attention. Unlike a text, they are largely traceless and incapable of providing a means by which any evidence of a will to be remembered can be "left behind." We consider inscription as having the privileged form for the transmission of a society's memories. Yet we can't underestimate the mnemonic importance and persistence of what is incorporated, 75, 95, 101-02.

5. Ibid., 96, 102.

6. Ibid., 39-40.

7. Ibid., 46-47.

8. Ibid., 93-95. The term *habit*, Connerton says, conveys the sense of "operativeness of a continuously practiced activity."

9. David D. Hall, ed. *Lived Religion in America: Toward a History of Practice* (Princeton, N.J.: Princeton University Press, 1997), vii.

10. Ibid. Lived religion as pursued in the case studies in the book build on other lines of inquiry, the sociological tradition of community studies, ritual studies, and cultural or symbolic anthropology associated in America with Clifford Geertz. The study of lived religion doesn't depend on any single method or discipline, ix-x.

11. Ibid., xi.

12. Ibid., 7.

13. MacIntyre, *After Virtue*, 221-23. In *After Virtue* MacIntyre laments the disorder of contemporary morality. Ever since Aristotelian teleology was discredited, he argues, moral philosophers have sought to provide some rational secular account of morality and have failed. Most of our modern morality is based on a set of fragmented survivals from the Aristotelian tradition. MacIntyre makes an appeal for a return to the classical Aristotelian tradition as an adequate grounding for moral philosophy. Aristotle's notion of telos and the tradition of the virtues have the potential for providing a unified vision for human culture.

CHAPTER 2

1. David Tracy, *The Analogical Imagination: Christian Theology and the Culture of Pluralism* (New York: Crossroad, 1981). While Tracy's vocabulary may sound unhelpfully "modern" I find his approach compatible with that of MacIntyre. In her book *Beyond Liberalism and Fundamentalism, How Modern and Postmodern Philosophy Set the Theological Agenda* (Valley Forge, Pa.: Trinity Press International, 1997), 103, 107, Murphy explains MacIntyre's assertion in his books *After Virtue* and *Three Rival Versions of Inquiry* that a tradition is an historically extended, socially embodied argument about how best to interpret and apply the formative text(s) of a tradition. A tradition fails on its own terms when a solution to an epistemological crisis cannot be found that measures up to the tradition's own internal standards of rationality. A tradition is justified insofar as it can be shown to make progress on its own terms while its live competitors fail to do so. My sense is that Tracy uses "classic" in much the same way and that one can look for commonalities among the particular expressions of a variety of traditions in order to look for a *more* universal understanding of what can confessionally be referred to as truth.

2. James W. Fowler discussing Tracy and Gadamer in *Faithful Change: The Personal and Public Challenges of Postmodern Life* (Nashville: Abingdon Press, 1996), 185-86.

3. Summarized by Ross T. Bender, *Education for Peoplehood: Essays on the Teaching Ministry of the Church* (Elkhart, Ind.: Institute of Mennonite Studies, 1997), 185, from Robert Friedmann, "The Doctrine of the Two Worlds," *The Recovery of the Anabaptist Vision*, Guy F. Hershberger ed. (Scottdale, Pa.: Herald Press, 1957), 105.

Walter Klaassen observes that the Anabaptists on the whole accepted the ancient Christian symbols which identified orthodox Christian belief. To a large extent they adhered to the basic theological affirmations of the ancient church, he said, and were heavily dependent on the tradition of the Christian church. This evidence shouldn't be obscured by highlighting their "orthopraxis." Without trinitarian faith there would have been no Anabaptism, he argues, pointing out the great significance currently of recognizing and maintaining links to the traditions of the Christian church which transcend the Mennonite churches. Recognition that the Anabaptist tradition was not a brand new departure but is very much a part of the rest of Christianity, however much that Christianity was criticized and rejected by 16th-century Anabaptists, is of fundamental importance, "Sixteenth-Century Anabaptism: A Vision Valid for the Twentieth Century?" *Conrad Grebel Review* 7 (Fall 1989): 245-46.

4. Thomas Finger, "The Constructive Appropriation of Scripture and Anabaptist Tradition," unpublished paper presented at conference entitled, "Gordon Kaufman's Theology as Imaginative Construction" (North Newton, Kan.: Bethel College, November 3-4, 1996).

5. Ibid.

6. John D. Roth, "Community as Conversation: A New Model of Anabaptist Hermeneutics" in *Anabaptist Currents: History in Conversation with the Present*, ed. Carl F. Bowman and Stephen L. Longenecker (Bridgewater, Va.: Penobscot Press, 1995), 52. In other words, Roth continues, the issue was one of hermeneutics, an issue to be discussed at greater length in a subsequent section.

7. Klaassen, "Sixteenth-Century Anabaptism," 250. The chief source for the believer's understanding is Scripture, he argues. Not, of course, for the specifics of sci-

ence and technology but for exposing the underlying superstitions of our time and learning what belongs in their place once they have been exposed. For every member to be a witness requires a massive job of what we normally call adult education.

8. Marlin Miller in Richard A. Kauffman and Gayle Gerber Koontz, editors, *Theology for the Church: Writings by Marlin E. Miller* (Elkhart, Ind.: Institute of Mennonite Studies, 1997), 143.

9. Summarized by John D. Roth, *Refocusing A Vision: Shaping Anabaptist Character in the 21st Century* (Goshen, Ind.: Mennonite Historical Society, 1995), viii.

10. Roth, 51.

11. In 1975 an essay was published in the Mennonite Quarterly Review with the title: "From Monogenesis to Polygenesis: The Historical Discussion of Anabaptist Origins," by James Stayer, Werner Packull and Klaus Depperman, *Mennonite Quarterly Review* 49, no. 2 (April 1975): 83-121. Mennonite historian, Walter Klaassen observes that it marked a turning point in the understanding of 16th-century Anabaptism. Rather than suggesting there was within the movement a common solid core of beliefs, with softer expression of the movement's main affirmations farther away from the center, and even degenerating into perversion at the circumference, this revised model differentiated between three groupings—the Swiss Brethren who were Zwinglian-humanist, the South German Anabaptists who were mystical-humanist and the Netherlands Anabaptists who were sacramentarian-apocalyptic. All three Anabaptist groups were part of a pervasive European protest movement of lay people against being controlled by the clergy. Anabaptism was the most visible churchly expression of the resulting anticlericalism, concluding that leadership would have to be lay. This gave a certain similarity among the various groups.

The earliest years of the movement 1524-1536, were years of considerable turmoil and searching for direction, suggests Klaassen. Consolidation came in Switzerland in 1527 with the Schleitheim Articles, in South Germany with the failure of Hans Hut's prediction of Christ's return at Pentecost, 1528, and in the Netherlands soon after the fall of Munster in June, 1535. After that there was a convergence among the groups as they developed. It was their popular anticlericalism which in large measure determined the shape they gave to their church structures, Klaassen, 241-43.

12. Roth, "Community as Conversation: A New Model of Anabaptist Hermeneutics," 52. How, asks Roth, might this reappraisal of virtually every assumption in the older historiography affect Anabaptist hermeneutics? We will explore this aspect further.

13. Miller, in Kauffman and Koontz, 143.

14. Ibid., 149.

15. Klaassen, 245.

16. Harold S. Bender, *The Anabaptist Vision* (Scottdale, Pa.: Herald Press, 1944), 20.

17. J. Lawrence Burkholder, "The Anabaptist Vision of Discipleship," in *The Recovery of the Anabaptist Vision*, Hershberger, ed., 136-37.

18. Miller, in Kauffman and Koontz, 144-45.

19. Ibid., 228.

20. Thomas N. Finger, "The Way to Nicea: Some Reflections from a Mennonite Perspective," *Journal of Ecumenical Studies*, 24, no. 2 (Spring 1987): 214. Finger cites

Mennonite historian, Walter Klaassen on this point.

21. Ibid., 215. Finger further observes that there are two ways of interpreting this dual phenomenon. The first regards the Anabaptists as forerunners of nondogmatic, ethical religion of the Enlightenment and, later, of the "modern" Western world. In this view, he suggests, Anabaptists were among the first to realize that the heart of religion is not belief in a deity beyond the world but the development of human capacities for moral action. Another view would suggest that Anabaptists, while orienting Christianity ("forwards") in a markedly ethical direction, preserved an indispensable ("backwards") link to certain traditional theistic affirmations. Due to their inability to pursue theology (impossible amidst savage persecution), however, and because their contemporaries took orthodox Christology for granted, Anabaptists were occupied with more crucial and disputed issues, he argues.

22. Ibid., 216-17. Finger argues that in general, believers' church movements are not best interpreted as movements away from outer authority to inner subjectivity but rather as attempts to turn from sub-Christian kinds of authority in order to come under the authentic, transcendent authority of Christ.

23. Miller, in Kauffman and Koontz, 39.

24. Ibid., 39.

25. Ibid., 40.

26. John Howard Yoder, *The Politics of Jesus* (Grand Rapids, Mich.: Eerdmans Publishing Co., 1972), 22.

27. *Confession*, pp. 65-66.

28. The concept of "indwelling" comes from Michael Polanyi, whose thought we will explore in Chapter 4. He suggests that we must indwell the particulars internal to our awareness in order to be able to do what we are consciously intending to do. See *The Tacit Dimension* (Gloucester, Mass.: Peter Smity, 1983).

29. Willard Swartley, "The Anabaptist Use of Scripture: Contemporary Applications and Prospects," in *Anabaptist Currents*, ed. Bowman and Longenecker, 67. The Anabaptist community was formed by reading the Bible from the perspective of a persecuted, suffering people, suggests Swartley. This is a different "lens" than the Catholic or established Protestant churches would have used. Since almost all the New Testament literature was preserved during the first three centuries by a persecuted, suffering church that kept only those writings that were worth dying for, it is no wonder that the suffering Anabaptists found Scripture to be so powerful in sustaining them, 70.

30. Ibid., 66-67.

31. Miller, in Kauffman and Koontz, 138, 144.

32. I John 2:2-6; Walter Klaassen, ed., *Anabaptism in Outline* (Scottdale, Pa.: Herald Press, 1981), 87.

33. Yoder and Horst cited in Swartley, "Anabaptist Use of Scripture," 70.

34. Finger, *Christian Theology*, vol. 2, 1989, 213-14.

35. Ted Koontz, "Grace to You and Peace: Nonresistance as Piety," in *Refocusing a Vision*, 88.

36. *Confession of Faith*, 69-71.

37. Lydia Harder, "Biblical Interpretation: A Praxis of Discipleship?" *Conrad Grebel Review* 10 (Winter 1992): 20.

38. Stuart Wood Murray, "Spirit, Discipleship, Community: The Contemporary

Significance of Anabaptist Hermeneutics," a thesis submitted in partial fulfillment of the requirements for the degree of Doctor of Philosophy, The Whitefield Institute, Oxford, July, 1992, 420-22.

39. Ibid. The assumption that Anabaptist hermeneutics was unsophisticated and has little to contribute to contemporary hermeneutical issues is a natural concomitant to the prevailing neglect and dismissal of Anabaptism, Murray suggests. The gradual rehabilitation of Anabaptism, however, and the discovery of its relevance to various topics and within diverse traditions justifies a reexamination of this assumption, 316.

John H. Yoder observes that it was "a basic novelty in the discussion of hermeneutics to say that a text is best understood in a congregation," "The Hermeneutics of the Anabaptists," in *Essays on Biblical Interpretation: Anabaptist-Mennonite Perspectives* ed. Willard Swartley (Elkhart, Ind.: Institute of Mennonite Studies), 27. And Lydia Harder has shown how this insight has much in common with current hermeneutical developments in liberation theology and interpretation theory, in "Hermeneutic Community: A Study of the Contemporary Relevance of an Anabaptist-Mennonite Approach to Biblical Interpretation," (Th.M. Thesis: Newman Theological College, 1984).

40. Ibid., "Summary of Thesis."

41. Ibid., 294. Murray suggests that the Anabaptist emphasis on obedience as a prerequisite for understanding Scripture meant that only a community of disciples could expect illumination. Unfaithfulness could make a congregation unable to function properly as a hermeneutic community. He acknowledges that this could involve a vicious circle, with communities interpreting Scripture in light of their understanding of faithfulness. It was here that the influence of other communities could play a role. Although this doesn't provide a complete safeguard against the vicious circle of subjectivity, it does offer some protection. The comparison of varying subjective approaches does result in a measure of objectivity. The hermeneutic community had a translocal dimension, 299.

42. Roth, "Community as Conversation: A New Model of Anabaptist Hermeneutics," 53. Roth notes that John Howard Yoder, for example, popularized the concept of the "hermeneutical community" as a distinctively Anabaptist approach to Scripture. In contrast to medieval Catholicism and the magisterial reformers, the Anabaptists interpreted Scripture as a communal exercise, thereby denying a prior authority to tradition, formal creedal statements, or the political interests of the state. C. J. Dyck has written of an Anabaptist "hermeneutics of obedience," arguing that early Anabaptists refused to separate proper Biblical interpretation from a life of obedience to God's will as revealed in Scripture. Others highlighted the Christocentric nature of Anabaptist hermeneutics, suggesting that the Anabaptists interpreted Scripture primarily through the lens of Christ's example and his teachings.

43. Ibid., 54-58. Roth also suggests that our understanding of Anabaptist hermeneutics would be enriched if greater consideration were given to the various contexts within which the Anabaptists read the Bible. Anabaptist theology did not emerge directly from Scripture, he acknowledges. While the importance of context has long been acknowledged in broader Anabaptist historiography, its implications for Anabaptist hermeneutics largely remain to be drawn, 58-59.

44. Ibid., 59-60.

45. Ibid., 60-62.
46. MacIntyre, *After Virtue*, 222-23.
47. Swartley, "The Anabaptist Use of Scripture," 73.
48. Ibid., 74-75.
49. Harder, "Biblical Interpretation: A Praxis of Discipleship?" 22. Harder elaborates on this discussion in her doctoral thesis, cited below.
50. Ibid., 22-23.
51. Lydia Harder, "A Hermeneutics of Discipleship: Toward a Mennonite/Feminist Approach to Biblical Authority" (Toronto: A doctoral thesis submitted to the Toronto School of Theology, 1993), 112, 114-15.
52. Ibid., 113, 298-99.
53. Murray, 424-28.
54. Murray, 332-33.
55. Miller, in Kauffman and Koontz, 41.
56. Ibid., 81.
57. Miller, summarizing Walter Klaassen, "Radical Politics: Anabaptism and Revolution," in *Anabaptism: Neither Catholic Nor Protestant* (Waterloo, Ont. Conrad Press, 1973), 78.
58. Richard B. Hays, *The Moral Vision of the New Testament: A Contemporary Introduction to New Testament Ethics* (San Francisco: HarperCollins, 1996, 245, summarizing Yoder, *Politics of Jesus*, 157-58.
59. Yoder, 1972, 157-61. Yoder refers extensively in his book to Hendrik Berkhof's book *Christ and the Powers* (Scottdale, Pa.: Herald Press, 1962).
60. Hays, 250-51, citing Yoder, *The Priestly Kingdom*, 43.
61. Ibid., 251, citing Yoder, *The Priestly Kingdom*, 69.
62. Ibid., 253, citing Yoder, *The Priestly Kingdom*, 92, 94.
63. Ibid., 196-97.
64. Ibid., 7, 212.
65. Clapp, in Phillips & Okholm, 90.
66. Dorothy Bass, ed., *Practicing Our Faith: A Way of Life for a Searching People* (San Francisco: Jossey-Bass Publishers, 1997). This discussion builds on MacIntyre's *After Virtue*. John Howard Yoder suggested what it means for a practice to qualify as "evangelical." It must communicate good news, he suggests. And among other things, it tells the world "what is the world's own calling and destiny, not by announcing either a utopian or a realistic goal to be imposed on the whole society, but by pioneering a paradigmatic demonstration of both the power and the practices that define the shape of restored humanity, *The Royal Priesthood*, 373.
67. Bass, 4-11. One significant additional source I've found comes from Jonas F. Soltis in Chapter V of the National Society for the Study of Education Yearbook, 1980, entitled "Education and the Concept of Knowledge." He describes a "sociocentric" view of knowledge which takes into account "the cultural nature of knowledge as a communal human construction that is both formed by and forms human beings". Central to this perspective is the recognition that "knowledge cannot be separated from knowers, that human beings construct different knowledge systems, and that all knowledge is imbedded in the fabric of social life". Knowledge making then, is more a communal rather than a private enterprise. And it includes in addition to learning lan-

guage, theories, etc. that we also learn recipes and skills for effective action. "The human capacity to do, to invent, to create, to make, to develop skills, arts, crafts, and dispositions in the service of 'humanness' is part and parcel of human knowledge. From the sociocentric perspective, knowledge is not just what is contained in heads and books but also in hands and actions as we take part in social living. . . . A sociocentric perspective invites our attention to those forms of human knowledge imbedded in human activities that embody the techniques and institutions we have developed to provide for our needs, satisfy our wants, and regulate our social lives. . . ." And he suggests, "our concept of knowledge has been broadened beyond what can be stated in words so as to include such legitimate categories as proper action and human skill," 97-98, 103.

CHAPTER 3

1. Werner Jaeger, *Paideia: The Ideals of Greek Culture* (New York: Oxford University Press; vol. 1, 1939; vol. 2, 1944; vol. 3, 1944). Jaeger draws primarily on Plato's *The Republic* for the aspects I cite. In addition he refers to all of Plato's writings, most notably *The Laws, Meno*, and *Apology*.

2. Jaeger, Volume I: *Archaic Greece; The Mind of Athens* (Oxford: Oxford University Press, Inc., 1939), v, ix.

3. Ibid., 286, 303.

4. Ibid., xiv, xxii, xxiv, xxviii. Plato developed a concept of the "ideal" as that which lies behind the shadow world of appearance in the true world of unchanging reality. An ideal for Plato meant an idea or concept of a thing which is perfect and never changes, Brubacher, 104. This sounds somewhat more abstracted than the earlier Greek notion discussed here by Jaeger as a "living ideal" that had grown up within their own history. The way in which I use "ideal" is not Plato's abstract notion of unchanging perfection but rather the historically constructed and identified aspirations that have emerged within a particular culture.

5. Ibid., xxvi, 287-88.

6. In Plato's description of the structure and functions of the State, he designated special roles to different groups within the State. As there are three facets to human nature, so he recognized three classes of society—the artisan, warrior, and philosopher classes. The artisan class was composed of those who were largely governed by their appetites; the warrior or guardian class by those in whom the spirit was dominant; and the philosopher class, by those who showed unusual intellectual capacity. In addition, each class was most closely associated with a particular virtue—the artisans with temperance, the guardians with bravery, the philosophers with wisdom. Justice was necessary to regulate and integrate the three classes (Brubacher 102-03).

It is primarily for the establishment of a distinct order of guardians that Plato undertakes a lengthy treatise on educational paideia, expanding into discussions on the education of women and the ruler in the ideal state. He justifies his detailed account of the guards' education by suggesting that it will help to illustrate his main theme in *The Republic*, that of how to achieve justice in the State. Jaeger says that while it appears that the big question of the nature of justice is the main theme of *The Republic*, the length and intensity of Plato's discussion of the question of paideia suggest that paideia is really the principal theme of the treatise in that it is connected with the method of gaining knowledge of standards and so, in a state that strives to realize the highest standard, becomes the chief concern. Plato's proposal to educate the guards through a system legally ordained by the state was a revolutionary reform. The natural way to educate both body and soul, he decides, is the traditional Greek system of paideia, divided into gymnastics and "music," and so he takes that as his basis for state directed education of the guards, Jaeger, Volume II, 209-10.

7. Jaeger, vol. 2, *In Search of the Divine Comedy*, 211, 224.
8. Ibid., 220, 214.
9. Ibid., 228-29.
10. Ibid., 216.
11. Ibid., 230-31.
12. Ibid., 294, 281-82.
13. Ibid., 294-95.
14. Ibid., 283-84.
15. Ibid., 285-86. Greek paideia and Greek philosophical theology were the two principal forms in which Greek thought influenced the world in those centuries when Greek art and science lay sleeping. Both were originally united in Homer, as human areté and the ideal of godhead. In Plato the unity reappears on another plane, Volume III, 261. The synthesis is clearest in his two great educational works, *The Republic* and *The Laws*. In Plato's thought there is no possible educational knowledge which doesn't find its origin, its direction, and its aim in the knowledge of God, according to Jaeger, based on what he calls the epilogue to all Plato's creative work, the *Epinomis*, which is an addition to *The Laws*. Plato explains that there are two sources for man's belief in the existence of the gods: knowledge of the orbits in which the heavenly bodies move; and the "eternal stream of being" in us, the soul. After a lifetime of effort to discover the true and indestructible foundations of culture, Plato's work ends in the Idea of that which is higher than man, and yet is man's true self. Greek humanism, in the form which it takes in Plato's paideia, is centered on God. The state is the social form given by the historical development of the Greek people to Plato in which to express this Idea. But as he inspires it with his new conception of God as the supreme standard, the measure of all measures, he changes it from a local and temporary organization on this earth to an ideal kingdom of heaven, summarizes Jaeger, vol. 3, *The Conflict of Cultural Ideals in the Age of Plato*, 262.

16. Werner Jaeger, *Early Christianity and Greek Paideia* (Cambridge: The Belknap Press of Harvard University Press, 1961).
17. Ibid., 10.
18. Ibid., 39, 62.
19. Ibid., 21, 41.
20. Ibid., 10.
21. Ibid., 60-64.
22. Ibid., 65-67.
23. Ibid., 81.
24. Ibid., 86-87.
25. Ibid., 88-90.
26. Ibid., 73-74.

27. Edward Farley, *Theologia: The Fragmentation and Unity of Theological Education* (Philadelphia: Fortress Press, 1983), xi, 152.

28. Ibid., 153.

29. Ibid., 170, 178. A moral virtue is a "habitus," a settled disposition of the will to act habitually in a morally excellent way—courageously, faithfully, honestly, prudently, etc., Kelsey, 34.

30. David Kelsey, *Between Athens and Berlin: The Theological Education Debate* (Grand Rapids: Eerdmans, 1993), 6. Kelsey's book *To Understand God Truly: What's Theological About a Theological School* (Louisville: Westminster John Knox Press, 1992) is also helpful in reflecting on theological education.

31. Ibid., 12.

32. Ibid., 20.

33. Ibid., 22, 48.

34. Ibid., 26.

35. Ibid., 227-28.

36. Lawrence A. Cremin, *Traditions of American Education* (New York: Basic Books, 1977), 19. Cited in Jack Seymour, Robert O'Gorman, and Charles Foster, *The Church in the Education of the Public: Refocusing the Task of Religious Education* (Nashville: Abingdon Press, 1984), 24.

37. Lawrence A. Cremin, *Public Education* (New York: Basic Books, 1976), 74. Cited in Seymour, 24.

38. Ibid., 57-77.

39. Seymour, 24, 28-29.

40. Rodney Sawatsky, "What Can the Mennonite Tradition Contribute to Christian Higher Education?" in *Models for Christian Higher Education*, Richard T. Hughes and William B. Adrian, eds., (Grand Rapids: Eerdmans, 1997), 195.

41. Ibid., 197-99. A qualifier is in order here to acknowledge that what we know of the ethic of Jesus we know by way of a community's critical retrieval and interpretation of that ethic.

42. Dwayne Huebner, "Spirituality and Knowing", in *Learning and Teaching the Ways of Knowing*, Elliot Eisner, ed. (Chicago: The University of Chicago Press, 1985), 160-73

43. Mark Schwehn, *Exiles of Eden* (New York: Oxford University Press, 1993), 23-25.

44. Ibid., 47-48.

45. Ibid., 48.

46. Ibid., 54-56.

47. Ibid., 41, 46-47.

48. Ibid., 94.

49. Sloan, 223-24. Also cited in Introduction.

50. David Tracy, "Can Virtue Be Taught? Education, Character and the Soul", in *Theological Perspectives on Christian Formation*, 376-77, 384.

Chapter 4

1. Sloan, *Faith and Knowledge*, 212. One fascinating study that illustrates this point comes from Jerome Bruner who argues that there are two irreducible modes of cognition, the "paradigmatic" (or logico-scientific) and the "narrative." Each mode comes spontaneously into existence in the functioning of human beings but each provides a different way of ordering experience, constructing reality, filtering perceptions, and organizing memory. The paradigmatic mode leads to good theory, tight analysis, empirical discovery, can be subjected to verification, and seeks to be context-free and universal. The narrative mode leads to good stories, gripping drama; truth is multifaceted and elusive, context sensitive and particular. Both modes seek to express truth but each judges their truth value differently. Efforts to reduce one to the other or ignore one at the expense of the other fail to capture the rich ways people "know." Jerome Bruner, "Narrative and Paradigmatic Modes of Thought," in Eisner, 97-115

2. Ibid., 219-20.

3. Ibid., 234-36. Sloan cautions, however, that the positive potentials of modern consciousness must be preserved: the capacity for clear thinking consciousness, individual identity and selfhood, and the potential for freedom that individuality and clear-consciousness make possible. The necessary transformation in knowing cannot be a return to premodern states of consciousness in which self is submerged in the Divine, in nature, or in the tribe and community. The needed transformation might best be thought of as the development of the imagination in the fullest sense, and he describes imagination as the involvement of the whole human being in the work of knowing.

Edward Farley also identifies intuitive imagination as by far the most important and the most neglected of all the components of knowing. Without intuitive imagination, he says, "the other hermeneutical perspectives fail to emerge. For it is the intuitive imagination—that central theme of romanticism—which grasps reality in its concreteness, its relationalities, its complexities; *The Fragility of Knowledge: Theological Education in the Church and the University* (Philadelphia: Fortress Press, 1988), 41.

4. Rebecca S. Chopp and Mark Lewis Taylor, eds., *Reconstructing Christian Theology* (Minneapolis: Fortress Press, 1994), 15-18.

5. Drusilla Scott, *Everyman Revived: The Common Sense of Michael Polanyi* (Lewes, Sussex: The Book Guild Limited, 1985 and Grand Rapids, Mich.: Eerdmans, 1995), vii.

6. Gelwick, *The Way of Discovery*, 31

7. Scott, 3-6.

8. Leslie Newbigin in Scott, iv-v.

9. Ibid., 6-7. Polanyi's best known published works include *Personal Knowledge* 1958; *Knowing and Being*, 1969; *Science, Faith and Society*, 1964; *The Tacit Dimension*, 1966; and, *Meaning* with Harry Prosch in 1975.

10. Gelwick, xv-xvi.

11. Scott, vii.

12. Gelwick, xvii, 132.

13. Michael Polanyi, *The Tacit Dimension* (Gloucester, Mass.: Peter Smith, 1983), 20.

14. Scott, 16, 26.
15. Ibid., 10.
16. Gelwick, 18-19.
17. Ibid., 56, 84.
18. Scott, 32. By "intuition" Polanyi means "a skill for guessing with a reasonable chance of guessing right; a skill guided by an innate sensibility to coherence, improved by schooling." Polanyi in "The Creative Imagination," *Chemical and Engineering News* 44 (April 1966): 89.
19. Michael Polanyi, *Personal Knowledge* (Chicago: University of Chicago Press, 1958), 135.
20. Scott, 36-40. The findings of Gestalt psychology gave reinforcement for Polanyi's view of knowledge. Polanyi transformed the Gestalt theory from psychology to philosophy. He transposed the findings of Gestalt psychology into a theory of knowledge, 57.
21. Michael Polanyi, *The Study of Man* (Chicago: University of Chicago Press, 1959), 19.
22. Ibid., vii-viii.
23. Ibid., viii. Gelwick suggests that it is Polanyi's aim that his view of the foundations of knowing will again renew the meaningfulness of traditional human ideals that were undercut by the scientific outlook and will enable humans to have a responsible place once again in the universe. Gelwick, 50.
24. Scott, 184.
25. Polanyi, *The Tacit Dimension*, 4.
26. Ibid., 15.
27. Ibid., 15-16.
28. Michael Polanyi, *Knowing and Being* (Chicago: University of Chicago Press, 1969), 147.
29. Scott, 71-72.
30. Polanyi, *The Tacit Dimension*, 52. Polanyi abandoned classic dichotomies: thought-action, practice-theoretical, mind-body, subject-object. In their places he put alternative logical structures such as subsidiary-focal, attending-*from*—attending-*to*, tacit-explicit, particular-comprehensive entity, proximal-distal. Thomas Langford and William Poteat, eds. *Intellect and Hope: Essays in the thought of Michael Polanyi* (Durham, N.C.: The Duke University Press, 1968), 10.
31. Polanyi, *The Tacit Dimension*, 15-16; and *Personal Knowledge*, 61.
32. Langford and Poteat, 66.
33. Ibid., 17.
34. Scott, 60-61.
35. Polanyi, *The Tacit Dimension*, 24.
36. Polanyi, *Personal Knowledge*, 311 with comments from Scott, 67.
37. Scott, 73. Polanyi took the idea of indwelling from theories of history which maintain that we come to understand history by dwelling in the actions of historical figures, "getting inside their skin."
38. Ibid., 73-74.
39. Polanyi, Michael, *Personal Knowledge*, 279.
40. Polanyi, *Personal Knowledge*, 311 and Scott, 76, 80.

41. Polanyi, *Knowing and Being*, 65.
42. Polanyi, *The Tacit Dimension*, 83.
43. Polanyi, *Knowing and Being*, 54.
44. Ibid., 66, italics added. There are several parallels between Wittgenstein and Polanyi. One is in their understanding of the nature of language. The most striking similarity between the two is that they "both see language as meaningful only within the wider context of culture, tradition, and ways of human living," Gelwick, 116.
45. Scott, 84. Scott further observes that the same is true for other kinds of knowledge: justice builds up a law code while allowing for its modification in the spirit of justice. Moral traditions are built up and preserved by a moral community while being modified by new moral insights of persons within the community. Art and music flourish in the same way—in communities dedicated to these values, upholding the traditions and styles that have meaning while accepting creative changes initiated by persons within them, 87.
46. Michael Polanyi, *Science, Faith and Society* (Chicago: The University of Chicago Press, 1964), 64.
47. Ibid., 56.
48. Ibid., 61, cited in Scott, 158.
49. Ibid., 59, cited in Scott, 163.
50. Polanyi, *The Tacit Dimension*, 92.
51. Ibid., 70.
52. Gelwick, 139.
53. Polanyi, *The Tacit Dimension*, 92.
54. Scott, 180-81.
55. Ibid., 182-83.
56. Polanyi, *Personal Knowledge,* 281.
57. Polanyi, *The Tacit Dimension*, 60-62.
58. Ibid., 80-92.
59. Gelwick, 132.
60. Scott, 186.
61. Ibid., 197-98.
62. Rebecca Chopp, *Saving Work: Feminist Practices of Theological Education* (Louisville, Ky.: Westminster John Knox, 1995), x-xi.
63. Ibid., 4-7.
64. Ibid., 9-11.
65. Ibid., 11-12.
66. Ibid., 13.
67. Ibid., 2-3, 14. In her book *The Power to Speak: Feminism, Language, God* (New York: N.Y., Crossroad, 1991), Chopp looks extensively at how language functions to transform. Susan Briehl, in a book review observes that it is a daring book because it develops new definitions of the Word of God and its proclamation using poststructuralist linguistic theory, feminist biblical hermeneutics, liberation theologies and recent theories of rhetoric, poetics, pragmatism, and feminism. Modern Christianity in reflecting the culture, contends Chopp, has reduced the Word of God to "the ultimate linguistic mirror" of the present monotheistic-patriarchal order and has restricted proclamation to giving comfort to individuals on Sunday morning. Marginalized

groups are forced to speak a language not their own, "Books," in *The Christian Century* 107, no. 14 (November 1990): 1070-71.

Richard Dietrich in another review observes that at the center of the book is the thesis that it is "the role, nature, and mission of Christianity, to provide Word and words of emancipatory transformation," discourses that not only correct the current "social-symbolic order" but must "rend and renew" it. The order can't be changed from within so much as from the margins. Feminist theology is at work on the margins, creating a new poetics of community (playful, graceful, gentle), and a new community of rhetoric (open and freeing). Dietrich makes the observation that while Chopp envisions a new poetics, she hasn't participated in it throughout the book. The book is not a playful, graceful book, but rather a most academic book—abstruse and Latinate, *Interpretation* 45, no 3 (July 1991): 324-26. Emancipatory transformation must take place—at least it must begin—on the level of language, Chopp contends. Rather than a language of order and control, we must cultivate a notion of the Word as perfectly open sign and Scripture as prototypes rather than archetype.

68. Ibid., 18.
69. Ibid., 21-22.
70. Ibid., 32. "Narrative" is used in philosophy to name the practice of lived experience. MacIntyre in *After Virtue* contends that narrative history is the most essential genre of describing human activity. Personal identity isn't fixed, but is constructed through narrative or, as he argues, narrative and identity presuppose each other.
71. Chopp, *The Power to Speak*, 12-13.
72. Chopp, *Saving Work*, 42-44.
73. Ibid., 50.
74. Ibid., 53-54.
75. Ibid., 55, 57, 61.
76. Ibid., 57-64. Chopp works with a "communicative" notion of justice, which emphasizes a view of justice focused on the rights and responsibilities of self-determination, highlighting voices of representation, deliberation, even self-definition.
77. Paul, Garrett, E., Review of *The Praxis of Suffering: An Interpretation of Liberation and Political Theologies*, (Maryknoll, N.Y.: Orbis Books), 1986 by Chopp in *Christian Century*. 104(2) (Jan 21, 1987): 61-62.
78. Chopp, *Saving Work*, 47.
79. Ibid., 51-53.
80. Ibid., 57-63.
81. Chopp's book *The Power to Speak* sees the church as the sacrament of God's grace in the world and makes a related claim about the church's proclamation as discourses of emancipatory transformation for the world, 4.
82. Ibid., 15. As in the term *praxis*, theorists use the term *practices* in somewhat different ways. MacIntyre and Michel Foucault, while differing in some aspects of their understanding of practices share a common focus on, as Chopp describes it, "the social construction of embedded patterns that produce both individual meaning and cultural organization," 16.
83. Ibid., 16. Kelsey also notes that practices have a history and are bearers of "traditions."
84. Ibid., 16-17.

85. Ibid., 68-69.
86. Chopp, *The Power to Speak*, 119-20.
87. Chopp, *Saving Work*, 41-42.
88. Ibid., 104. Chopp mentions Howard Gardner's seven kinds of intelligence and among others the book Belenky et al., *Women's Ways of Knowing*, to illustrate her point.
89. Ibid., 73. "Praxis" refers to integrations of theory *and* practice that intend an emancipative transformation. "Praxis" is a more complex term than "practices," focusing as it does on theory *and* practice in union toward an end, *Reconstructing Christian Theology*, Chopp and Taylor, 15.
90. Ibid., 76-77.
91. Ibid., 81-82.
92. Ibid., 82-83.
93. Chopp and Sheila Greeve Davaney, eds., *Horizons in Feminist Theology: Identity, Tradition and Norms*, (Minneapolis: Fortress Press, 1997), 15. In the book Chopp and other writers focus attention on the debates within feminist theory and feminist theologians' relationship to them. The book is an attempt to focus on theory and the role it should play in feminist thought. The acknowledgment is made that this is not a return to the grand theories of old but a commitment to a critical analysis that seeks to make clear the often implicit and unacknowledged presuppositions that shape feminist proposals. It's a self-conscious attempt to take responsibility for the assumptions held and their repercussions, 1-3.

One assumption challenged is the tendency of feminists to refer to *woman* or *women* as unified, inclusive concepts and to appeal to women's experience as the source and norm of feminist thought. The notions of woman and women's experience have been called into question and, with them, the whole edifice of feminist commitments and strategies. The volume examines these theoretical changes and their impact on feminist theology. How should women rethink subjectivity or identity in the face of the dissolution of feminists' historical appeal to women's experience, 5-7? Thinkers in this volume argue that identity is not just the function of some positive or unchanging essence. Rather identity is wrought "in the midst of multiple cultural and natural relations." It is also the product of what is excluded, left outside, left unsaid. Identity is the result of both inclusion and exclusion, 9-10.

94. *Saving Work*, 83.
95. Ibid., 86.
96. Murray notes areas of agreement and disagreement between liberation theology and an Anabaptist approach to hermeneutics. His discussion relates in significant ways to our comparison between a feminist and an Anabaptist approach to epistemology.

Both liberation theologians and the Anabaptists sought to enfranchise ordinary, uneducated believers and to oppose the monopoly of professional interpreters. Both regarded hermeneutics as a communal activity, with a local community functioning as the hermeneutic community. In Anabaptism, congregations of baptized believers comprised this hermeneutic community. In Latin America, base communities have operated in this way. The emphasis within both movements has been on application rather than intellectual interpretation. Both have operated with a "hermeneutics of justice" rather than a "hermeneutics of order." The Anabaptists' primary concern was to obey Scripture regardless of the social consequences. Both groups have been drawn to the Gospels and to the historical Jesus, although liberation hermeneutics cannot be regarded as Christocentric in the way Anabaptist hermeneutics was. The parallels between the two are quite extensive. Murray cites others to support his interpretation including Willard Swartley's "Liberation Theology, Anabaptist Pacifism and Munsterite Violence: Hermeneutical Comparisons and Evaluation," in Daniel Schipani, ed., *Freedom and Discipleship* (Maryknoll, N.Y.: Orbis, 1989).

There are several issues, however, on which Anabaptist and liberation theology's hermeneutics differ. Those include the observation that Latin American liberation theology remains predominantly a scholarly phenomenon, despite all its pretensions to being a popular movement. By comparison, Anabaptist hermeneutics, although dependent in part on educated first-generation leaders, was more representative of the ways in which ordinary congregations interpreted Scripture. Anabaptist hermeneutics points to the continuing need for a genuine enfranchisement of ordinary believers and for an "ideological suspicion" of grids imposed on Scripture from whatever political or sociological perspective. Another difference is the nature of the local hermeneutical communities. Among Anabaptists, Scripture was interpreted by "believers' churches," where everyone had expressed a commitment to Jesus Christ and had been baptized as believers. The focus of biblical interpretation was ecclesiocentric and oriented towards discipleship and mission. The base communities are not "believers' churches."

It seems that liberation theology's belief in the "hermeneutical privilege of the poor" implies that poverty and oppression in themselves equip base communities in the interpretation of Scripture, whatever the spiritual experience of the interpreters. Among Anabaptists, regeneration and the activity of the Holy Spirit were regarded as primary. Although the experience of suffering and powerlessness was significant, according to the Anabaptist leaders, it was persecution for following Christ, suffering in relation to discipleship, rather than political oppression, that was in view.

A final area of difference between Anabaptism and liberation theology concerns the principle of *sola scriptura*. Anabaptist hermeneutics were rooted in the Reformation commitment to the authority and sufficiency of Scripture. From the perspective of Anabaptist hermeneutics, the question needs to be asked: does liberation hermeneutics treat Scripture as authoritative or is its use of Scripture eclectic? Does Scripture act as the primary source of revelation and arbiter of liberationist ideas and practices, or is it consulted merely to discover stories and texts that are illustrative of principles derived from ideological or situational sources? Murray, "Spirit, Discipleship, Community," 350-61.

97. Nancey Murphy, *Beyond Liberalism and Fundamentalism: How Modern and Postmodern Philosophy Set the Theological Agenda* (Valley Forge, Pa.: Trinity Press International, 1997), ix-x.

98. Murphy, Nancey, *Reconciling Theology and Science: A Radical Reformation Perspective* (Kitchener, Ontario: Pandora Press, 1997), 78.

99. Murphy, *Beyond Liberalism & Fundamentalism*, 95 and in most of her books. Of the theologians she notes who have consciously adopted a nonfoundational approach she recognizes the Yale school, including Hans Frei, Paul Holmer, David Kelsey, and George Lindbeck, professors or former professors at Yale, and some of their students, including Ronald Thiemann, William Werpehowski, William Placher,

Charles Wood, and Kathryn Tanner. Also she mentions Stanley Hauerwas in this connection. Others who've come to nonfoundational positions by other routes include James Wm. McClendon, Jr. through study of J. L. Austin's philosophy of language and John Howard Yoder, apparently simply from reflection on the nature of biblical, ethical, and theological reasoning, and herself, through familiarity with nonfoundational philosophy of science. Some, she said, would call Karl Barth the first great anti-foundationalist theologian, though he could certainly be read as a "scriptural foundationalist."

100. Ibid., 87.

101. Ibid., 94.

102. Ibid., 89. Lakatos compares what he calls "research programs" and shows how they can be compared on the basis of how they change over time in response to problematic empirical discoveries. Murphy argues that his methodology can be used in theology, suggesting that competing theological programs can be compared on the basis of "their relative progress or degeneration," over time. MacIntyre's insights parallel those of Lakatos, she contends, 101-03.

103. Edward A. Yonan, Book Review of Murphy's *Theology in the Age of Scientific Reasoning* in *Journal of Religion* 72, no 4 (October 1992): 601-02.

104. Nancey Murphy, *Reconciling Theology and Science*, 1-2. Murphy argues for a non-dualistic account of the person. As we go up the hierarchy of levels from physics and chemistry to biology—from nonliving to living—we do not need to add any new substance such as a vital force. "Life is a result of the special *organization of nonliving matter*," she suggests, 3. See Murphy and George Ellis, *On the Moral Nature of the Universe: Theology, Cosmology and Ethics* (Minneapolis: Fortress Press, 1996) for a much more extensive discussion of the relationship of theology and science.

105. Murphy describes what she refers to as "boundary questions," which are questions that arise at one level of the hierarchy but can only be answered by turning to a higher level. There are many questions, she argues, that can only be answered by referring to factors at a lower level. And there are questions that can be answered only by reference to factors described at higher levels of analysis, Ibid., 2, 15.

106. Ibid., 2, 25.

107. Ibid., 28-29.

108. Ibid., 29.

109. Murphy, *Beyond Liberalism & Fundamentalism*, 103-04. Murphy observes that relativistic worries associated with holist epistemology come from recognition that standards of rationality don't stand outside the history of traditions but develop within them so every tradition will appear to be justified on the basis on its own standards. MacIntyre's answer is that this isn't the case. A tradition fails on its own terms when a solution to an epistemological crisis cannot be found that measures up to the tradition's own internal standards of rationality. He addresses this in his book *Three Rival Versions of Moral Inquiry: Encyclopaedia, Genealogy, and Tradition* (Notre Dame: University of Notre Dame Press, 1990), 92.

110. Murphy, "A Theology of Education," 4. MacIntyre's definition of practice, on which many of the authors cited in this book rely is this: By a "practice" I am going to mean any coherent and complex form of socially established cooperative human activity through which goods internal to that form of activity are realized in the course of

trying to achieve those standards of excellence which are appropriate to, and partially definitive of, that form of activity, with the result that human powers to achieve excellence, and human conceptions of the ends and goods involved, are systematically extended.

111. Murphy, *Beyond Liberalism and Fundamentalism*, 104-05.

112. Murphy, Nancey, Stanley Hauerwas, and Mark Nation, eds., *Theology Without Foundations: Religious Practice and the Future of Theological Truth* (Nashville: Abingdon Press, 1994), 266-67. Elsewhere Murphy notes that Frei, also (like Lindbeck) of the Yale school of biblical scholars, asks why for centuries the biblical narratives were read realistically, assuming that they are about what they first seem to be about, and yet in modern theology they have been taken to be about something else—the history *behind* the text, or the religious self-awareness of Jesus, etc. By pointing to the significant change in how the texts are read, Frei led toward an attempt to recover the traditional reading strategies, which Murphy observes, is compatible with the change from foundational to nonfoundational epistemology, *Beyond Liberalism and Fundamentalism*, 96.

113. Murphy, *Beyond Liberalism and Fundamentalism*, 105. Among the many definitions of experience Murphy finds this one most apt: "active participation in events or activities, leading to the accumulation of knowledge or skill," and also "the totality of such events in the past of an individual or group," 106.

114. Ibid., 106.

115. Murphy, *Reconciling Theology and Science*, 90.

116. Ibid., 82-83.

117. Ibid., 1, 80-81. It is important to note again at this point that Murphy relies extensively on MacIntyre's tradition-based epistemological concerns which grow out of his work in ethics. In *After Virtue* he argued that it is not possible to evaluate an ethical theory apart from the tradition in which it has developed.

118. Murphy, "A Theology of Education," 12.

119. Ibid., 13 citing *Zygon: Journal of Religion and Science*, 29 No. 2 (1994): 205-29. She cites Holmes Rolston, "Nature is . . . cruciform . . . a theater where life is learned and earned by labor, a drama where even the evils drive us to make sense of things. Life is advanced not only by thought and action, but by suffering, not only by logic but by pathos . . . . God is not in a simple way the Benevolent Architect, but is rather the Suffering Redeemer. . . . The abundant life that Jesus exemplifies and offers to his disciples is that of a sacrificial suffering through to something higher . . . . The cruciform creation is, in the end, deiform, godly, just because of this element of struggle, not in spite of it. . . . God rescues from suffering, but the Judeo-Christian faith never teaches that God eschews suffering in the achievement of the divine purposes. To the contrary, seen in the paradigm of the cross, God too suffers, not less than his creatures, in order to gain for his creatures a more abundant life." Murphy also cites James McClendon who emphasizes that "faithful, costly, and redemptive suffering in Christian love is a necessary ingredient" in the continuation of the story of God and God's community. "In an analogous way," Murphy continues, "all sentient beings participate in the suffering that comes from the fact that what God created is not God, it is other than God. Only through God's slow travail does that which is closer to God emerge from that which is totally other," *Reconciling Theology and Science*, 74.

120. Ibid., 14-15 and *Reconciling Theology and Science*, 76.
121. Murphy, *Reconciling Theology and Science*, 85-87.
122. Murphy, "A Theology of Education," 9.
123. Ibid., 6. Murphy gives credit to James McClendon Jr. and to John Howard Yoder for seminal thinking related to the principalities and powers. Murphy illustrates how the Radical Reformation tradition is distinct from the several traditions that MacIntyre recognizes: the outworn Enlightenment or Encyclopaedist tradition, the Nietzschean tradition, and MacIntyre's own Aristotelian-Thomist tradition. The Anabaptist tradition, she suggests, seems peculiarly well suited to address the current crisis in academia. With the Nietzscheans we can recognize the tendency of the will-to-power to obscure the truth and provide guidance for workable social and epistemic practices aimed at developing the capacity to live (and think and do research) without the assertion of power.
124. Ibid., 6. This argument is not far from the argument presented by feminist writers working with a counter-hegemonic agenda. Patti Lather writes that the task of counter-hegemonic groups is the development of counter-institutions, ideologies, and cultures that provide an ethical and epistemological alternative to the dominant hegemony, a lived experience of how the world can be different, in "Critical Theory, Curricular Transformation and Feminist Mainstreaming," Boston University *Journal of Education* 166, no. 1 (March 84): 55-56.
125. Ibid., 15.
126. Yoder's concept of "revolutionary subordination" is discussed at length in his *Politics of Jesus* and in Yoder's chapter in *Authentic Transformation*. In response to the question whether the *Haustafeln* of the New Testament represent a kind of divine ratification of every individual's social station he responds by arguing that rather than Paul calling for persons to smash the oppressive structures in which they found themselves, each should voluntarily accede to one's subordinate role but do so as a free ethical agent. Paul isn't calling for a new world regime which violently replaces the old, but rather showing how the old and the new order exist concurrently on different levels. It is because Christ has made all persons free that the slave is on the same level as the freed person, *Politics*, 190-91. Subordination is a dimension of the life of everyone inasmuch as everyone is in a position of subordination to someone else. The duty of the subordinate person according to the New Testament and that of the person in power are the same—both are called to be subordinate to one another. It is the reciprocity of subordination that is unique in Paul's approach and is "revolutionary" according to Yoder, *Authentic Transformation*, 79, 282.
127. Murphy, "A Theology of Education," 7,8, and far more extensively in *Theology in the Age of Scientific Reasoning* (Ithaca: Cornell University Press, 1990), ch. 5.
128. Ibid., 9.
129. Murphy, *Theology in the Age of Scientific Reasoning*, 152.
130. Ibid., 157.
131. Ibid., 133-58.
132. Ibid., 146-47. For the Anabaptists the principle of consistency with Scripture (particularly the New Testament) took such a prominent place in their decision-making that discussion of these matters by contemporary historians often falls under the topic of "Anabaptist hermeneutics." Judgment always took place in the context of a

need for guidance in questions concerning a local congregation's practice. John Howard Yoder points out that since the Holy Spirit was promised to the church in the context of the reconciling approach to wayward members (Matt. 18:19-20; John 20:22-23) the mandate and enablement to discern the will of God were seen as provisions not primarily for scholars, but for the concrete congregation struggling with differing visions of what obedience meant in its own time and place. This is not to say that scholarship had no place in the community; only that it must be relevant to shaping the community's common life.

133. Ibid., 149-50.
134. Ibid., 150.
135. Murphy, "A Theology of Education."

CHAPTER 5

1. Chopp, *Saving Work*, 73. Chopp is referring to an image she got from Megan Beverly, "Preaching from a Feminist Perspective: 'A Crazy Quilt'" (manuscript, 1992).

2. Murphy, *Beyond Liberalism and Fundamentalism*, 94.

3. George Lindbeck makes the observation that the spiritual formation most contemporary students desire is not the internalization of a comprehensive and coherent religious outlook and correlated practices that a communal tradition provides. They would rather think of an eclectically constructed, individual vision. But for reasons which are widely discussed (Bellah's *Habits of the Heart*) it is doubtful that even religious geniuses proceed in this fashion. The biblical prophets, and Jesus himself, were deeply immersed in their own tradition. Jesus was a spiritually mature Jew, and only because of this, humanly speaking, a religiously creative individual, Lindbeck in *Theological Perspectives on Christian Formation*, Jeff Astley, Leslie J. Francis and Colin Crowder, eds. (Grand Rapids: Eerdmans, 1996), 290.

4. Chopp and Davaney, *Horizons in Feminist Theology*, 192-97.

5. The assertion that ways of knowing are morally directive comes from Mark R. Schwehn, *Exiles From Eden,* 94.

6. Sloan, 232-233.

7. F. Michael Connelly and D. Jean Clandinin, "Personal Practical Knowledge and the Modes of Knowing: Relevance for Teaching and Learning," in *Learning and Teaching the Ways of Knowing*, Elliot Eisner, ed. (Chicago: The National Society for the Study of Education, 1985), 182-97. The authors suggest that the narrative unities which make up a person's life experience and contain experiential elements are "on call" for the purpose of teaching. They suggest that a teacher who wants her students to feel "at home" will make it possible for them to feel comfortable within the cultural rhythms she's established in her classroom. She will pay attention to a learner's narrative experience and seek to "give back" that experience to the students so that it may be reflected upon, valued, and enriched.

8. Sloan, 219, 234, citing Edward Farley, Professor of Theology at The Divinity School, Vanderbilt University and author of *The Fragility of Knowledge: Theological Education in the Church and the University,* and *Theologia: The Fragmentation and Unity of Theological Education.*

9. Murphy, *Reconciling Theology and Science*, 74-75.

10. Murphy, *Moral Nature of the Universe*, 138.

CHAPTER 6

1. For a perspective on the concept of "ideal" as I use it refer to Chapter 3, footnote 4 or the glossary.

2. David Tennant, "Anabaptist Theologies of Childhood and Education—Child Rearing," *Baptist Quarterly* (Oct. 1984): 360-61 and William Klassen, "The Role of the Child in Anabaptism," in Harry Loewen, ed., *Mennonite Images* (Winnipeg: Hyperion Press, 1980), 31.

3. Thieleman J. van Braght, *The Bloody Theater or Martyrs Mirror of the Defenseless Christians,* 12th ed., trans. Joseph F. Somm, 1886 (Scottdale, Pa.: Herald Press, 1979).

4. Stanley Hauerwas, "The Family as a School for Character," *Religious Education* 80, no. 2 (Spring 1985).

5. Rodney Clapp, *Families at the Crossroads: Beyond Traditional & Modern Options* (Downers Grove, Ill.: InterVarsity Press, 1993), 68, 84-85.

6. Marjorie J. Thompson, *Family, The Forming Center* (Nashville: Upper Room Books, 1996), 26.

7. Robert Coles, *The Moral Intelligence of Children* (New York: Random House, 1997), 5, 58-59.

8. Don S. Browning, et al., eds. *From Culture Wars to Common Ground: Religion and the American Family Debate* (Louisville: Westminster John Knox Press, 1997), 23, 307.

9. Ibid., 308.

10. Ibid., 273.

11. Murphy, "A Theology of Education." Murphy was referring specifically to higher education in her address but I think her observations are relevant to tradition-based education at any level.

12. Caleb D. Miller, "If Mennonites Really Got Serious About Church Discipline," *Gospel Herald* (Oct. 11, 1994), 2.

13. J. Howard Kauffman, "Boundary Maintenance and Cultural Assimilation of Contemporary Mennonites," *The Mennonite Quarterly Review* 51, no. 3 (July, 1997): 240.

14. Some of the insights mentioned in the practices above were gleaned from Bass, *Practicing Our Faith,* from the *Mennonite Confession of Faith*, or inspired by Mary Pipher's book *The Shelter of Each Other: Rebuilding Our Families*, (New York: Ballantine Books, 1996).

15. Sara Little discusses a variety of action/reflection models in her book *To Set One's Heart: Belief and Teaching in the Church* (Atlanta: John Knox Press, 1983), 76-85. She discusses one model that uses a four-phase process called AAAR, signifying Awareness, Analysis, Action, Reflection. This process can intentionally be used to guide teaching and learning. Another approach is known as "Shared Praxis," popularized by Thomas Groome, though largely inspired by Paulo Freire. For Groome, "praxis" is preferred over "practice" as it refers to "reflective action," or a group "sharing in dialogue their critical reflection on present action in light of the Christian Story

and its Vision toward the end of lived Christian faith," *Christian Religious Education* (San Francisco: Harper & Row, 1980), 184.

Glossary

1. *Confession of Faith in a Mennonite Perspective* (Scottdale, Pa.: Herald Press, 1995) The introduction says that "Statements of what Mennonites believe have been among us from earliest beginnings. A group of Anabaptists, forerunners of Mennonites, wrote the Schleitheim Articles in 1527. Since then, Mennonite groups have produced numerous statements of faith. This *Confession of Faith in a Mennonite Perspective* takes its place in this rich confessional history. The historic creeds of the early Christian church, which were assumed as foundational for Mennonite confessions from the beginning, are basic to this confession as well." 7.

SELECT BIBLIOGRAPHY

Alcoff, Linda, and Elizabeth Potter, eds. *Feminist Epistemologies*. New York: Routledge, 1993.

Aristotle. *The Nicomachean Ethics*. T.rans. and introduction David Ross. Oxford: Oxford University Press, 1980.

Astley, Jeff, Leslie J. Francis, and Colin Crowder, eds. *Theological Perspectives on Christian Formation*. Grand Rapids, Mich.: Eerdmans, 1996.

Bass, Dorothy C., ed. *Practicing Our Faith: A Way of Life for a Searching People*. San Francisco: Jossey-Bass Publishers, 1997.

Belenky, Mary Field, Blythe McVicker Clincy, Nancy Rule Godberger, and Jill Mattack Tarule. *Women's Ways of Knowing: The Development of Self, Voice, and Mind*. New York: Basic Books, 1986.

Bender, Harold S. *The Anabaptist Vision*. Scottdale, Pa.: Herald Press, 1944.

Bender, Ross Thomas. *Education for Peoplehood: Essays on the Teaching Ministry of the Church*. Elkhart, Ind.: Institute of Mennonite Studies, 1997.

―――. *The People of God: A Mennonite Interpretation of the Free Church Tradition*. Scottdale, Pa.: Herald Press, 1971.

Bowman, Carl F., and Stephen L. Longenecker. *Anabaptist Currents: History in Conversation with the Present*. Bridgewater, Va.: Penobscot Press, 1995.

Boys, Mary. *Educating in Faith: Maps and Visions*. Kansas City, Mo.: Sheed & Ward, 1989.

Boys, Mary, ed. *Education for Citizenship and Discipleship*. New York: The Pilgrim Press, 1989.

Browning, Don S., Bonnie J. Miller-McLemore, Pamela D. Couture, K. Brynoff Lyon, and Robert M. Franklin. *From Culture Wars to Common Ground: Religion and the American Family Debate*. Louisville: Westminster John Knox, 1997.

Brubacher, John S. *A History of the Problems of Education*. New York: McGraw-Hill Book Co., 1966.

Bruner, Jerome. *On Knowing: Essays for the Left Hand*. Cambridge: The Belknap Press of Harvard University Press, 1962.

Cartwright, Michael G., ed. *The Royal Priesthood: Essays Ecclesiological and Ecumenical—John Howard Yoder*. Grand Rapids: Eerdmans, 1994.

Chopp, Rebecca S. *Saving Work: Feminist Practices of Theological Education*. Louisville: Westminster John Knox Press, 1995.

———. *The Power to Speak: Feminism, Language, God*. New York: Crossroad, 1991.

———. *The Praxis of Suffering: An Interpretation of Liberation and Political Theologies*. Maryknoll, N.Y.: Orbis Books, 1986.

Chopp, Rebecca S., and Sheila Greeve Davaney, eds. *Horizons in Feminist Theology: Identity, Tradition, and Norms*. Minneapolis: Fortress Press, 1997.

Chopp, Rebecca S., and Mark Lewis Taylor. *Reconstructing Christian Theology*. Minneapolis: Fortress Press, 1994.

Clapp, Rodney. *A Peculiar People: The Church as Culture in a Post-Christian Society*. Downers Grove, Ill.: InterVarsity Press, 1996.

———. *Families at the Crossroads: Beyond Traditional & Modern Options*. Downers Grove, Ill.: InterVarsity Press, 1993.

Code, Lorraine. *What Can She Know? Feminist Theory and the Construction of Knowledge*. Ithaca: Cornell University Press, 1991.

Coles, Robert. *The Call of Service: A Witness to Idealism*. Boston: Houghton Mifflin Company, 1993.

———. *The Moral Intelligence of Children*. N.Y.: Random House, 1997.

Confession of Faith In a Mennonite Perspective. Scottdale, Pa.: Herald Press, 1995.

Connerton, Paul. *How Societies Remember*. Cambridge: Cambridge University Press, 1989.

Cremin, Lawrence A. *American Education: The Colonial Experience, 1607-1783*. New York: Harper & Row, 1970.

———. *Public Education*. New York: Basic Books, 1976.

———. *Traditions of American Education*. New York: Basic Books, 1977.

———. *The Transformation of the School: Progressivism in American Education, 1876-1957*. New York: Alfred A. Knopf, 1962.

Douglas, Mary. *Natural Symbols*. Middlesex, England: Penguin Books Ltd., 1970.

Driver, Tom F. *The Magic of Ritual: Our Need for Liberating Rites that Transform Our Lives & Our Communities*. San Francisco: HarperSanFrancisco, 1991.

Dykstra, Craig, and Sharon Parks, eds. *Faith Development and Fowler*. Birmingham: Religious Education Press, 1986.

Eisner, Elliot, ed. *Learning and Teaching the Ways of Knowing*. Chicago: The National Society for the Study of Education, 1985.

Farley, Edward. *Ecclesial Man: A Social Phenomenology of Faith and Reality*. Philadelphia: Fortress Press, 1975.

———. *Theologia: The Fragmentation and Unity of Theological Education*. Philadelphia: Fortress Press, 1983.

Finger, Thomas N. *Christian Theology: An Eschatological Approach*, Volume I & II. Scottdale, Pa.: Herald Press, 1985 & 1989.

Fowler, James W. *Faithful Change: The Personal and Public Challenges of Postmodern Life*. Nashville: Abingdon Press, 1996.

_____. *Stages of Faith: The Psychology of Human Development and the Quest for Meaning.* San Francisco: Harper & Row, 1981.

Friedman, Robert. *The Theology of Anabaptism.* Scottdale, Pa.: Herald Press, 1973.

Fulkerson, Mary McClintock. *Changing the Subject: Women's Discourses and Feminist Theology.* Minneapolis: Fortress Press, 1994.

Gelwick, Richard. *The Way of Discovery: An Introduction to the Thought of Michael Polanyi.* New York: Oxford University Press, 1977.

Hall, David D. ed. *Lived Religion in America: Toward a History of Practice.* Princeton: Princeton University Press, 1997.

Harder, Leland, ed. *Perspectives on the Nurturing of Faith.* Elkhart, Ind.: The Institute of Mennonite Studies, 1983.

Harder, Lydia. "A Hermeneutics of Discipleship: Toward a Mennonite/Feminist Approach to Biblical Authority." Doctoral thesis submitted to Toronto School of Theology, Toronto, 1993.

Hauerwas, Stanley. *A Community of Character.* Notre Dame: University of Notre Dame Press, 1981.

Hauerwas, Stanley, and Alasdair MacIntyre, eds. *Changing Perspectives in Moral Philosophy.* Notre Dame: University of Notre Dame Press, 1983.

Hauerwas, Stanley, Nancey Murphy, and Mark Nation eds. *Theology Without Foundations: Religious Practice and the Future of Theological Truth.* Nashville: Abingdon Press, 1994.

Hawkley, Ken, ed. *Mennonite Higher Education: Experience and Vision, A Symposium on Mennonite Higher Education.* Sponsored by the Council on Higher Education of The General Conference Mennonite Church, June 26-28, 1992.

Hays, Richard B. *The Moral Vision of the New Testament.* San Francisco: Harper, 1996.

Hershberger, Guy F. ed. *The Recovery of the Anabaptist Vision.* Scottdale, Pa.: Herald Press, 1957.

Hertzler, Daniel. *Mennonite Education: Why and How? A Philosophy of Education for the Mennonite Church.* Scottdale, Pa.: Herald Press, 1971.

Huebner, Harry, ed. *The Church as Theological Community: Essays in Honor of David Schroeder.* Winnipeg, Manitoba: Canadian Mennonite Bible College, 1990.

Hughes, Richard T., and William B. Adrian eds. *Models for Christian Higher Education: Strategies for Survival and Success in the Twenty-First Century.* Grand Rapids: Eerdmans, 1997.

Jaeger, Werner. *Early Christianity and Greek Paideia.* Cambridge: The Belknap Press of Harvard University Press, 1961.

_____. *Paideia: The Ideals of Greek Culture—Archaic Greece, The Mind of Athens.* Volume I. New York: Oxford University Press, 1939.

_____. *Paideia: The Ideals of Greek Culture—In Search of the Divine Center.* Volume II. New York: Oxford University Press, 1944.

_____. *Paideia: The Ideals of Greek Culture—The Conflict of Cultural Ideals in the Age of Plato.* New York: Oxford University Press, 1944.

Kauffman, Richard A., and Gayle Gerber Koontz, eds. *Theology for the Church: Writings by Marlin E. Miller*. Elkhart, Ind.: Institute of Mennonite Studies, 1997.
Kauffman, J. Howard and Leo Driedger, eds. *The Mennonite Mosaic: Identity and Modernization*. Scottdale, Pa.: Herald Press, 1991.
Keller, Evelyn Fox. *Reflections on Gender and Science*. New Haven: Yale University Press, 1985.
Kelsey, David H. *Between Athens and Berlin: The Theological Education Debate*. Grand Rapids: William B Eerdmans Publishing Company, 1993.
———. *To Understand God Truly: What's Theological About A Theological School*. Louisville: Westminster John Knox Press, 1992.
Klaassen, Walter. *Anabaptism: Neither Catholic Nor Protestant*. Waterloo, Ontario: Conrad Press, 1973.
Kraybill, Donald B. *Ethnic Education: The Impact of Mennonite Schooling*, San Francisco, Calif.: R & E Research Associates, Inc., 1977.
———. *Mennonite Education: Issues, Facts, and Changes*. Scottdale, Pa.: Herald Press, 1978.
Langford, Thomas A., and William H. Poteat, eds. *Intellect and Hope: Essays in the Thought of Michael Polanyi*. Durham, N.C.: Duke University Press, 1968.
Lindbeck, George A. *The Nature of Doctrine: Religion and Theology in a Postliberal Age*. Philadelphia: The Westminster Press, 1984.
Little, Sara. *To Set One's Heart: Belief and Teaching in the Church*. Atlanta: John Knox Press, 1983.
Loder, James. *The Transforming Moment*. Colorado Springs: Helmers & Howard, 1989.
Loewen, Harry, ed. *Mennonite Images*. Winnipeg, Man.: Hyperion Press, 1980.
Loewen, Howard John. *One Lord, One Church, One Hope, and One God: Mennonite Confessions of Faith*. Elkhart, Ind.: Institute of Mennonite Studies, 1985.
Luhmann, Niklas. *Ecological Communication*. Chicago: The University of Chicago Press, 1986.
MacIntyre, Alasdair. *After Virtue*. Notre Dame: University of Notre Dame Press, 1981.
———. *Three Rival Versions of Moral Inquiry: Encyclopaedia, Genealogy, and Tradition*. Notre Dame: University of Notre Dame Press, 1990.
Martin, Jane Roland. *Changing the Educational Landscape: Philosophy, Women, and Curriculum*. New York: Routledge, 1994.
Martin, John R. *Ventures in Discipleship*. Scottdale, Pa.: Herald Press, 1984.
Minnich, Elizabeth Kamarck. *Transforming Knowledge*. Philadelphia: Temple University Press, 1990.
Murphy, Nancey. *Anglo-American Postmodernity: Philosophical Perspectives on Science, Religion, and Ethics*. Boulder, Colo.: Westview Press, 1997.
———. *Beyond Liberalism & Fundamentalism: How Modern and Postmodern Philosophy Set the Theological Agenda*. Valley Forge, Pa.: Trinity Press International, 1996.
———. *Reconciling Theology and Science: A Radical Reformation Perspective*. Kitchener, Ontario: Pandora Press, 1997.

_____. *Theology in the Age of Scientific Reasoning*. Ithaca: Cornell University Press, 1990.

Murphy, Nancey, and George F. R. Ellis. *On the Moral Nature of the Universe: Theology, Cosmology, and Ethics*. Minneapolis: Fortress Press, 1996.

Murray, Stuart Wood. "Spirit, Discipleship, Community: The Contemporary Significance of Anabaptist Hermeneutics." A doctoral thesis submitted to the Whitefield Institute, Oxford, 1992.

Niebuhr, H. Richard. *Christ and Culture*. New York: Harper & Row, 1951.

Phillips, Timothy R., and Dennis L. Okholm. *The Nature of Confession: Evangelicals & Postliberals in Conversation*. Downers Grove, Ill., InterVarsity Press, 1996.

Polanyi, Michael. *Knowing and Being: Essays*. Chicago: The University of Chicago Press, 1969.

_____. *Personal Knowledge: Towards a Post-Critical Philosophy*. Chicago: The University of Chicago Press, 1958.

_____. *Science, Faith and Society*. Chicago: The University of Chicago Press, 1964.

_____. *Scientific Thought and Social Reality: Essays*. New York: International Universities Press, 1974.

_____. *The Study of Man*. Chicago: The University of Chicago Press, 1959.

_____. *The Tacit Dimension*. Gloucester, Mass.: Peter Smith, 1983.

Redekop, Calvin, ed. *Mennonite Identity: Historical and Contemporary Perspectives*. Lanham, Md.: University Press of America, 1988.

Redekop, Calvin. *Mennonite Society*. Baltimore: The Johns Hopkins University Press, 1989.

_____. *The Free Church and Seductive Culture*. Scottdale, Pa.: Herald Press, 1970.

Rorty, Richard. *Philosophy and the Mirror of Nature*. Princeton: Princeton University Press, 1979.

Roth, John, ed. *Refocusing a Vision: Shaping Anabaptist Character in the Twenty-First Century*. Goshen, Ind.: Mennonite Historical Society, 1995.

Sawatsky, Rodney. *Authority and Identity: The Dynamics of the General Conference Mennonite Church*. North Newton, Kan.: Bethel College, 1987.

_____. *Commitment and Critique: A Dialectical Imperative*. Waterloo, Ontario: Conrad Grebel College, 1982.

_____. *History and Ideology: American Mennonite Identity Definition Through History*. Ann Arbor, Mich.: UMI Dissertation Services, 1977.

Schipani, Daniel, ed. *Freedom and Discipleship*. Maryknoll, N.Y.: Orbis, 1989.

Schwehn, Mark. *Exiles of Eden*. New York: Oxford University Press, 1993.

Scott, Drusilla. *Everyman Revived: The Common Sense of Michael Polanyi*. Grand Rapids: Eerdmans, 1985.

Seymour, Jack L., Robert O'Gorman, and Charles Foster. *The Church in the Education of the Public: Refocusing the Task of Religious Education*. Nashville: Abingdon Press, 1984.

Sloan, Douglas. *Faith & Knowledge: Mainline Protestantism and American Higher Education*. Louisville, Ky.: Westminster John Knox, 1994.

Snyder, Arnold C. *An Introduction to Anabaptist History and Theology.* Kitchener, Ontario: the author, 1994.

Sobrino, Jon. *The Principle of Mercy: Taking the Crucified People from the Cross.* Maryknoll: Orbis Books, 1994.

Swartley, Willard, ed. *Explorations of Systematic Theology from Mennonite Perspectives.* Elkhart, Ind.: Institute of Mennonite Studies, 1984.

Thompson, Marjorie, J. *Family, The Forming Center.* Nashville: The Upper Room, 1996.

Tillich, Paul. *Theology of Culture.* New York: Oxford University Press, 1959.

Toews, Paul. *Mennonites in American Society, 1930-1970: Modernity and the Persistence of Religious Community.* Scottdale, Pa.: Herald Press, 1996.

Toulmin, Stephen. *Cosmopolis: The Hidden Agenda of Modernity.* New York: The Free Press, 1990.

Tracy, David. *The Analogical Imagination: Christian Theology and the Culture of Pluralism.* New York: Crossroad, 1981.

Troeltsch, Ernst. *Writings on Theology and Religion.* Louisville: Westminster John Knox Press, 1990.

van Braght, Thieleman J. *The Bloody Theater or Martyrs Mirror of the Defenseless Christians.* Trans. Joseph F. Sohm in 1886. Scottdale, Pa.: Herald Press, 1979.

Waltner, Erland, ed. *Jesus Christ and the Mission of the Church: Contemporary Anabaptist Perspectives.* Newton, Kan.: Faith and Life Press, 1990.

Weaver, Alain Epp, ed. *Mennonite Theology in Face of Modernity: Essays in Honor of Gordon D. Kaufman*, North Newton, Kan.: Bethel College, 1996.

Yoder, John Howard, Glen Stassen, and D. M. Yeager. *Authentic Transformation: A New Vision of Christ and Culture.* Nashville: Abingdon Press, 1996.

Yoder, John Howard. *The Politics of Jesus.* Grand Rapids: William B. Eerdmans Publishing Company, 1972.

_____. *The Priestly Kingdom: Social Ethics as Gospel.* Notre Dame: Notre Dame Press, 1984.

The Index

A

Anabaptist/s, 14, 23, 133-134. *See also* Mennonites, education
  descriptive overview, 38-42
  discipleship, 39-48, 135-137. *See also* discipleship
  ecclesiology, 42, 54-57, 71, 104, 135. *See also* church, community
  hermeneutical community, 42, 48-54. *See also* community, discernment
  radical reformers, 38-40, 55, 76, 93, 106, 113-114
  spirituality, 47, 153-154
    abiding in Christ, 47-48, 135-141, 147, 151, 154, 157
  theology, 38
    classic distinctives, 37, 40, 48, 117, 134, 136, 148
    implicit, 18, 38
    Jesus as norm, 18, 45, 76-77, 104-105, 111, 116, 134, 137, 140-142, 154
    and Scripture, 45-46, 50, 76. *See also* Scripture
    and tradition, 93, 104-105, 123-124. *See also* tradition
  ways of knowing, 15, 18. *See also* knowing—Anabaptist ways of
Aristotle, 24, 88
Augustine
  and Polanyi, 82, 85, 90-91

B

Basil of Caesarea, 65
Bass, Dorothy, 58
Bender, H. S., 40, 43

Body. *See also* rituals, practices, habits, knowledge
  bodily practices, 24, 100-101, 134, 143, 147, 155-156
  roots of thought, 85, 127
  and embodiment, 17-18, 42, 45, 74, 89, 94, 140
  as moral value, 101
  of practices, 93, 100, 103, 117, 134
  of tradition, 42, 110, 122, 125
  of the Word, 57-58, 105
  knowledge grounded in, 85-86, 127, 138, 143
  remembering in the, 26
  and social memory, 25, 143, 156
  spirituality of, 95, 100-101
Browning, Don, 150
Burkholder, J. Lawrence, 43

C

Cappadocian fathers, 65
Celts, 158-159
Chopp, Rebecca, 23, 80, 119-132
  biographical intro, 94-96
  ekklesia, women-church, 98-99, 125, 131
  emancipatory praxis, 100-102, 105, 120-124, 131
  narrativity, 96-98, 125
  practices of theological education, 99-101
  theology as:
    "saving work," 101-103, 120, 125, 129
    paradigmatic quilt, 101, 120, 136

201

Church, 18, 148-150, 154. *See also* community, ecclesiology
  and Christian narrative, 17, 148, 165
  as community of disciples, 55, 57, 71-72, 98, 104, 113, 135, 148-149
  congregational locus of interpretation, 48, 157
  ekklesia, women church, 96-99
  Mennonite congregational profile, 27
  and science, 83, 88
Church of the Brethren, 107, 111
Classic, 37. *See also* Anabaptist theology classic distinctives
  religious, 73
  paideia, 60-61, 67-68
Clement of Alexandria, 65
Community/ties, 165. *See also* church, particularity-based interpretation, 48-49, 53, 58, 80, 92, 123, 131, 147
  distinctive, 13-18, 42, 57, 71, 134, 136, 141, 143, 152-156, 164
  counter-cultural, 57-59, 70-71, 98, 153
  hermeneutical, 42, 48-54. *See also* discernment, Polanyi "society of explorers"
  and who participates, 48, 52, 54, 58, 123, 132, 157
  arguments about, 50-51
  "ideal type", 49
  limitations of, 50-53
  of obedience and suspicion, 52
  ideals, 74, 141
  and knowledge construction, 75, 121, 127, 130, 141. *See also* knowledge
  other particular Christian, 15, 133, 151, 164
  and paideia, 60, 68, 148, 153. *See also* paideia
  tradition-based, 15, 35, 70, 153. *See also* education
Confession of Faith in Mennonite Perspective, 153-154
  discipleship, 45
  Christian spirituality, 47
Connerton, Paul, 23-25
Contextualization, 14, 157. *See also* knowledge
  and feminist theological education, 95-96, 103
  narrative context, 16, 139
  and paideia, 60
Conversation. *See also* discernment
  about education and knowing, 14-15, 18-19, 23-24, 37, 80, 133, 164
  and home-based faith, 31, 34, 150
  about an ideal, 50-51, 54
Cremin, Lawrence, 70
Critical/Critique, 164
  Berlin model of, 68-69
  education as both tradition-based and, 17. *See also* education
  of paideia, 62, 74-77
  retrieval:
    of paideia, 60, 70
    of Anabaptist legacy, 42, 52, 117, 147
    of traditions, 19, 146
  thinking, 143, 145-146, 155-156
Culture/cultural, 158, 162, 166. *See also* transformation
  Christian, 67, 143
  family, 150, 154, 158
  indwelling, 87. *See also* indwelling
  knowledge and truth rooted in, 16, 139. *See also* knowledge
  and practice, 27

D

Denck, Hans, 46
Discernment. *See also* community—hermeneutical, conversation, epistemology
  communal, 48, 54, 59, 80, 92, 103, 114-117, 121, 126, 130, 133, 136, 142, 154, 156-157, 164
    as "Society of Explorers", 94, 131, 156-157. *See also* Polanyi, Society of Explorers
  theory of, 109
    Christian epistemic practice, 109, 114, 131, 142. *See also* Murphy
  tradition and experience in, 54, 105, 110, 121-122, 126, 132, 154-157, 164
Descarte, 86
  mind-body dualism, 101, 103, 127, 143
Discipleship, 39, 48-49, 59, 135, 141, 154. *See also* Anabaptist, education
  normative, 47
  relevance for education, 42, 47
    immersion in Scripture, 46, 135. *See also* Scripture
    indwelling Jesus story, 42, 45-48, 154
    Jesus as model, 44, 45, 140, 144, 154
    patterning lives on Jesus, 39, 42, 43, 59
Dykstra, Craig, 14, 58, 100

E

Eastern Mennonite Seminary, 162
Ecclesiology, 42, 71, 135. *See also* church
  Anabaptist, 42. *See also* Anabaptist
  tradition for transformation, 54-56
Education, 70, 166. *See also* practices
  Anabaptist distinctives relevant for, 42, 47, 54-59, 139, 151-152
  ecology of institutions, 70, 148, 153
  and Greek paideia, 61-63, 68, 70-75, 98. *See also* paideia
    Athens and Berlin, 68-69
    alternative paideia, 71-74
    early Christian notions of, 64
  priorities, 15, 24, 73.
    imagination as center of, 128-129, 144
    moral formation, 112-113, 117-118, 126
  settings, 147
    church, 148, 153-158, 162-163
    family, 148-158, 162-163
    school, 151-158, 162-163
  strategies, 151-153
    communal moral discernment, 154-157
    indwell narratives and practices, 154-156
    reimage ideals, 152-153
    revitalize core practices, 148, 157-162
  theory construction, 23, 37, 42, 59, 79, 81, 94, 103, 119, 133-134, 137-139, 164
  tradition-based, critical, 14, 17-18, 37, 57, 60, 64, 71, 78, 92, 94, 108, 116-119, 134, 148, 151-153, 164
  vision and mission, 15, 17, 19, 70, 137, 141-142, 153-154, 164. *See also* transformation
Edwards, Jonathan, 114-115

Ellis, George, 111
Enlightenment, 15. *See also* post-modernity
Epistemology. *See also* knowledge, knowing, truth, discernment, practices
    Christian epistemic practice, 109, 117. *See also* Murphy
    distinctive sixteenth- century, 46
    and education, 78
    and ethics, 42, 58, 75, 100, 103, 120, 126, 146-147, 158
        knowing and doing, 47-48, 93, 125, 135, 138, 139, 147
    and Polanyi, 82, 92. *See also* Polanyi
    tradition-based, 109, 116
    in crisis, 110, 116, 121-123
Ethics/ethical. *See also* practices, virtues, truth, knowing, praxis
    and epistemology, 42, 58, 100, 120, 137, 147, 158. *See also* epistemology
    implications for knowing, 75, 125-126
    theological knowing, 103
    as ideological grid, 104-105, 123-124. *See also* emancipatory praxis
    of Jesus, 72, 146, 155, 158
    new family, 150
    and theology in academy, 111, 112, 117
    nonviolence, 111-112, 117
    and science, 111

F
Family, 13, 148-163
Farley, Edward, 60, 67-68, 120, 128
Finger, Tom, 18, 44, 47
Fiorenza, Elizabeth Schüssler, 52
Formation/formative
    communal, 14-15, 18, 24-25, 136, 141, 149
    of human personality, paideia, 65, 74, 98, 142
    in godliness, theologia, 68, 97
    in secular academy, 75
    moral, 112, 118, 126, 146, 151
    personal, 14, 24-25, 98, 136, 154
    practices, 58, 76, 126, 133-134, 147-148, 155-157
    texts, 46, 54, 66-67, 72, 76, 109-110, 117-118, 122, 140, 146-147, 151, 155
    narratives, 148, 155
Foundation/Foundationalism
    philosophical approach to knowledge, 14, 107, 116, 119-121, 136
    Jesus as, 43, 136-137
Frameworks. *See also* tradition
    authoritative traditional, 89-91, 94, 122-123, 130-132, 144
    and self determination 123, 131-132, 142
    conceptual, 15, 134
    of discipline and originality, 89, 142
    ideals provide, 50, 54
Friedmann, Robert, 38

G
Gadamer, Hans Georg, 37
Gregory of Nazianzus, 65
Gregory of Nyssa, 65-67

H
Habits/habitual
    and moral character, 24-25
    rhythm of daily practices, 25-26, 127, 143, 147, 155
    and tacit knowledge, 85-86, 143
    and virtue, 24-25

Habitus, 166
  and paideia, 60, 68, 74, 77
  in theological education, 68, 97
Harder, Lydia, 47, 52
Hauerwas, Stanley, 148
Hays, Richard, 57
Hermeneutical community. *See* community—hermeneutical, discernment, Anabaptists
Holy Spirit, 18, 48-49, 54, 66-67, 76, 94, 99, 104, 108-109, 114-115, 122, 131, 135, 140-142, 154-157, 162-163
Horst, Irvin, 46
Huebner, Dwayne, 73

I
Ideals, 167
  conversation about, 50-51, 54
  core, 134, 153
  false, 83, 125, 146
  "ideal type" of hermeneutical community, 49-51, 54
  paideia and "living ideals", 60-63, 67, 142, 153-154
  Christ as, 142
  the Good, 62-66, 72, 74
  poetry, music, rhythm as, 61-63, 73-74
  reimage, 152-153
  of a tradition, 51, 141, 150
Identity, 13, 16
Ignatius of Loyola, 115
Imagination, 79, 129-131, 155. *See also* knowing, knowledge
  in discernment, 94, 156
  imaginative integration, 86, 128, 144
  intuitive, 128, 142, 144
  as root of knowledge, 128, 139
  shaped by Sripture, 45, 127, 154

Indwelling, 86, 154-156. *See also* discipleship, Polanyi, story
  authoritative tradition, 94
  Jesus story, 45-46, 93, 155
  same as teacher, 91, 93, 154-155
  particulars of subliminal knowledge, 86, 143, 154
  of tradition, 86-87, 92, 140
  tacit knowledge, 89, 143
Intuition, 83-84, 120, 129. *See also* knowing, knowledge
  bodily roots, 86, 143
  in discernment, 94, 156
  intuitive imagination, 128, 142, 144
  of non-sensory realities, 79
  as root of knowledge, 128

J
Jaeger, Werner, 60-62, 65-67, 72

K
Kelsey, David, 60, 67-69, 100
Klassen, Walter, 39
Knowing. *See also* epistemology, knowledge, truth, discernment
  Anabaptist ways of, 15, 18, 46, 48, 58, 113, 117, 138-139, 146-147
  by apprenticeship to tradition/teacher, 93, 156
  and doing. *See* epistemology
  and loving, 138-139
  and ethics, 100, 103, 126
  morally directive, 75, 125-126
  how and what we know, 15, 78-79
  multiple ways of, 79, 85-86, 94, 119, 125-128, 139, 144-145
  personal, participatory, 16, 42, 84, 125, 128, 143

rationalist paradigm, 79
Knowledge. *See also* epistemology, knowing, truth, discernment, community
   bodily roots or substratum of, 24, 26, 75, 100-101, 134, 143
   intuitive, traditional and other roots of, 94, 127-128, 130, 139-140, 143, 145
   construction of, 78-79, 133
   in community, 75, 80, 121, 125, 130, 141-142
   as particular and perspectival, 14, 92
   rooted in culture, 16, 139
   tradition-based, 35, 82, 85, 151
   art, poetry, myth, religion as providing, 86, 128
   personal, 83-85, 92, 120, 127, 156. *See also* Polanyi
   tacit, 86, 127-128, 143. *See also* Polanyi
   as a web, 107, 110, 119, 121, 136
Koontz, Ted, 47
Kuhn, Thomas, 107

L
Lakatos, Imre, 107-108
Lindbeck, George, 17, 46

M
MacIntyre, Alasdair, 16, 23, 35, 51, 100, 107-109, 113, 120
Martyrs Mirror, 146, 154
McLaren, Brian, 158
Memory, 13
   bodily social, 25-26, 143, 156
   communal, 26
Mennonites, 14-15, 18, 23, 40, 54, 71, 133-134, 152, 159. *See also* Anabaptist
   changes in "lived religion", 26
   congregational profile, 27
   family/church-based practices, 29-34
   critique of tradition, 23-24, 41, 50, 52-53
   and higher education, 118
   loss of faith practices, 15, 23-24, 133
Menno Simons, 43, 46, 137, 144
Miller, Marlin, 40-46, 55
Modeling:
   on Jesus, 17, 44, 93. *See also* discipleship
Modernity, 15, 79, 136, 145
Murphy, Nancey, 23, 71, 80, 119-132
   biographical intro, 105-106
   ethics and theology in academy, 111-112. *See also* ethics, theology
   power renouncing practices, 113-117, 126, 131. *See also* practices
   Christian epistemic practice, 114-115, 126, 131. *See also* discernment
   on MacIntyre, 16
   postmodernity, 14. *See also* postmodernity
   knowledge as web, 107, 110, 119, 121, 136
   Radical Reformation heritage, 113-114, 131. *See also* Anabaptist
   science and theology, 108-109
   tradition and present experience, 109-110, 122. *See also* tradition
Murray, Stuart, 48-49, 53

N

Narratives. *See also* story, contextualization
  Anabaptist-Mennonite, 18, 105, 135, 145
  discarding of, 15
  formative, 148, 155. *See also* formative texts
  provide identity/meaning, 16, 97
    feminist narrativity, 97-98, 105, 120, 125, 129
    "in action", 127, 143
    of Jesus, 38, 143
    tradition-based, 16, 35, 139
    transformative, 57, 97
Nietzsche, 113

O

Obedience, 49, 112, 137-138
  hermeneutics of, 52-54
Origin, 65

P

Paideia. *See also* education, ideal
  classical Greek notions of, 18, 60-64, 68-69, 75
    ideal of, 61-64, 72-74
    philosophical critique, 62
    preconditions for growth, 62-64
    social purpose, 62-63, 70, 72
  early Christian notions of, 64-67, 70
    imitation of Christ, 64-67
    true, divine paideia, 65-66
    and theological education, 67-69
    Athens and Berlin, 68-69
  alternative, 70, 76-77, 142, 148
    embodiment of Christ "ideal", 74, 142
    idolatries critiqued, 76-77

preconditions for growth, 74, 76, 143, 150
  tradition-based counter-culture, 70-72, 147, 153
Paradigm, 119-120, 136
  Anabaptist, proposed, 137, 152-153, 155
  Chopp, theology as quilt, 101, 120-121, 136
  Murphy, web of knowledge, 107, 111, 119, 121, 136
  Polanyi, heuristic philosophy, 83-84, 120, 136
Particular/particularity, 17, 27, 95, 149, 155. *See also* community
  Christian communities, 15, 18, 151, 154
  cultural inheritance, 87, 92, 122, 139, 143
  peoplehood, 13, 27
  tradition, 116, 118, 122, 139
  paideia, 72
  tested in public, 37
Plato, 23-24, 60-63, 74-76
Polanyi, Michael, 23, 80, 119-132, 156
  biographical intro, 81-83
  heuristic discovery as paradigm, 83-84, 120, 136
  indwelling, 86-87, 89-92, 154-156
  personal knowledge/responsibility, 81-85, 92, 120, 125-128, 156
    false objectivity, 82, 84, 125
    scientism, science, 83, 85, 88-91, 122, 128, 130, 144
  roots of knowledge, 82. *See also* knowledge, knowing
    bodily, intuitive, traditional, 82, 83, 120
    tacit knowledge, 85-86, 89-91

Society of Explorers, 83, 88, 92, 94, 120, 130, 142, 154. *See also* discernment
  authority and tradition, 88-92, 142
  discipline and originality, 89-92, 132, 142
  tradition, 90. *See also* tradition
  basis for discovery, 89, 91, 120, 122
  purpose of, 90-91, 122, 130
  apprenticeship to, 89-93, 122, 130, 156
Popper, Karl, 107
Postmodernity, 13-14, 17-18, 37, 51, 71, 110, 116, 158-159
Practices, 58-59, 147, 167. *See also* body, education, epistemology
  Anabaptist-Mennonite, 18, 27, 40, 154
  being discarded, 15, 23-24, 133
  unity of faith and, 18, 103
  congregational profile of, 24, 27
  power-renouncing, 113, 118, 126, 147, 151, 164
  discernment, 114, 117 *See also* Murphy, Christian epistemic
  community/church-based, 15, 29-34, 158
  family-based, 13, 28-34, 148-150, 154, 158
  formative. *See* formation/practices
  habituated, patterned, 25-26, 74, 77, 143, 155-156
  as "lived religion", 27
  provide identity/meaning. 16, 100, 160
  particular traditions and, 17, 35, 72. *See also* particularity
  embody traditions, 18, 42, 45, 122. *See also* body
  revitalized core, 148, 157-164
  and Scripture, 45, 135
  for entering "world of Bible", 110, 116, 127, 147
  as sites of learning, 58, 99-101, 103, 125, 127, 147
  practicing as knowing, 48, 58, 125, 158
  truth derived from, 100, 147, 154. *See also* truth
  in theological education, 95-96, 100. *See also* Chopp, Murphy
Praxis, 167
  emancipatory. *See* Chopp

Q
Quakers, 111
Quine, W. V. O., 107, 110, 121

R
Rational thinking, 15, 79, 86, 145-146, 156
  Enlightenment and, 15
  scientific, 83, 91, 122
  like theological, 108
  tradition-dependent, 16, 71, 73, 109, 113, 118, 122
Reality
  beyond language conventions, 17, 76, 94, 120, 130-131, 140
  underlying tradition, 90, 129, 145
  noumenal, immaterial, 79, 128
  perspectives on, 14, 58, 74, 108, 112, 128, 146-147, 155, 157, 164
  from alternate perspective, 112, 117-118, 126, 146, 149, 151, 155
  ways of knowing and, 119, 144

Remembering, 13, 14. *See also* body, memory
  in common, 25-26
Ritual/s, 161. *See also* body and social memory
  ceremonies/ bodily practices, 26, 134, 147
  and Christian worship, 90, 92, 150
  narratives in action, 127
  of a particular religion, 122
  Celtic, 159
Roth, John, 39-40, 49-51
Rousseau, 149

S
Sabean, David, 50
Sawatsky, Rodney, 71
Schwehn, Mark, 73-75
Scripture, 38, 156. *See also* practices, Anabaptist
  Anabaptist:
    immersion in, 45-46, 74, 76, 93, 135, 144, 155
    and protestant reformation view of, 39
    shared conviction about, 41, 45-46, 48-49
    as world creating, 58, 127, 129, 135-136, 145, 154
    as authoritative, 104-105, 110, 135
    and Christian paideia, 66-67
    and present experience, 110, 131. *See also* tradition and experience
Seymour, Jack, 71
Sloan, Douglas, 120
Story/story-telling, 152, 160-161. *See also* narrative
  alternative, 149
  that "aspire to truth," 16
  of Israel, of Jesus, 17
  indwelling Jesus, 42, 45-46, 155
Swartley, Willard, 45-46, 51-52

T
The Meno, 74-75
Theology, 163
  Anabaptist-Mennonite implicit, 18, 37-38, 111, 151
  Celtic, 158-159
  and ethics as priority, 112, 116-117, 141
  reweaving doctrinal web, 110
  and science, 105, 108-109, 111, 116
  in academy and church, 111
  theological education, 19
  and paideia, 67.
  and theologia, 68
  Athens and Berlin, 68
  as "saving work", 95-96, 100-103, 120, 129
  theologians and Polanyi, 82, 91
Tracy, David, 37, 77
Tradition, 167. *See also* body, knowing, knowledge, epistemology, practices, truth
  apprenticeship to, 122, 130, 139
  and original discovery, 89, 91, 120, 123, 140, 144, 151
  creative dissent of, 89, 92, 94, 122, 124, 130, 140
  maintained and revitalized, 76, 90, 93, 109, 122-124, 140, 164
  authority of, 89, 91, 94, 130, 132
  Greek paideia as, 61, 74, 142
  indwelling the particulars of, 86-87, 92
  patriarchal distortions of, 102, 123-124, 140, 146

as potent legacy, 14, 16, 41, 152
  spiritual qualities of, 73, 75,
    94, 140-141
  and present experience, 54, 105,
    110, 121, 126, 129, 132, 137,
    140
  preserves an ideal, 51, 54
  socially embodied argument, 51,
    109-110, 117, 122, 127, 140,
    142
  traditional frames of reference,
    90-91, 94, 122-123, 132, 149.
    See also frameworks
  traditional roots of knowledge,
    82, 85, 127, 139
  for transformation, 54, 56, 104,
    145-146
  of the virtues, 16, 35, 141. See also
    virtues
Tradition-based, 168
  critical education, 14, 17-18, 37,
    57, 60, 64, 78, 92-96, 108, 116-
    119, 134, 148, 152-153, 164
  rationality, morality, 16, 71, 73,
    109, 113, 118, 122
  counter-cultural paideia, 70
Transformation
  as Anabaptist mission, 54, 140,
    148, 154
  of culture, 42, 148
  and feminist theology, 95-99,
    102, 132
  as purpose of education, 17, 94,
    168
  social, 55
  of ways of knowing, 79, 128, 139,
    144
Truth. See also practices
  Anabaptist ways of knowing, 15,
    18, 76, 117, 126, 147
  assumptions about, 15, 88, 120-
    121, 140, 145
  strategies of, 121, 128
  communal discernment of, 42,
    48-49, 103, 114, 126, 130-
    131. See also discernment
  criteria for judging, 114-115,
    117, 131, 142. See also practice,
    power-renouncing
  Greek notions of, 62-63, 74
  as perspectival and confessional,
    14
  rooted in culture, 16
  of poetry, art, morality, philoso-
    phy, law, 85-86, 125
  from "saving work", 100, 102. See
    also Chopp
  derived from practice, 100, 125,
    132, 147, 154, 157
  of tradition, 89, 92, 113, 139
  universal understanding of, 37,
    92, 122

V
Veverka, Fayette, 18
Virtues, 169
  Aristotle, intellectual and moral,
    24-25
  and higher education, 75
  and power-renouncing practices,
    113-114, 117, 146-147, 164.
    See also Murphy
  relationship to paideia, 60-66
  culturing of, 68, 76, 151, 154,
    156
  tradition of, 16, 35, 141, 143
  training in habit, 24-25. See also
    habits

W
Wenger, J. C., 46

Y
Yoder, John Howard, 45, 55-56, 113

The Author

Sara Wenger Shenk is Associate Dean and Associate Professor of Christian Education at Eastern Mennonite Seminary, Harrisonburg, Virginia. She is an author of four books on themes related to family spirituality and culture and is a frequent speaker on educational themes.

Shenk spent much of her life negotiating cultural change, which has contributed to her reflection on practices and the intentional shaping of a wholesome, identity forming culture. She grew up in Ethiopia, and she and her husband began their family while studying and working with theological education in the former Yugoslavia. Sara is also the founding pastor of Immanuel Mennonite Church in northeast Harrisonburg, a multi-ethnic congregation with significant neighborhood ministries.

www.ingramcontent.com/pod-product-compliance
Lightning Source LLC
Chambersburg PA
CBHW020355170426
43200CB00005B/175